Contents

S0-AYP-256

Contents

Strategy Workshop

As you listen to the story "A Mummy Mystery," by Andrew Clements, you will stop from time to time to do some activities on these practice pages. These activities will help you think about different strategies that can help you read better. After completing each activity, you will discuss what you've written with your classmates and talk about how to use these strategies.

Remember, strategies can help you become a better reader. Good readers

- use strategies whenever they read

- use different strategies before, during, and after reading

- think about how strategies will help them

Name _____

Strategy I: Predict/Infer

Use this strategy before and during reading to help make predictions about what happens next or what you're going to learn.

Here's how to use the Predict/Infer Strategy:

1. Think about the title, the illustrations, and what you have read so far.
2. Tell what you think will happen next—or what you will learn.
3. Thinking about what you already know on the topic may help.
4. Try to figure out things the author does not say directly.

Listen as your teacher begins "A Mummy Mystery." When your teacher stops, complete the activity to show that you understand how to predict what the story might be about and what the mystery might be.

Think about the story and respond to the question below.

What do you think the story is about, and what might the mystery be?

_____

_____

_____

_____

_____

As you continue listening to the story, think about whether your prediction was right. You might want to change your prediction or write a new one below.

_____

_____

_____

_____

_____

Name _____

Strategy 2: Phonics/Decoding

Use this strategy during reading when you come across a word you don't know.

Here's how to use the Phonics/Decoding Strategy:
1. Look carefully at the word.
2. Look for word parts you know and think about the sounds for the letters.
3. Blend the sounds to read the words.
4. Ask yourself: is this a word I know? Does it make sense in what I am reading?
5. If not, ask yourself what else can I try? Should I look in a dictionary?

Listen as your teacher continues the story. When your teacher stops, use the Phonics/Decoding Strategy.

Now write down the steps you used to decode the word *Dynasty*.

_____

_____

_____

_____

_____

_____

_____

_____

_____

_____

Remember to use this strategy whenever you are reading and come across a word that you don't know.

Name _____

Strategy 3: Monitor/Clarify

Use this strategy during reading whenever you're confused about what you are reading.

Here's how to use the Monitor/Clarify Strategy:

- Ask yourself if what you're reading makes sense—or if you are learning what you need to learn.
- If you don't understand something, reread, use the illustrations, or read ahead to see if that helps.

Listen as your teacher continues the story. When your teacher stops, complete the activity to show that you understand what's happening in the story.

Think about the mummy and respond below.

1. Describe what happened with the mummy's hand.

_____

_____

_____

_____

2. Can you tell from listening to the story how everyone reacts to the mummy's hand moving? Why or why not?

_____

_____

_____

3. How can you find out what made the mummy's hand move?

_____

_____

_____

_____

Name _____

Strategy 4: Question

Use this strategy during and after reading to ask questions about important ideas in the story.

Here's how to use the Question Strategy:

- Ask yourself questions about important ideas in the story.
- Ask yourself if you can answer these questions.
- If you can't answer the questions, reread and look for answers in the text. Thinking about what you already know and what you've read in the story may help you.

Listen as your teacher continues the story. Then complete the activity to show that you understand how to ask yourself questions about important ideas in the story.

Think about the story and respond below.

Write a question you might ask yourself at this point in the story.

_____

_____

_____

_____

_____

_____

If you can't answer your question now, think about it while you listen to the rest of the story.

Name _____

Strategy 5: Evaluate

Use this strategy during and after reading to help you form an opinion about what you read.

Here's how to use the Evaluate Strategy:

- Tell whether or not you think this story is entertaining and why.
- Is the writing clear and easy to understand?
- This is a mystery story. Did the author make the characters believable and interesting?

Listen as your teacher continues the story. When your teacher stops, complete the activity to show that you are thinking of how you feel about what you are reading and why you feel that way.

Think about the story and respond below.

1. Tell whether or not you think this story is entertaining and why.

_____

_____

_____

_____

2. Is the writing clear and easy to understand?

_____

_____

_____

_____

3. This is a mystery story. Did the author make the characters interesting and believable?

_____

_____

_____

_____

Name _____

Strategy 6: Summarize

Use this strategy after reading to summarize what you read.

Here's how to use the Summarize Strategy:
- Think about the characters.
- Think about where the story takes place.
- Think about the problem in the story and how the characters solve it.
- Think about what happens in the beginning, middle, and end of the story.

Think about the story you just listened to. Complete the activity to show that you understand how to identify important story parts that will help you summarize the story.

Think about the story and respond to the questions below:

1. Who is the main character?

_____

_____

_____

2. Where does the story take place?

_____

_____

_____

3. What is the problem and how is it resolved?

_____

_____

_____

_____

Now use this information to summarize the story for a partner.

Name _____

Courage

The characters in this theme show courage in dangerous or challenging situations. After reading each selection, complete the chart below to show what you learned about the characters.

	Hatchet	Passage to Freedom
What challenge does the main character face?		
Where does the challenge take place?		
In what ways does the main character show courage?		
What do you think the character learns from his or her experience?		

Name _____

Courage

	Climb or Die	The True Confessions of Charlotte Doyle
What challenge does the main character face?		
Where does the challenge take place?		
In what ways does the main character show courage?		
What do you think the character learns from his or her experience?		

What have you learned about courage in this theme?

_____

_____

2   Theme 1: **Courage**

Name _____

Words in the Wild

Answer each of the following questions by writing a vocabulary word.

1. Which word tells what you should seek in a rainstorm so you won't get wet? ___shelter___

2. Which word describes what a snake is doing when it moves across the ground? ___Slithering___

3. Which word names a tool used to chop wood?
   ___hatchet___

4. Which word describes small pieces of wood needed to build a fire? ___Kindling___

5. Which word means "very frightened"?
   ___terrified___

6. Which word names the sharp spines a porcupine uses to defend itself? ___quills___

7. Which word means "the process of staying alive"?
   ___survival___

8. Which word describes a feeling a person has when he or she keeps trying to do something but cannot do it?
   ___fustration___

Write two questions of your own that use vocabulary words from the list above.

9. ___Which word means "very scared"?___

10. ___Which word is a place where you won't get wet when it rains?___

Name _____

Details Chart

Page(s)	Brian feels _____.	Details that show how Brian feels
30	terrified	• he hears a growl • there is a smell that makes him think of dead people
32–33	painful	• the eight quills in his leg seem like dozens • his pain spreads • catches his breath when he pulls the quills out
33–34	sad	• He thinks, "I can't take this" and "I can't do this." • He cries until he is cried out.
34–35	frustrated	• He doesn't know what the dream is telling him
36–37	curious	• realizes the hatchet can make sparks • recognizes the message about fire from his dreams • begins to make sparks to start a fire
38–41	determined	• looks for something to use for fuel
43	satisfied	he makes the fire

4   Theme 1: **Courage**

What Really Happened?

These sentences tell about Brian and the things that happen to him in the story. Write T if the sentence is true. Write F if the sentence is false. If the sentence is false, correct it to make it true.

1. __F__ Brian wakes up when he hears a bear growling outside his shelter.

   He only hears growling. Not a bear

2. __F__ Brian's leg gets injured when he kicks out in the darkness and hits the hatchet.

   He hits the animal.

3. __T__ After crying for a long time, Brian realizes that feeling sorry for yourself changes nothing.

   _____

4. __F__ Seeing his father and his friend Terry in a dream makes Brian feel happy.

   He feels flustrated and angry

5. __F__ In Brian's dream, his friend Terry shows him a path out of the forest.

   Terry points to the fire.

6. __T__ Brian thinks that throwing his hatchet to protect himself from wild animals is a bad idea.

   _____

7. __T__ By hitting the hatchet against a hard black rock, Brian is able to make sparks.

   _____

Name _____

Seeing the Solution

Read the story. Then complete the activity on page 7.

The Water Tree

Paul and I had been hiking for six hours. We came upon a dry creekbed that ran through the desert. Paul frowned, and I sighed. "I hope this isn't the creek we've been trying to reach," I said.

"See, Tom, I told you we should have brought more water," said Paul. Between the two of us, we had only about a third of a bottle left. Our clothes were wet with sweat and our throats were dry, but we dared not drink any more water yet. Even if we headed back right away, it was at least a six-hour hike back to our campground.

Paul and I just stared at the dry creekbed. "Check the map," I said to Paul. "Is there any other water within a mile of here?" I thought that even if there was another creek nearby, it might be dry too.

"There's nothing but lava rocks and an occasional cactus for another three miles," he reported grimly as he pulled out his map. Then his eyes lit up. "Wait a second, Tom," he said in a much happier voice. "A cactus!" He grinned and slapped me on the back.

"A cactus what?" I said. I wondered how he could be so excited about desert plants at a time like this.

"Don't you remember what we learned at camp last summer?" Paul asked. Then my own face curled into a smile. At camp they had shown us how to get water from a cactus.

"Do you have a knife?" I asked. "I have a handkerchief we can use to strain the water from the cactus flesh." Within minutes we were squeezing water out of a prickly pear cactus into our water bottles, through a funnel fashioned from a sun visor. We didn't get much water per squeeze, but there were more than enough cacti around. We'd make it back to camp with water to spare.

Name _____

Seeing the Solution continued

Answer these questions about the story on page 6.

1. How do Paul and Tom feel when they reach the dry creekbed? Why?

   They feel tired because there was no water.

2. What details in the first paragraph help you figure out how the boys feel?

   Paul frowned, and I sighed.

3. What kind of danger are the boys in? What details help you understand the danger?

   The boys cannot find water. They find a creekbed for water only that they find it dry.

4. How does Paul feel when he remembers that they can get water from a cactus? How do you know his feelings change?

   Paul feels happier. It says that he grinned and slapped Tom's back.

5. How do the boys make use of what they have to get water?

   They use their knife to cut the cactus and a handkerchief to squeeze out the water.

6. Do you think that the task of filling the water bottles will be a fast one or a slow one? Why?

   A slow one because the text says there wasn't much water per squeeze.

Name _____

Suffixes Aflame

**Circle the words with the suffixes -*ful*, -*less*, and -*ly* in the flames.
Use the circled words to complete the story.**

OXV**POWERLESS**ABLE
BRIEFLYHMBRQZTEND
CAREFULLYTOAND
FINALLYOAD**BEAUTIFUL**
SER**MEANINGLESS**JUS
SKILLFULBLIYLFRCH
INCREDIBLYXGAN
HANDFULOZZMEK

Brian's strange dream at first seemed ___meaningless___, until he
realized that he needed a fire. In one ___handful___ after another,
he gathered tiny bits of ___beautiful___ white birch bark. He made
a nest out of the ___powderless___ fine bits of bark, but it stayed alight
only ___briefly___. He seemed ___powerless___
to keep the flame going. ___Finally___, he discovered how to fan
the flames with his breath. In time, he would become ___skillful___
at building a fire.

Which word has *two* suffixes?

___hopefully___

Name _____

Short Vowels

A short vowel sound is usually spelled *a, e, i, o,* or *u* and is followed by a consonant sound.

/ă/ cr**a**ft   /ĕ/ d**e**pth   /ĭ/ f**i**lm   /ŏ/ b**o**mb   /ŭ/ pl**u**nge

Write each Spelling Word under its short vowel sound.

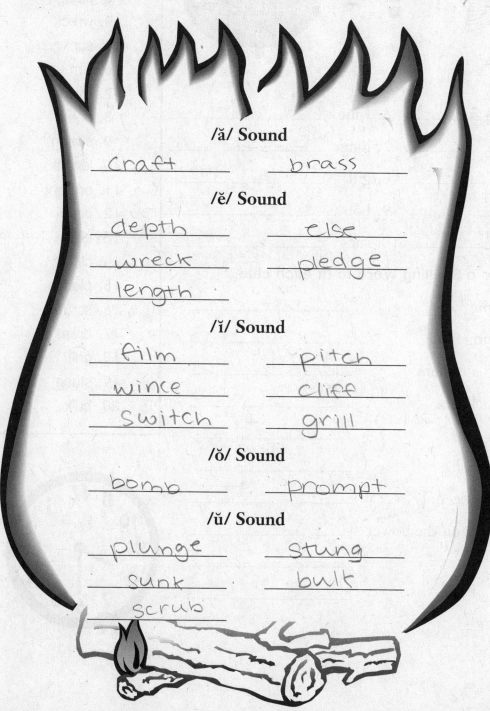

/ă/ Sound
craft   brass

/ĕ/ Sound
depth   else
wreck   pledge
length

/ĭ/ Sound
film   pitch
wince   cliff
switch   grill

/ŏ/ Sound
bomb   prompt

/ŭ/ Sound
plunge   stung
sunk   bulk
scrub

Spelling Words

1. depth
2. craft
3. plunge
4. wreck
5. sunk
6. film
7. wince
8. bomb
9. switch
10. length
11. prompt
12. pitch
13. else
14. cliff
15. pledge
16. scrub
17. brass
18. grill
19. stung
20. bulk

Name _____

Spelling Spree

Change the Word Write a Spelling Word by adding one letter
to each word below.

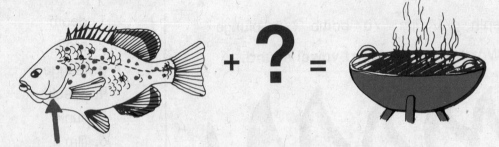

Spelling Words

1. depth
2. craft
3. plunge
4. wreck
5. sunk
6. film
7. wince
8. bomb
9. switch
10. length
11. prompt
12. pitch
13. else
14. cliff
15. pledge
16. scrub
17. brass
18. grill
19. stung
20. bulk

1. ledge _pledge_
2. bass _brass_
3. sun _sunk_
4. itch _pitch_
5. raft _craft_

6. wine _wince_
7. lunge _plunge_
8. gill _grill_
9. bob _bomb_
10. sung _stung_

Word Detective Write a Spelling Word to fit each clue.

11. great size or volume _bulk_
12. the measure of being long _length_
13. something used in a camera _film_
14. an overhanging rock face _cliff_
15. other or different _else_
16. what's left after a crash _wreck_
17. the quality of being deep _depth_
18. a device used to turn on the power _switch_
19. to clean very well _scrub_
20. right on time _____

Name _____

Proofreading and Writing

Proofreading Circle the five misspelled Spelling Words in this journal entry. Then write each word correctly.

I spent all day today starting a fire. Building a fire is a real craft! I began by trying to light pieces of a torn twenty-dollar bill. Then I decided to swich to strips of birch bark. I gathered some pieces of the right lenth and width and made them into a ball. I lit the ball with the sparks made by striking my hatchet against the rock wall. It was hard work, but I don't know what els I could have used to start the fire. I still winse when I think about another night without one. My next goal is to figure out how to make a gril that I can cook on.

1. _switch_
2. _length_
3. _else_
4. _wince_
5. _grill_

Spelling Words

1. depth
2. craft
3. plunge
4. wreck
5. sunk
6. film
7. wince
8. bomb
9. switch
10. length
11. prompt
12. pitch
13. else
14. cliff
15. pledge
16. scrub
17. brass
18. grill
19. stung
20. bulk

✏️━━━ **Write an Opinion** What do you think about the way the writer of this journal entry went about building a fire? Was there anything about his or her behavior that you admired? Is there anything you would have done differently?

On a separate piece of paper, write a paragraph in which you give your opinion of the writer's way of doing things. Use Spelling Words from the list.

Theme 1: **Courage**   11

Name _____

A Search for Meaning

Your friend doesn't know the meaning of some words in a story she's reading. Use context clues to help her figure out the underlined words, and then fill in the chart.

From a safe distance, Marcy squatted low and watched the burning storage barn. The flames were consuming one section after another, as though the building were an enormous meal. The fire left almost nothing behind, so she thought all the building materials must be flammable. She was gratified to hear sirens in the distance. Her 911 call had been heard.

Word	Clues from Context	Meaning
squatted		to bend you knees down low
consuming		
flammable		
gratified		

Name _____

What Is a Spiny Pig?

Kinds of Sentences A **declarative** sentence makes a statement. It ends with a **period**. An **interrogative** sentence asks a question. It ends with a **question mark**. An **imperative** sentence gives an order or makes a request. It ends with a **period**. An **exclamatory** sentence shows excitement or strong feeling. It ends with an **exclamation point**.

Add the correct end punctuation to each sentence. Then label each sentence *declarative, interrogative, imperative,* **or** *exclamatory.*

1. Porcupines are rodents.   _declaritive_

2. They have long, sharp quills.   _declaritive_

3. Treat all animals with respect.   _imperative_

4. Have you ever seen a porcupine?   _interrogative_

5. How big the tail is!   _exclamatory_

6. Do porcupines have fine or coarse fur?   _Interrogative_

7. Please let me see your porcupine quill.   _imperative_

8. What a sharp tip it has!   _exclamatory_

9. Did you know the word *porcupine* means "spiny pig" in Latin?
   interrogative

10. *Porcupine* comes from Latin *porcus* (meaning "pig") and *spina*
    (meaning "spine").   _declarative_

Name _____

Campfires Need . . .

Subjects and Predicates The **subject** of a sentence tells whom or what the sentence is about. The **complete subject** includes all the words in the subject. The **simple subject** is the main word or words of the complete subject.

The **predicate** tells what the subject does, is, has, or feels. The **complete predicate** includes all the words in the predicate. The **simple predicate** is the main word or words of the complete predicate.

Draw a line between the complete subject and the complete predicate in each sentence below. Then write the simple subject and the simple predicate on the lines.

1. Brianna \ needed kindling for a fire.

   Simple subject: _Brianna_

   Simple predicate: _needed_

2. A fire \ needs oxygen.

   Simple subject: _fire_

   Simple predicate: _needs_

3. A roaring fire \ will keep them warm.

   Simple subject: _fire_

   Simple predicate: _will keep_

4. The first spark \ has faded quickly.

   Simple subject: _spark_

   Simple predicate: _has faded_

5. I \ am learning about building safe campfires.

   Simple subject: _I_

   Simple predicate: _am learning_

Name _____

This and That

Combining Sentences A good writer avoids writing too many short,
choppy sentences. Combine short sentences by creating **compound
subjects** or **compound predicates.**

Moose live in these woods.
Caribou live in these woods too.

Compound Subject
Moose and caribou live in these woods.

I ate quickly.
I gulped my juice.

Compound Predicate
I ate quickly and gulped my juice.

Combine subjects or predicates in each group of sentences below.

Example: I sighed. Then I sat down.

I sighed and sat down.

1. Rebecca was prepared for an emergency.
   The other hikers were prepared for an emergency.

   Rebecca and the other hikers were prepared for an emerge

2. The scout built the fire.
   The scout stoked the fire.

   The scout built and stoked the fire.

3. Hatchets should be used with caution.
   Axes should be used with caution.
   Other sharp tools should be used with caution.

   Hatchets, axes, and other sharp tools should be used wit
   caution

4. The birch trees swayed in the wind.
   The birch trees creaked in the wind.

   The birch trees swayed and creaked in the wind.

5. Conrad will gather wood.
   Sam will gather wood.

   Conrad and Sam will gather wood.

Theme 1: **Courage**   15

Name _____

Writing Instructions

In *Hatchet*, Brian is stranded alone in the Canadian wilderness. The only tool he has is a hatchet. How could Brian explain to someone else how he used the hatchet to start a fire? **Instructions** tell readers how to do or make something. Good written instructions clearly explain the materials needed and the order in which the steps are to be followed.

Use this page to plan and organize your own written instructions. First, choose a process you would like to explain. Then list the materials that are needed. Finally, write each step in the process, giving details that readers will need to know.

How to _____

Materials	
Steps	**Details**
Step 1	
Step 2	
Step 3	
Step 4	
Step 5	

Using the information you recorded, write your instructions on a separate sheet of paper. You can either number each step or use sequence words such as *first, next,* and *finally*. Include diagrams or pictures to help readers picture this process.

Name _____

Using Sequence Words and Phrases

Following steps correctly is a matter of life or death for Brian in *Hatchet*. A careful writer gives clear instructions so that a reader can complete the steps in a process. Sequence words and phrases in instructions help readers understand a process and keep track of the order of steps.

The following page is from a first-aid manual. The instructions tell readers how to treat puncture wounds like those Brian suffered from the porcupine quills in his leg. In the blanks provided, add sequence words and phrases from the list to make the connection between steps clearer. Remember to capitalize sequence words as needed.

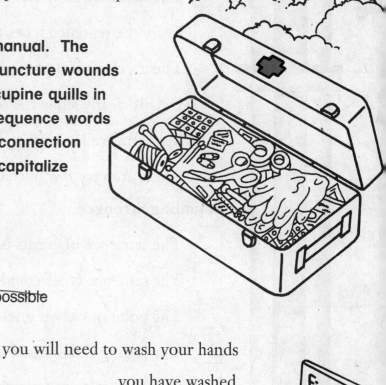

Sequence Words and Phrases

~~first~~	~~after~~	by the time
during	prior to	~~finally~~
before	~~then~~	~~as soon as possible~~

_____First_____, you will need to wash your hands with soap and water. _____After_____ you have washed your hands, remove the object with a pair of tweezers. _____Then_____ control any bleeding with direct pressure and elevation. Wash the puncture wound thoroughly with soap and water. _____Finally_____, cover the wound with a sterile dressing.

Check with a doctor to find out whether a tetanus shot is needed. If you see any signs of infection, such as pus, pain, redness around the wound, or a fever, call the doctor back _____as soon as possible_____.

Name _____

Revising Your Story

Reread your story. What do you need to make it better? Use this page to help you decide. Put a checkmark in the box for each sentence that describes your story.

Loud and Clear!

- [ ] The sequence of events is clear.
- [ ] I vary the sentence types to make my story read smoothly.
- [ ] The narrative is in my own voice and is interesting to read.
- [ ] Details clearly show the setting.
- [ ] My narrative has a satisfying ending that makes sense.
- [ ] There are very few mistakes.

Sounding Stronger

- [ ] The sequence of events is sometimes confusing.
- [ ] The sentence types could be more varied.
- [ ] The point of view is unclear.
- [ ] The setting is described in a general way.
- [ ] The ending isn't resolved well.
- [ ] Errors make parts of the story hard to follow.

Turn Up Volume

- [ ] My plot is a series of disconnected events.
- [ ] The sentence types are all the same.
- [ ] There is no consistent point of view.
- [ ] My story has no clear setting or conflict.
- [ ] Too many mistakes make the story hard to read.

Name _____

Improving Your Writing

Varying Sentences **Rewrite the paragraphs in the spaces provided. Each paragraph should include at least one example of each type of sentence: declarative, interrogative, imperative, and exclamatory.**

Backstage Pass
NO SENTENCE VARIATION
I shook hands with Whole New Crew! I was at their concert! I went backstage! I met Jeff! I met Pinky! I met Wanda! I met Therese! At first, I was so excited I could hardly breathe! And guess what — they ignored me! After a while it got boring! So we went home!

Backstage Pass
SENTENCE VARIATION
I shook hands with whole new crew! I was at their concert. I went backstage. I met Jeff. I met Pinky. I met Wanda. I met Therese. At first, I was so excit I could hardly breathe! And guess what? — th ignored me! After a while it got boring. So we went home.

Jalapeño Biscuits
NO SENTENCE VARIATION
Do I know how to make biscuits? Sort of. Did I put in the flour, butter, and baking powder? I did. Did I add jalapeño peppers? Accidentally. What did it taste like? It was sort of good. Then why did I end up running to get a drink of water? Because it was so HOT.

Jalapeño Biscuits
SENTENCE VARIATION
_____
_____
_____
_____
_____
_____

Early Start
NO SENTENCE VARIATION
The coach said to meet at 6 A.M. for Saturday's game. Anyone late would not play, the coach said. On Friday, I set my alarm for 5. I went to the field. Everyone was there — except the coach. We finally found her. Her car had broken down. She said, "I guess I don't get to play."

Early Start
SENTENCE VARIATION
_____
_____
_____
_____
_____

Name _____

Spelling Words

Most of the Spelling Words on this list are often misspelled because they are **homophones,** words that sound alike but have different meanings and spellings. Look for familiar spelling patterns to help you remember how to spell the words on this page. Think carefully about the parts that you find hard to spell in each word.

Write the missing letters and apostrophes in the Spelling Words below.

Spelling Words

1. your
2. you're
3. their
4. there
5. they're
6. its
7. it's
8. wouldn't
9. we're
10. to
11. too
12. that's
13. knew
14. know

1. y _o_ _u_ _r_ _____
2. you _'_ _____ _r_ _e_ _____
3. th _____ _e_ _____ _i_ _____ r
4. th _e_ _____ r _e_ _____
5. th _____ _e_ _____ _y_ _____ re
6. it _s_ _____
7. it _'_ _____ _s_ _____
8. w _o_ _____ _u_ _____ _l_ dn't
9. we _'_ _____ _r_ _e_ _____
10. t _o_ _____
11. t _o_ _____ _o_ _____
12. tha _t_ _____ _'_ _s_ _____
13. k _n_ _____ ew
14. _k_ _____ _n_ _____ ow

Study List **On a separate piece of paper, write each Spelling Word. Check your spelling against the words on the list.**

Name _____

Spelling Spree

Homophone Blanks The blanks in each of the following sentences can be filled with homophones from the Spelling Word list. Write the words in the correct order.

1–3. I think that _____ sitting over _____ on _____ blanket.
4–5. If you don't hurry, _____ going to miss _____ bus.
6–7. The pizza's still _____ hot _____ eat.
8–9. Since _____ so hot today, the school is letting _____ students go home early.

1–3. _they're, there, their_
4–5. _you're, your_
6–7. _too, to_
8–9. _it's, its_

Word Addition Write a Spelling Word by adding the beginning of the first word to the end of the second word.

10. than + Pat's
11. we'll + score
12. knack + flew
13. work + shouldn't
14. knight + grow

10. _that's_
11. _we're_
12. _knew_
13. _wouldn't_
14. _know_

Spelling Words

1. your
2. you're
3. their
4. there
5. they're
6. its
7. it's
8. wouldn't
9. we're
10. to
11. too
12. that's
13. knew
14. know

Name _____

Proofreading and Writing

Proofreading Circle the five misspelled Spelling Words in this poster. Then write each word correctly.

1. your
2. you're
3. their
4. there
5. they're
6. its
7. it's
8. wouldn't
9. we're
10. to
11. too
12. that's
13. knew
14. know

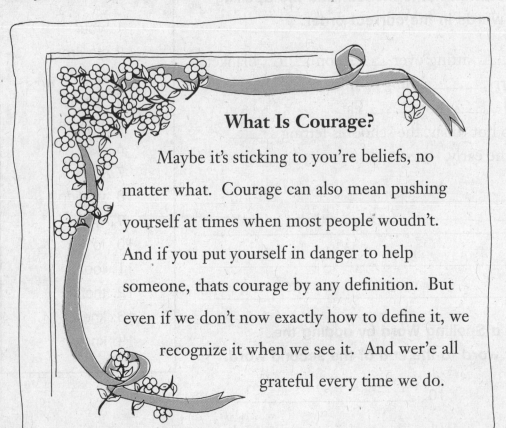

What Is Courage?

Maybe it's sticking to you're beliefs, no matter what. Courage can also mean pushing yourself at times when most people woudn't. And if you put yourself in danger to help someone, thats courage by any definition. But even if we don't now exactly how to define it, we recognize it when we see it. And wer'e all grateful every time we do.

1. _____ 4. _____

2. _____ 5. _____

3. _____

✏️➤ **Writing Headlines** Suppose that a newspaper were going to write articles covering the events that take place in each of the selections in this theme. What would some good headlines be?

On a separate piece of paper, write a headline for each selection in the theme. Use Spelling Words from the list.

Name _____

The Official Word

Read the word in each box below from *Passage to Freedom*.
Then write a word from the list that is related in meaning.
Use a dictionary if necessary.

bosses
documents
envoy
organization
choice
approval
victims

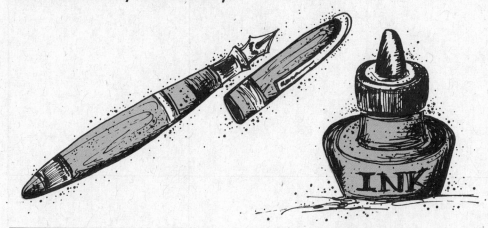

superiors	government	visas
_____	_____	_____

refugees	diplomat	decision
_____	_____	_____

permission
_____

Choose *three* words from the list above. Write a short paragraph
about what Hiroki Sugihara's father did in *Passage to Freedom*.

_____

_____

_____

_____

_____

Name _____

Judgments Chart

	Facts from the Selection	Own Values and Experiences	Judgment
What kind of person is Mr. Sugihara?			
Is Mr. Sugihara's decision right or wrong?			
What kind of a person is Hiroki's mother?			

Name _____

Award for a Hero

Complete the fact sheet below about Chiune Sugihara.
Then on a separate sheet of paper design an award that
honors Mr. Sugihara.

FACT SHEET

Who Chiune Sugihara was:	_____
Where he was from:	_____
	_____
Where he was working at the beginning of World War II:	_____
	_____
What his job was:	_____
	_____
	_____
Why people needed his help:	_____
	_____
What conflict he faced:	_____
	_____
	_____
	_____
What decision he made:	_____
	_____
	_____
Why he is remembered:	_____
	_____

Name _____

Judge for Yourself

Read the passage. Then answer the questions on page 27.

A South African Hero

In 1918, Nelson Mandela was born into a royal African family in South Africa. He was raised to be a chief, but instead chose to become a lawyer. He hoped to help blacks win equal rights in South Africa. At the time, the country was ruled by a white minority that discriminated against blacks. This policy was later called *apartheid*.

In the 1940s, Mandela earned his law degree. He helped set up the first black law firm in South Africa. He also joined the African National Congress (ANC), a group that worked to end apartheid. Mandela soon became a top official in the ANC and a leader of nonviolent protests.

The government cracked down on the ANC, however, and responded to peaceful protests with violence. In 1960, Mandela decided to abandon nonviolence and support armed struggle against apartheid. "The government left us no other choice," he said. Arrested several times for his work, he was tried for treason in 1963. At his trial, Mandela declared, "I have cherished the ideal of a democratic and free society. . . . It is an ideal which I hope to live for and to achieve. But if needs be, it is an ideal for which I am prepared to die."

Mandela was sentenced to life in prison and spent the next twenty-seven years behind bars. The struggle for equal rights in South Africa continued, however, and people around the world called for an end to apartheid. The government offered to free Mandela in exchange for his cooperation, but he refused. Finally, in 1990, the government released him from prison. He later won the Nobel Peace Prize and became South Africa's first black president. As president, Mandela called for peace and harmony in South Africa and tried to ensure equal rights for all South Africans.

Name _____

Judge for Yourself continued

Answer these questions about the passage on page 26.

1. What was important to Nelson Mandela as a young man?

   Peace and apartheid was important to Nelson
   Mandela as a young man.

2. What facts from the passage reveal his values as a young man?

   He won the Nobel Peace Prize and
   became South Africa's first black president.

3. Circle three words you would use to describe Nelson Mandela.

   (selfless)   (compassionate)   uninspired
   powerless   alienated   (determined)

4. Write each word you circled below. Then tell why you made that
   judgment about Mandela's character. Use facts from the passage to
   support your judgment.

Word	Reasons for Judgment
selfless	He wants to help others with the apartheid.
compassionate	He cares about others and just not himself.
determind	He wants to get rid of apartheid and won't stop trying.

5. How have your own experiences and beliefs helped you make a
   judgment about Nelson Mandela's character and actions?

   _____

   _____

Theme 1: **Courage**   27

Name _____

Sugihara Syllables

Write each underlined word on the line below. Add slashes between the syllables of each word. Then write another sentence using the word correctly.

1. My father was a Japanese <u>diplomat</u> working in Lithuania.

   _____

   _____

   _____

2. <u>Hundreds</u> of refugees gathered outside our house.

   _____

   _____

   _____

3. They needed <u>visas</u> to leave the country.

   _____

   _____

   _____

4. My father <u>replied</u> that he would help each one of the refugees.

   _____

   _____

   _____

5. My life changed <u>forever</u> because of my father's action.

   _____

   _____

   _____

TRACK 9

Name _____

Long Vowels

A long vowel sound may be spelled vowel-consonant-*e* or with two vowels written together.

/ā/ g**aze**, tr**ait**   /ē/ th**eme**, pr**each**, sl**ee**ve   /ī/ str**ive**

/ō/ qu**ote**, r**oam**   /yōō/ m**ute**

Write each Spelling Word under its long vowel sound.

1. theme
2. quote
3. gaze
4. pace
5. preach
6. strive
7. trait
8. mute
9. sleeve
10. roam
11. strain
12. fade
13. league
14. soak
15. grease
16. throne
17. fume
18. file
19. toast
20. brake

/ā/ Sound

_____

_____

_____

_____

_____

/ī/ Sound

_____

_____

/ō/ Sound

_____

_____

_____

_____

_____

/ē/ Sound

_____

_____

_____

_____

/yōō/ Sound

_____

_____

Theme 1: **Courage**   29

Name _____

Spelling Spree

The Third Word Write the Spelling Word that belongs with each group of words.

1. pocket, collar, _sleeve_
2. association, group, _league_
3. vapor, gas, _fume_
4. feature, quality, _____
5. crown, castle, _throne_
6. advise, counsel, _preach_
7. passage, excerpt, _____

Code Breaker Some Spelling Words have been written in code. Use the code below to figure out each word. Then write the words correctly.

CODE: J X B M S L T O W K E G C N I Z H
LETTER: A B D E F G H I K L M O R S T U V

8. LCMJNM _grease_   12. XCJWM _brake_
9. ITMEM _theme_   13. IGJNI _toast_
10. SOKM _file_   14. NGJW _soak_
11. SJBM _fade_   15. CGJE _roam_

Spelling Words

1. theme
2. quote
3. gaze
4. pace
5. preach
6. strive
7. trait
8. mute
9. sleeve
10. roam
11. strain
12. fade
13. league
14. soak
15. grease
16. throne
17. fume
18. file
19. toast
20. brake

Name _____

Proofreading and Writing

Proofreading Circle the five misspelled Spelling Words in this screenplay. Then write each word correctly.

Mr. Sugihara enters his home. He walks to a chair and collapses into it. He sits (muet) for a few seconds, and then he speaks.

MR. SUGIHARA: I've been filling out visas all day at an incredible (pase.) I don't know how much longer I can take the (strane.) . . . *(His voice begins to fade as his head droops to his chest.)*

MRS. SUGIHARA: *(She looks at her husband.)* I know, but you must think of the people. You can't just leave them to roam the countryside. They need a place to go.

MR. SUGIHARA: *(He slowly lifts his head and meets his wife's (gaiz.))* You're right, of course. I should (striv) to help as many as I can. If I don't, what will happen to them?

1. mute
2. pace
3. strain
4. gaze
5. strive

Spelling Words

1. theme
2. quote
3. gaze
4. pace
5. preach
6. strive
7. trait
8. mute
9. sleeve
10. roam
11. strain
12. fade
13. league
14. soak
15. grease
16. throne
17. fume
18. file
19. toast
20. brake

Write a Persuasive Letter You have a chance to send Mr. Sugihara a letter on behalf of the refugees. You know he is unsure of what action to take. What will you write to convince him to help them?

On a separate piece of paper, write a persuasive letter to Mr. Sugihara. Include several reasons why he should help the refugees. Use Spelling Words from the list.

Name _____

Word-Order Sets

For each set of words, decide which two would be the guide words if all three words were on a dictionary page. On each "page," write the guide words in the correct order on the first line, and the other word on the line below.

office	ceiling	gown	refugees	emergency
offer	celery	government	refuse	embody
offside	celebration	gourmet	refrigerator	embraced

offer _____ offside

office

ceiling _____ celery

celebration

gourmet _____ gown

government

refridgerator _____ refuse

refugees

embody _____ emergency

embraced

Name _____

Safety and Freedom

Conjunctions A **conjunction** is a word that connects words or sentences. The words *and*, *but*, and *or* are conjunctions.

In each sentence below, add a conjunction. Then on the line, write *words* or *sentences* to show what the conjunction joins.

Example: The escape was risky ___and___ frightening.
___words___

1. The diplomat had courage, ___and___ he had compassion.
   ___sentences___

2. He knew it was risky, ___but___ he helped the people.
   ___sentences___

3. His children could not see their friends ___or___ teachers.
   ___words___

4. His wife ___and___ family members agreed to help.
   ___words___

5. The women, men, ___and___ children escaped to a safer place.
   ___words___

Theme 1: **Courage** 33

Name _____

Should We Run, or Should We Hide?

Compound Sentences A **compound sentence** is two simple sentences
joined by a comma and a conjunction (*and*, *but*, or *or*).

Add a comma followed by *and*, *but*, **or** *or* **to combine the simple
sentences below into compound sentences.**

> **Example:** Our escape was dangerous. We made it safely.
>
> Our escape was dangerous, but we made it safely.

1. World War II brought many hardships. People showed great courage.

   World War II brought many hardships, but
   people showed great courage.

2. Have you read any books about that war? Did you see any movies
   about it?

   Have you read any books or movies about
   that war?

3. Bombs fell in many places. They did not fall in America.

   Bombs fell in many places, but they did not
   fall in America.

4. My great-grandfather was in the Navy. He showed me his uniform.

   My great-grandfather was in the Navy, and he
   showed me his uniform

5. Our town built a war memorial in the park. My class went to see it.

   Our town built a war memorial in the park and
   my class went to see it.

Name _____

I Can Speak Italian, but I Can't Speak Japanese

Combining Sentences: Compound Sentences Sometimes combining short, choppy sentences into longer sentences makes your writing more interesting. Use a comma and *and*, *but*, or *or* to combine sentences.

Lee has written a letter to Aunt Lucy. Revise the letter by combining simple sentences to make compound sentences. Insert your marks on, above, and below the line, as shown in the example. The last sentence will not change.

Tomorrow I'd like to go to the zoo. I'd like to visit Mel.
, or

Dear Aunt Lucy,

I think I'd like to be a diplomat someday. I don't know

where I'd like to live. Italy would be an interesting place to

live. I might live in Japan. You taught me to speak Italian.
or but

I don't know anyone who can teach me Japanese. Maybe I

could study it in school. I could study Japanese history too.

My teacher visited Japan. He showed us beautiful pictures.
and

The next time I visit, may I see your photos of Italy?

Love,
Lee

Name _____

Writing a Memo

Chiune Sugihara was a diplomat in Lithuania in 1940. He probably wrote different forms of business communication, such as letters, reports, and memos. A **memo** is a brief, informal message that is sent from one person to others in the same company, group, or organization.

Imagine that you are Mr. Sugihara. Plan and organize a memo to your superiors in the Japanese government about the plight of the Jewish refugees from Poland. Follow these steps:

1. Name the person or persons to whom you are writing the memo.
2. Tell who is writing the memo.
3. Write the date.
4. Identify the subject of the memo.
5. Write the body of the memo. Begin by stating your reason for writing. Use clear, direct language and a business-like tone. Be brief but include all the important information. If you want a response, end by asking a question or by requesting that a specific action be taken.

To: Dad

From: Merci

Date: 9/3/15

Subject: Group Meeting

On Saturday, I will go to the park a 2:00 - 4:00. It is for a group meeting.

Copy your memo on a separate sheet of paper and exchange it with a classmate. Then, using the format above, write a response memo from the officials in the Japanese government to Chiune Sugihara in which you deny him permission to grant visas to the Polish refugees.

Name _____

Capitalizing and Punctuating Sentences

To communicate effectively, a writer must write sentences correctly. When you write, remember to begin all sentences with a capital letter and to capitalize the names of people and places. Also, remember to end sentences with a period, a question mark, or an exclamation mark.

Proofread the following memo. Look for errors in capitalizing and punctuating sentences. Use these proofreading marks to add the necessary capital letters and end punctuation.

⊙   Add a period.   ! ∧   Add an exclamation mark.

≡   Make a capital letter.   ? ∧   Add a question mark.

To: Mrs. Masue Okimoto, Office Manager

From: Mr. Kenji Hamano

Date: August 25, 1940

Subject: Request for Office Supplies

my assistant boris Lavhas informed me that we need to restock some

office supplies will you kindly send the items listed below ?

1. two hundred visas and permission forms

2. one dozen fountain pens

3. two dozen bottles of ink

please ship these supplies to my office in lithuania immediately ⊙

thank you for your prompt action in this matter ⊙

Name _____

Complete the Climb

Complete each sentence about mountain climbing with the correct word from the list.

Vocabulary

carabiners
pitons
foothold
desperate
improvising
belay
ice ax
overcome
functioned
fatigue

1. Metal spikes with a hole at the end through which you

   pass a rope are called _____.

2. Metal rings you use to attach rope to pitons are called

   _____.

3. To cut into the ice and support your upper body while

   climbing, you might use an _____.

4. In order to remain steady on your feet, it is important to

   find a secure _____.

5. If you and another climber are helping each other climb up the

   mountain while attached to the same rope, you are

   on _____.

6. Do not push yourself too hard, or you may experience

   extreme _____.

7. If you get lost and feel nearly hopeless that help will arrive,

   you feel _____.

8. If you don't have the proper equipment, you might look for other

   tools you have and try _____.

9. If you climb cautiously and with safety in mind, you will never

   have to face an obstacle you won't be able to _____.

10. Safe climbers have always _____

    as role models for others.

Name _____

Event Chart

1. **Page 75** At first Danielle hits the rock with Dad's hammer. Then she

   _____

2. **Page 77** The hammers work. Next, Jake and Danielle

   _____

3. **Page 78** Danielle gets to the top of the trench first. Then she

   _____

4. **Pages 80–81** Jake and Danielle are happy to be at the top. Then they realize

   _____

5. **Page 82** Crying, Jake and Danielle hug each other. Then Danielle pushes Jake
   away. Suddenly, Jake realizes that she is

   _____

6. **Page 84** Through the clouds, they see

   _____

7. **Pages 84–85** Danielle is getting weaker. When they finally knock on the
   weather station door,

   _____

8. **Page 86** Jake improvises by _____ As a

   result, _____

Name _____

Interview with the Ice Climbers

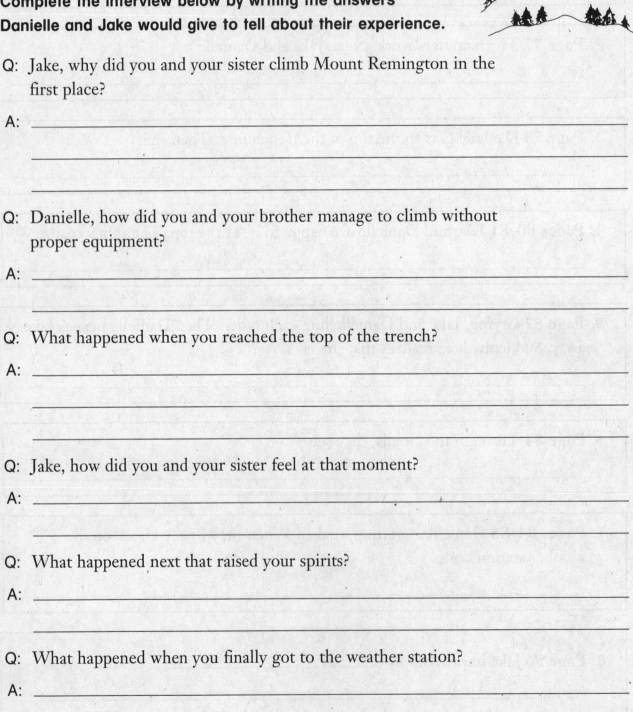

**Complete the interview below by writing the answers
Danielle and Jake would give to tell about their experience.**

Q: Jake, why did you and your sister climb Mount Remington in the
first place?

A: _____

_____

_____

Q: Danielle, how did you and your brother manage to climb without
proper equipment?

A: _____

_____

Q: What happened when you reached the top of the trench?

A: _____

_____

_____

Q: Jake, how did you and your sister feel at that moment?

A: _____

_____

Q: What happened next that raised your spirits?

A: _____

_____

Q: What happened when you finally got to the weather station?

A: _____

_____

Name _____

Then What Happened?

Read the passage. Then complete the activity on page 42.

A Day Hike

"I'm so glad you're okay!" Elaine's dad said as he hugged her close. "But what were you thinking, wandering off like that?"

The events of the past hour came rushing back to Elaine. She had been hiking along behind her mom and dad, enjoying the mountain scenery and warm summer day. Then she had stopped to look at some wildflowers. The flowers spread away from the path and down into a meadow. Elaine had wandered off the trail and into the meadow. While her parents had continued hiking up the trail, Elaine had lain on her stomach, peering at hundreds of pink, yellow, and blue blossoms.

A few minutes later she had heard a sound. When she looked up, she couldn't believe her eyes. Fifty yards away stood a mountain lion, staring straight at her! Elaine had frozen, her heart pounding. Should she lie still? Should she run? Then she remembered what her parents had told her the summer before. "If you ever see a mountain lion," they had said, "stay as still as you can. Sudden moves could cause the lion to attack."

Elaine had stayed as still as she could. The lion had watched her for a moment, and then had begun to edge closer. At that moment, her mom and dad had rushed up. As they ran into the meadow, the lion turned and slipped away into the woods. That was when Elaine had collapsed into her father's arms.

Name _____

Then What Happened? continued

Complete the sequence chart to show the order of events in the passage on page 41. Begin the chart with an event that happened the year before the events described in the passage.

```
┌─────────────────────────────────────────────────────────┐
│ _____     │
│ _____     │
└─────────────────────────────────────────────────────────┘
                            ↓
┌─────────────────────────────────────────────────────────┐
│ _____     │
│ _____     │
└─────────────────────────────────────────────────────────┘
                            ↓
┌─────────────────────────────────────────────────────────┐
│ _____     │
│ _____     │
└─────────────────────────────────────────────────────────┘
                            ↓
┌─────────────────────────────────────────────────────────┐
│ _____     │
│ _____     │
└─────────────────────────────────────────────────────────┘
                            ↓
┌─────────────────────────────────────────────────────────┐
│ _____     │
│ _____     │
└─────────────────────────────────────────────────────────┘
                            ↓
┌─────────────────────────────────────────────────────────┐
│ _____     │
└─────────────────────────────────────────────────────────┘
                            ↓
┌─────────────────────────────────────────────────────────┐
│ _____     │
│ _____     │
└─────────────────────────────────────────────────────────┘
```

Now go back to the passage and underline the sentences that tell where two different events happened at the same time. Circle the sequence words that helped you to figure this out.

Name _____

Prefix Clues

**Underline the word in each sentence that has the prefix *un-* or *re-*.
Then write a meaning for the word on the line below the sentence.**

Prefix	Meaning
un-	not
re-	again, back, backward

1. The hikers agreed to reassemble at the summit.

   _____

2. Some of them were unprepared for such a long hike.

   _____

3. They reconsidered their plan and turned back.

   _____

4. Jake felt unsteady on the narrow ledge.

   _____

5. He had renewed energy after eating a banana.

   _____

6. Danielle rearranged the contents of her bag, looking for the map.

   _____

7. Only when the bag was completely unpacked did she find the map.

   _____

8. When they reexamined the map, they saw that they did not have far to go.

   _____

9. Since the day was clear, they had an unobscured view of the valley.

   _____

10. Despite the unusually warm weather, it was cold on the summit.

   _____

Name _____

More Vowel Spellings

Remember these less common spellings for some long and short
vowel sounds:

/ē/ *i*-consonant-*e* (rout**ine**)   /ī/ *y* (c**y**cle)

/ĕ/ *ea* (sw**ea**t)   /ĭ/ *y* (rh**y**thm)   /ŭ/ *o*-consonant-*e* (sh**ove**)

Write each Spelling Word under its vowel sound.

Spelling Words

1. cycle
2. sweat
3. rhythm
4. rely
5. pleasant
6. routine
7. cleanse
8. shove
9. reply
10. meant
11. sponge
12. apply
13. threat
14. myth
15. deny
16. leather
17. rhyme
18. thread
19. meadow
20. ravine

/ĕ/ Sound

_____

/ē/ Sound

_____

_____

/ī/ Sound

_____

_____

_____

_____

_____

/ĭ/ Sound

_____

_____

/ŭ/ Sound

_____

Name _____

Spelling Spree

Word Changes Write a Spelling Word to fit each clue.

1. Drop two letters from *really* to write a word meaning "to depend."
2. Change a letter in *moth* to write a synonym for *legend*.
3. Drop a consonant from *shovel* to write a word meaning "to push."
4. Replace a consonant in *great* with two letters to write a synonym for *danger*.
5. Change a letter in *repay* to write a synonym for *respond*.
6. Replace two letters in *circle* with one to write a shorthand word for riding a bike.
7. Add a consonant to *peasant* to write a word meaning "enjoyable."
8. Replace a consonant in *leader* with two letters to write a word that names a clothing material.

1. _____   5. _____

2. _____   6. _____

3. _____   7. _____

4. _____   8. _____

Word Addition Write a Spelling Word by adding the beginning of the first word to the end of the second word.

9. throne   +   bread   = _____

10. deal   +   funny   = _____

11. approach +   fly   = _____

12. swing   +   defeat   = _____

13. rat   +   thyme   = _____

14. spoke   +   range   = _____

 + = **?**

Theme 1: **Courage**   45

Proofreading and Writing

Proofreading Circle the six misspelled Spelling Words in this travel poster. Then write each word correctly.

You Need a Vacation!

Get away from the daily routeen and head for the mountains! You will clenz your body and your mind with a week of restful hiking and climbing. Follow well-marked trails to a pleasant meddow. Test your climbing skills as you explore a scenic ravene. Delight in the beauty and rythm of nature. You'll discover that the mountains are the place you were ment to be!

---

1. _____   4. _____

2. _____   5. _____

3. _____   6. _____

Spelling Words

1. cycle
2. sweat
3. rhythm
4. rely
5. pleasant
6. routine
7. cleanse
8. shove
9. reply
10. meant
11. sponge
12. apply
13. threat
14. myth
15. deny
16. leather
17. rhyme
18. thread
19. meadow
20. ravine

Write a Comparison and Contrast How does the portrayal of hiking and climbing in the poster above compare with the experience that Danielle and Jake had in the selection? Is one more realistic than the other? Is there anything missing from both accounts?

On a separate piece of paper, write a paragraph in which you compare and contrast the two descriptions. Use Spelling Words from the list.

46   Theme 1: **Courage**

Dictionary Deciphering

Read the dictionary entries. Follow each numbered instruction.

des•o•late (dĕs′ ə lĭt) *adj.* Having few or no inhabitants; deserted: *an abandoned shack on a desolate road.* —*v.* (dĕs′ ə lāt′). *des•o•lat•ed, des•o•lat•ing, des•o•lates.* To make lonely, forlorn, or wretched: *The loss of our old dog desolated us.* —**des′o•late•ly** *adv.*

im•pro•vise (ĭm′ prə vīz′) *v.* **im•pro•vised, im•pro•vis•ing, im•pro•vis•es. 1.** To invent or perform without preparation: *The comics improvised several scenes based on audience suggestions.* **2.** To make on the spur of the moment from materials found nearby: *The hikers improvised a bridge out of fallen logs.* —**im′pro•vis′•er** *n.*

stag•ger (stăg′ ər) *v.* **stag•gered, stag•ger•ing, stag•gers. 1.** To move or stand unsteadily; totter. **2.** To begin to lose confidence or sense of purpose; waver.

tex•ture (tĕks′ chər) *n.* **1.** The structure of the interwoven threads or strands of a fabric: *Burlap has a coarse texture.* **2.** The appearance and feel of a surface: *The plaster gives the wall a rough texture.*

1. Write a sample sentence for the first definition of *stagger*.

   I staggered toward the building.

2. Write a sentence using the noun *improviser*.

   My friend is a very good improvisor.

3. Write a sentence using the second definition of *texture*.

   The texture of syrup is very thick.

4. Write a sentence using the adjective *desolate*.

   This is a desolate island.

Name _____

After I Prepared, I Climbed the Mountain

Complex Sentences A clause contains both a subject and a predicate. An independent clause can stand by itself as a sentence. A subordinate clause cannot stand by itself as a sentence. A **complex sentence** has at least one subordinate clause and one independent clause.

A subordinate clause contains a subordinating conjunction. Here are some subordinating conjunctions:

after	because	since	when
although	before	unless	whenever
as	if	until	while

Join the two sentences using the subordinating conjunction shown in parentheses. Write the new complex sentence on the line.

1. You should not try to climb a mountain. You have prepared properly. (until)

   You should not try to climb a mountain until you have prepared properly

2. They begin climbing. Skilled climbers check their equipment. (before)

   Skilled climbers check their equipment before they begin climbing.

3. They reached the peak. They enjoyed the view. (when)

   They enjoyed the view when they reached the peak,

4. Danielle and Jack reached their goal. They could improvise. (because)

   Danielle and Jack reached their goal because they could improvise

5. I want to visit the weather station. I climb Mount Washington. (if)

   I want to visit the weather station if I climb Mount Washington.

Name _____

Before I Climbed

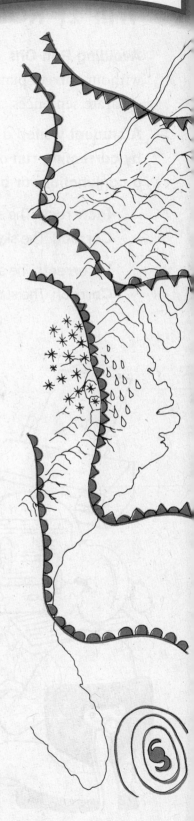

Correcting Fragments A **sentence fragment** does not express a complete thought. Correct a fragment by adding a subject or a predicate or both.

A **run-on sentence** expresses too many thoughts without correct punctuation. Correct a run-on sentence by creating separate sentences, a compound sentence, or a complex sentence.

Read the following sentence fragments or run-on sentences. Correct the problem, and write a new sentence on the line. There is more than one way to fix each sentence.

1. Because the weather can change quickly.

    _____

    _____

2. Meteorologists predict the daily weather, they make long-range forecasts.

    _____

    _____

3. This weather station has recorded the highest wind speeds. And the coldest temperatures in the state.

    _____

    _____

4. Visitors learn how a barometer works they get a tour of the weather station.

    _____

    _____

5. When the next storm comes.

    _____

    _____

Name _____

Will It Rain?

Avoiding Run-Ons A **run-on sentence** expresses too many thoughts
without correct punctuation. Correct a run-on sentence by creating
separate sentences, a compound sentence, or a complex sentence.

**A student visited a weather station and wrote the following. Revise it
by correcting run-on sentences. You might need to add punctuation,
a conjunction, or both. Here are two examples:**

> **Incorrect:** The sky is cloudy I think it will rain.
> **Correct:** The sky is cloudy. I think it will rain.

> **Incorrect:** The sun came out it was still cold.
> **Correct:** The sun came out, **but** it was still cold.

I want to be a weather forecaster someday. a big
storm would be exciting. A snowstorm can cause traffic
accidents. high winds can bring down power lines. I
would want to be accurate. an accurate forecast helps
people prepare for bad weather. I might be a scientist at
a weather station. I might work at a television station.
Because I want to be a weather scientist I will study
science.

Name _____

Writing a Friendly Letter

A **friendly letter** is a letter that you write to a friend to share news about what is happening in your life.

Use this page to help you plan and organize a friendly letter. Either write a letter that Jake or Danielle might have written to a friend about climbing to the Mount Remington weather station, or write a letter to a friend of yours in which you share a recent experience or adventure of your own. Follow these steps:

1. Write a **heading** (your address and the date) and a **greeting** (*Dear* and the person's name followed by a comma).
2. Write the **body** of your letter below the greeting. Begin by writing something that shows you care about the friend to whom you are writing. At the end of the letter, ask your friend to write back soon.
3. Write an informal **closing** such as *Love* or *Your friend* followed by a comma in the lower right corner. Then sign your name under the closing.

Heading _____

_____

_____

Greeting _____

Body _____

_____

_____

_____

_____

Closing _____

Signature _____

When you finish your friendly letter, copy it onto a clean sheet of paper. If you wrote your letter to a friend, address an envelope and mail it!

Name _____

Voice

Every writer has a **voice**, or a unique way of saying things. This voice
reflects the writer's personality and manner of expression. You can express
your own personal voice in writing by using the following techniques:

► Make what you say sound like you.

► Include expressions and figures of speech you might use when speaking.
When Danielle reaches the summit of Mount Remington and does not
see the weather station, for example, she tells Jake "We're dead" to
express her feelings of hopelessness.

► Write in a way that reflects your thoughts and feelings.

**Think about how you express yourself in different situations. What do
you usually say if you are upset or frustrated? On the lines below, write
expressions and figures of speech that you might use to convey different
feelings.**

My Personal List of Expressions and Figures of Speech

_____   _____

(to express fear)   (to express worry)

_____   _____

(to express relief)   (to express confusion)

_____   _____

(to express joy)   (to express surprise)

_____   _____

(to express doubt)   (to express helplessness)

_____   _____

(to express sympathy)   (to express excitement)

**When you revise your friendly letter, use several of these expressions
and figures of speech to reflect your personal voice. By adding some
of these expressions, you can make what you say sound more like
you — as if you are speaking directly to your friend.**

Name _____

A Test of Courage

Use these words to complete the sentences below.

Vocabulary

ascent
entangled
seasoned
endeavored
rigging
ratlines
treacherous

1. Are you a _____ sailor, or is this
   your first voyage?

2. To prove that you will be an able sailor, you must climb to
   the top of the _____.

3. To start your climb, grab one of the _____,
   the small ropes that form a ladder.

4. As you continue your _____
   upward, be careful not to become entangled in the ropes.

5. Rain and wind make the climb even more _____
   than it usually is.

6. I have _____ to give you guidance, but you
   must find courage within yourself to make the climb.

**Use two vocabulary words in a short description of what it might
feel like to make the climb described above.**

_____

_____

_____

Name _____

Predictions Chart

selection details + personal knowledge + THINKING = prediction

Selection Details page 99	**Personal Knowledge**
▶ Charlotte must climb the tallest mast to prove her worth. _____ _____	_____ _____ _____

Prediction: _____

Selection Details page 105	**Personal Knowledge**
▶ Charlotte makes it to just below the top gallant spar. _____ _____	_____ _____ _____

Prediction: _____

Selection Details page 107	**Personal Knowledge**
▶ Charlotte begins her climb down. _____ _____	_____ _____ _____

Prediction: _____

Selection Details page 105	**Personal Knowledge**
▶ Captain Jaggery appears on deck. _____ _____	_____ _____ _____

Prediction: _____

Name _____

A Day on the *Seahawk*

Answer the questions about the setting, characters, and plot of
The True Confessions of Charlotte Doyle.

1. Where is Charlotte when the story begins?

   _____

2. What does she have to do to become a member of the crew?

   _____

3. Why doesn't Charlotte start over again after she realizes she has begun to climb the wrong set of rigging?

   _____

4. After the ship dips, how does Charlotte feel about her decision to climb?

   _____

5. How long does it take Charlotte to climb to a point on the mast that a seasoned sailor could reach in two minutes?

   _____

6. Why is climbing near the top of the mast more difficult than climbing closer to the bottom?

   _____

7. Why is climbing down the rigging more difficult than climbing up?

   _____

8. How does the crew react when Charlotte finally returns safely to the deck?

   _____

Name _____

You Guessed It!

Read the story. Then complete the activity on page 57.

The Deep End

Manning flopped around in his bed like a fish. A moment before, he had been sinking to the bottom of a swimming pool. He heard muffled shouts coming from above. He flailed his arms, but it was no use. He just kept sinking. His father's voice roused him from his dream. "Are you ready for your first day of lifeguard training?" Manning groaned.

Rough and Ready Summer Camp was just about the only place around that gave summer jobs to teenagers younger than eighteen. Manning needed money for a backpacking trip to the Rocky Mountains in the fall. He needed to buy a train ticket to Montana. He needed a new backpack and new hiking boots. He needed a job!

He had applied for the position of assistant counselor. He got the job, but was then dismayed to find out that, like all counselors at the camp, he needed to go through lifeguard training. He was a capable swimmer, but he had one discomfort that had been with him all his life: he did not like to be in deep water. In fact, being in water over his head terrified him.

At ten o'clock training began at Taft Pool. The trainer announced that first they would take a swimming test—ten laps of freestyle. "When I blow my whistle, dive in and start swimming," he said. "This is not a race," he added, "it's a test of your endurance."

Manning's heart was pounding. He knew he'd be fine in the shallow water, but what would happen when he reached the deep end? "Swimmers, on your mark!" the trainer called. Manning got into diving position. At the shrill sound of the whistle, he took a deep breath and dove. His body hit the water smoothly, and he fell into an even stroke.

"Just breathe," he told himself as he swam toward the deep end. He concentrated on his stroke. To his relief, he didn't panic as he passed the five-foot marker on the side of the pool. Nor did he panic when he passed the eight-foot marker. By the time he reached the far side of the pool, he was just hitting his best rhythm. He flipped himself around and started back toward the shallow end.

56   Theme 1: **Courage**

Name _____

You Guessed It! continued

Answer these questions about the passage on page 56.

1. Do you think Manning will successfully complete lifeguard training? Why or why not?

   _____

   _____

2. What information in the story might lead you to predict that Manning will not complete the training?

   _____

   _____

3. At which point in the story might you change your prediction?

   _____

   _____

4. What do you think Manning will do with the money he earns as assistant counselor?

   _____

   _____

5. The following statements are generally true in real life. Which statement helps you predict that Manning will most likely succeed in lifeguard training? Circle it.

   A. People often avoid what they fear.
   B. People will often face a difficult challenge to get something they really want.
   C. Good friends help each other through hard times.

Name _____

Book Report Rewrite

Underline each contraction or possessive in this book report. Then, on the lines below, rewrite the report, replacing each contraction or possessive with its longer form.

> The True Confessions of Charlotte Doyle
> by Avi
>
> Charlotte dresses in sailor's garb and asks to be accepted as a crew member. "You're a girl" is Dillingham's reply. "What'll the captain say?" Charlotte doesn't want to think about the task she must perform, but she's determined.
> Charlotte's climb is terrifying, but it's nothing compared to her descent. I'd highly recommend this book to adventure lovers. The book's author has also written many other entertaining stories.

_____

_____

_____

_____

_____

_____

_____

Name _____

The /ou/, /o͝o/, /ô/, and /oi/ Sounds

Remember these spelling patterns for the /ou/, the /o͝o/, the /ô/, and the /oi/ sounds:

/ou/ *ou* st**ou**t   /ô/ *au, aw, ough, augh*
/o͝o/ *oo* bl**oo**m   v**au**lt, squ**aw**k, s**ough**t, n**augh**ty

                                /oi/ *oi, oy* av**oi**d, ann**oy**

Write each Spelling Word under its vowel sound.

/ou/ Sound

_____

_____

_____

_____

_____

/o͝o/ Sound

_____

_____

_____

_____

/ô/ Sound

_____

_____

_____

_____

_____

_____

/oi/ Sound

_____

_____

_____

Spelling Words

1. bloom
2. stout
3. droop
4. crouch
5. annoy
6. vault
7. squawk
8. avoid
9. sought
10. naughty
11. mound
12. groove
13. foul
14. hoist
15. gloom
16. trout
17. noun
18. roost
19. clause
20. appoint

Name _____

Spelling Spree

Find a Rhyme **Write a Spelling Word that rhymes with the underlined word.**

1. If you _____ down, you can see the kangaroo's <u>pouch</u>.

2. The baseball player <u>found</u> his glove near the pitcher's _____.

3. Please <u>pause</u> while I find the _____ in this sentence.

4. I think I can see this bird's _____, if you give me a <u>boost</u>.

5. Every plant in the gardener's <u>room</u> was starting to _____.

6. Don't <u>pout</u> just because you didn't catch a _____ today.

1. _____   4. _____

2. _____   5. _____

3. _____   6. _____

Word Search **Find nine Spelling Words in the Word Search below. Circle each word as you find it, and then write the words in order.**

S H O I S T E R N O U N I N G A V O I D A N

S F O U L S T E G R O O V E D U N V A U L T R U

G L O O M D I A P P O I N T A N A U G H T Y A R N

7. _____   12. _____

8. _____   13. _____

9. _____   14. _____

10. _____   15. _____

11. _____

Spelling Words

1. bloom
2. stout
3. droop
4. crouch
5. annoy
6. vault
7. squawk
8. avoid
9. sought
10. naughty
11. mound
12. groove
13. foul
14. hoist
15. gloom
16. trout
17. noun
18. roost
19. clause
20. appoint

Name _____

Proofreading and Writing

Proofreading Circle the five misspelled Spelling Words in this part of a letter. Then write each word correctly.

> Dear Mother,
>
> A most unusual event took place onboard today. Miss Charlotte Doyle, a young woman who saught to join the crew, managed to hoist herself to the top of the royal yard. Many of the crew had expected her to fail, and her success seemed to anoy more than a few of them. One sailor's response was to let his shoulders droup noticeably. Another let loose a rude squak and said, "She was just lucky." Personally, I think Miss Doyle has a stowt heart and will be a valuable addition to the ship.

1. bloom
2. stout
3. droop
4. crouch
5. annoy
6. vault
7. squawk
8. avoid
9. sought
10. naughty
11. mound
12. groove
13. foul
14. hoist
15. gloom
16. trout
17. noun
18. roost
19. clause
20. appoint

1. _____ 4. _____

2. _____ 5. _____

3. _____

━━━ **Write a Character Sketch** What does Charlotte Doyle's behavior tell you about her? What do you think about her ability to make herself climb to the top of the royal yard?

On a separate piece of paper, write a character sketch in which you describe Charlotte. Use Spelling Words from the list.

Name _____

Word Family Matters

Decide which word best completes each sentence. Write the word in the blank.

1. The puppy barked ____horribly____ when our older dog was let out at night.

2. My ____advice____ to you is to hike with a friend.

3. I hope you ____enjoy____ your school vacation.

4. I don't ____normally____ eat six cookies at lunchtime.

5. Why does my brother ____normalize____ everything I say?

Now write a sentence using two words you haven't used yet.

_____

_____

Name _____

Charlotte and the Navy

Common and Proper Nouns A **common noun** names a person, a place,
a thing, or an idea. A **proper noun** names a particular person, place,
thing, or idea. Each important word in a proper noun is capitalized.

**Determine which nouns in the following sentences are proper nouns
and which are common nouns. List the nouns in the proper columns
below the sentences.**

    Example: New Mexico is a state in the United States.

        Proper Nouns   **Common Nouns**

        New Mexico   state

        United States

1. Charlotte Doyle wanted to be a sailor.
2. My big sister joined the U.S. Navy.
3. Her ship is called *The Piedmont*.
4. Last year, she sailed to Hawaii.
5. The crew is sailing in the Atlantic Ocean now.

    Proper Nouns   **Common Nouns**

_____   _____

_____   _____

_____   _____

_____   _____

_____   _____

Name _____

Foxes and Deer

Singular and Plural Nouns A **singular noun** names one person, place, thing, or idea. A **plural noun** names more than one person, place, thing, or idea. To form the plural of most nouns, simply add -s or -es to the singular form. Some nouns have the same singular and plural forms, and some nouns have unusual plural forms. Study the examples below.

Singular	Plural	Singular	Plural
ship	ship**s**	chur**ch**	church**es**
walt**z**	waltz**es**	d**ay**	day**s**
Jone**s**	Jones**es**	di**sh**	dish**es**
sol**o**	solo**s**	scar**f**	scar**ves**
bo**ss**	boss**es**	fo**x**	fox**es**
coun**ty**	count**ies**	deer	**deer**

Compare the spelling pattern of each singular noun below to the ones in the list above. Then write the correct plural form. You may use a dictionary.

Singular   Plural

1. box   _____

2. city   _____

3. toss   _____

4. leaf   _____

5. watch   _____

6. cap   _____

7. ash   _____

8. yes   _____

9. zoo   _____

10. toy   _____

Ms. Doyle and President Kim

Capitalization and Punctuation of People's Titles A title before a person's name is capitalized. When a title is abbreviated, it is followed by a period.

> **Examples:** I will introduce **Ms.** Clara Kindowsky.
> The press interviewed **President** Carter.

Rewrite each sentence below. Use correct punctuation and capitalization for titles.

1. The sailors saluted captain Smith and lieutenant Lee.

   _____

   _____

2. A member of the crew approached Capt Smith and dr. Tilton.

   _____

   _____

3. Dr Tilton visited ensign Johnson, who was sick.

   _____

   _____

4. I recommend either mr. Kim or Mrs Ortiz for the position.

   _____

   _____

5. Mrs Ellison and principal Lesnikoski stood in the hallway.

   _____

   _____

Theme 1: **Courage**   65

Name _____

Writing an Opinion Paragraph

An **opinion** is a strong belief or conclusion that may or may not be
supported by facts and reasons. For example, Zachariah in *The True
Confessions of Charlotte Doyle* expresses his opinion of Charlotte, saying,
"You're as steady a girl as ever I've met." As you read a story, you will
form your own opinions about its characters.

**As you read *The True Confessions of Charlotte Doyle*, think about this
question: *Do you think Charlotte should have been allowed to prove
her competence as a sailor by climbing to the top of the royal yard,
or should someone have stopped her from performing this hazardous
feat?***

**Then use this diagram to record your opinion and to write facts and
examples that support it.**

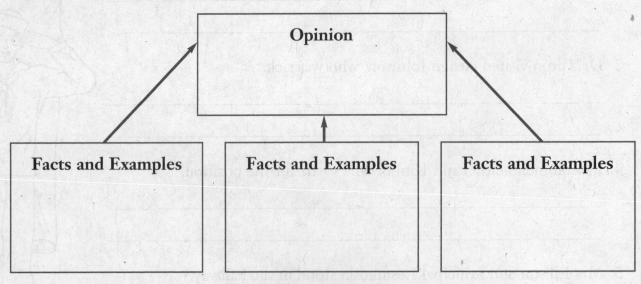

Opinion

Facts and Examples   Facts and Examples   Facts and Examples

**Using the information you recorded in the diagram, write an opinion
paragraph on a separate sheet of paper. In the first sentence, state
your opinion in response to the question above. In the body of the
paragraph, write two to three reasons why you think and feel the way
you do. Support your opinion with facts and examples. Then end
your paragraph with a concluding sentence that restates your opinion.**

Combining Sentences with Appositives

One way to improve your writing is to combine two short sentences into one by using an appositive. An **appositive** is a word or group of words that immediately follows a noun and identifies or explains it. Appositives are usually set off from the rest of the sentence by commas. Here is an example of before and after:

Charlotte Doyle was a thirteen-year-old girl. She joined the crew of the *Seahawk*.

Charlotte Doyle, **a thirteen-year-old girl,** joined the crew of the *Seahawk*.

Revise the following sentences from Captain Jaggery's ship's log. Combine each pair of short, choppy sentences into a single sentence with an appositive.

Charlotte Doyle is a young passenger. She wants to work aboard the Seahawk.

_____

Today two members of the crew described a test of worth that Charlotte had to pass. Zachariah and Foley are the crew members who described the test.

_____

_____

The men asked Charlotte to climb to the top of the royal yard. The royal yard is the tallest mast of the ship.

_____

_____

Ewing gave Charlotte some helpful advice. He is a seasoned sailor.

_____

Happily, Charlotte passed the test with flying colors. The test was a difficult physical and mental challenge.

_____

_____

Name _____

Choosing the Best Answer

Use the test-taking strategies and tips you have learned to help you answer these multiple-choice questions. You may go back to *Hatchet* if you need to. This practice will help you when you take this kind of test.

Read each question. In the answer row, fill in the circle that corresponds to the best answer.

1   What was the first clue Brian had that there was a living creature in the shelter with him?

   A   He heard it growl.

   B   He saw it in the darkness.

   C   He smelled it.

   D   He felt it touch his feet.

2   What happened when Brian kicked the porcupine?

   F   The porcupine sailed out of the shelter.

   G   The porcupine stuck quills into Brian's leg.

   H   The porcupine hid in the corner of the shelter.

   J   The porcupine knocked Brian's hatchet off some rocks.

3   What was the important rule of survival that Brain learned?

   A   Never kick at something that you can't see.

   B   A hatchet is the most valuable tool you can have.

   C   Feeling sorry for yourself doesn't work.

   D   Sleeping in a cave can be dangerous.

4   When Brain was dreaming, what did he see Terry pointing to?

   F   a park bench   **H**   a grocery sack

   G   a hatchet   **J**   a fire

ANSWER ROWS 1 (A) (B) (C) (D)   3 (A) (B) (C) (D)
                      2 (F) (G) (H) (J)   4 (F) (G) (H) (J)

Name _____

Choosing the Best Answer

continued

5   What kind of tools did Brian think about making to help him push
    an animal away?

    A   a crutch or a broom

    B   a shovel or a rake

    C   a knife or a hatchet

    D   a staff or a lance

6   In the dream, what had Terry been trying to tell Brian?

    F   Brian could make a fire with the hatchet.

    G   Brian could find charcoal in the cave.

    H   Brian could pick wild raspberries outside the cave.

    J   Brian should never let go of the hatchet.

7   What did Brian find in his pocket that he used to get the fire started?

    A   matches

    B   a magnifying glass

    C   a twenty dollar bill

    D   charcoal

8   What was the missing ingredient that Brian needed to have a fire?

    F   oxygen

    G   sparks

    H   paper

    J   wood

ANSWER ROWS 5 Ⓐ Ⓑ Ⓒ Ⓓ   7 Ⓐ Ⓑ Ⓒ Ⓓ
                 6 Ⓕ Ⓖ Ⓗ Ⓙ   8 Ⓕ Ⓖ Ⓗ Ⓙ

Name _____

Spelling Review

Write Spelling Words from the list to answer the questions.

1–8. Which eight words have the /ă/, /ĕ/, /ĭ/, /ŏ/, or /ŭ/ sound?

1. _____   5. _____

2. _____   6. _____

3. _____   7. _____

4. _____   8. _____

9–30. Which twenty-two words have the /ā/, /ē/, /ī/, /ō/, /yōō/, /ou/, /ōō/, /ô/, or /oi/ sound?

9. _____   20. _____

10. _____   21. _____

11. _____   22. _____

12. _____   23. _____

13. _____   24. _____

14. _____   25. _____

15. _____   26. _____

16. _____   27. _____

17. _____   28. _____

18. _____   29. _____

19. _____   30. _____

Spelling Words

1. ravine
2. wince
3. squawk
4. gaze
5. league
6. vault
7. bulk
8. avoid
9. theme
10. sought
11. depth
12. throne
13. hoist
14. strive
15. routine
16. prompt
17. stout
18. mute
19. reply
20. strain
21. roam
22. meant
23. annoy
24. craft
25. naughty
26. rhythm
27. sponge
28. sleeve
29. foul
30. bloom

Name _____

Spelling Spree

Puzzle Play Write a Spelling Word to fit each clue.

1. a plant's flower

2. a muscle injury

3. screech

4. a jacket's arm covering

5. a steady look

6. a recurring pattern of sound or movement

7. disobedient

Now write the boxed letters in order. They will spell a mystery word that is a synonym for *courage*.

Mystery Word:

1. vault
2. theme
3. sleeve
4. squawk
5. meant
6. throne
7. rhythm
8. stout
9. strain
10. hoist
11. sponge
12. bloom
13. naughty
14. annoy
15. gaze

Word Switch Write a Spelling Word to replace each underlined word or word group in these sentences.

8. The gold coins were kept in a locked storage area for valuables. _____

9. The ruler's chair was inlaid with gems. _____

10. Movers used a crane to haul up the piano to the top floor. _____

11. We discussed the subject of the book. _____

12. I intended to give her your message, but I forgot. _____

13. The ship was tied to the dock with strong and sturdy ropes. _____

14. The fly's constant buzzing began to irritate me. _____

15. Please wipe off the table. _____

Buzz!

Name _____

Proofreading and Writing

Proofreading Circle the six misspelled Spelling Words in this letter to the editor. Then write each word correctly.

    As a usual routene, I don't write letters to newspapers. (The bulck of my writing is reserved for homework!) I must, though, tell the public about a very special person.

    Last Saturday, the weather was really fowle. Since my baseball leage practice was canceled, I decided to test my new hiking rain gear. In the hills near town, I slipped and fell into a deep gully. Gushing rainwater swept me along, and I was struck muete with terror! Suddenly, a stranger's arms grabbed me and began to hoist me to solid ground. I can never thank that person enough for my rescue. From now on, I will stryve to be as courageous as he is!

1. bulk
2. mute
3. prompt
4. craft
5. league
6. avoid
7. roam
8. ravine
9. reply
10. foul
11. depth
12. routine
13. wince
14. sought
15. strive

1. _____ 3. _____ 5. _____

2. _____ 4. _____ 6. _____

Just the Opposite Write the Spelling Word that means almost the opposite of each word or words.

7. to grin _____   12. confront _____

8. stand still _____   13. late _____

9. found _____   14. lack of ability _____

10. hilltop _____   15. to ask _____

11. width _____

▬▬▬▬ **Write an Interview Script** On a separate sheet of paper, write the script of an interview with a real or imagined hero. Use the Spelling Review Words.

Name _____

Comparing Poems About Friends

Choose two poems from *Poems About Friends*. Compare and contrast them by answering the questions in the chart. Add questions of your own to the chart too.

	Poem #1 Title:_____	**Poem #2** Title:_____
What is the subject of the poem?		
What words in the poem help you see, feel, hear, etc.?		
Does the poet use words for sound or rhyme? Give examples.		
Does the poem remind you of something from your own life? Explain.		
What is the mood or tone?		

Which poem did you like more? Why?

_____

_____

_____

_____

Name _____

Comparing Poems About Family

Choose two poems from *Poems About Family*. Compare and contrast them by answering the questions in the chart. Add questions of your own to the chart too.

	Poem #1 Title:_____	Poem #2 Title:_____
What is the subject of the poem?		
What words in the poem help you see, feel, hear, etc.?		
Does the poet use words for sound or rhyme? Give examples.		
Does the poem remind you of something from your own life? Explain.		
What is the mood or tone?		

Which poem did you like more? Why?

_____

_____

_____

Name _____

What Really Happened?

Each selection in this theme attempts to explain a mystery. After reading each selection, complete the chart below and on the next page to show what you learned about these mysteries.

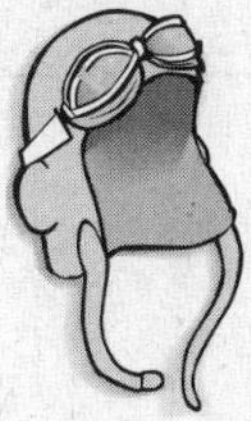

	Amelia Earhart: First Lady of Flight	The Girl Who Married the Moon	Dinosaur Ghosts
What mystery does the selection attempt to explain?			
What do you think the author's purpose was in writing the selection?			
What kind of writing is the selection an example of?			

Name _____

What Really Happened?

	Amelia Earhart: First Lady of Flight	The Girl Who Married the Moon	Dinosaur Ghosts
How did the author attempt to explain the mystery?			
Why do you think the mystery fascinates people?			

What are some different ways in which people try to explain mysterious events?

_____

_____

Name _____

A Tragic Disappearance

Use these words to complete the paragraph below.

One of the greatest mysteries in the history of ___aviation___ is the ___disappearence___ of famed pilot Amelia Earhart and her ___navigator___ Fred Noonan. When Amelia ___taxied___ down the ___runway___ and took off toward Howland Island on the second of July, 1937, she seemed certain to ___accomplish___ her goal of flying around the world at the equator. She had been giving an ___accounting___ of her experiences to newspapers, and her words were an ___inspiration___ to millions of people everywhere. She was also keeping a ___journal___, in which she recorded her thoughts. During that day's flight, radio operators lost contact with Amelia after she sent a confusing ___transmission___ over the radio. She and Noonan never reached their goal. It may never be known for sure what happened.

Vocabulary

- accounting
- journal
- runway
- disappearance
- aviation
- taxied
- inspiration
- accomplish
- navigator
- transmission

Name _____

Fact and Opinion Chart

Passage	Fact or Opinion?	How I Can Tell
Page 148: She had read the note but believed Noonan had made an error.		
Page 148: Noonan had been right that it was necessary to turn south in order to get to Dakar.		
Page 151: Earhart's plane ran out of gas and crashed at sea.		
Page 152: Amelia Earhart was spying for the U.S. government.		
Page 153: The Japanese did not let the U.S. search party into their waters, or onto the islands they controlled, to look for Amelia and Fred.		
Page 154: When Goerner showed the islanders photographs of several women, all of them picked Earhart as the woman they had seen.		
Page 154: Amelia had been brainwashed and was "Tokyo Rose."		
Page 156: Amelia was "a tragedy of the sea."		

Mystery Fact Sheet

Fill in the fact sheet below with important information from the selection.

The pilot: _____

The navigator: _____

The goal: _____

Where their plane disappeared: _____

_____

What Happened?

The Theories	Supporting Evidence	Evidence Against
1. They ran out of gas and crashed into the ocean.		
2. They were spies for the United States.		
3. Amelia was still alive.		
4. Amelia crashed on Nikumaroro.		

Name _____

Focus on Facts

Read the passage. Then complete the activity on page 83.

Jacqueline Cochran, American Aviator

Jacqueline Cochran was a record-breaking female aviator. Though not as famous as Charles Lindbergh or Amelia Earhart, she certainly deserves to be.

Jacqueline was born in the early 1900s in Pensacola, Florida. She had a poor childhood in a lumber mill town. By age thirteen, she was working as a hair cutter in a beauty salon. Eventually, she moved to New York City and started her own cosmetics company. This was a courageous and admirable achievement. So that she could sell her products in more places, she learned to fly. "At that moment, when I paid for my first lesson," Cochran said, "a beauty operator ceased to exist and an aviator was born."

Soon Jacqueline was the leading female pilot in the United States. In September of 1938, with just enough gas for another few minutes of flying, she won the transcontinental Bendix Race. This was a truly incredible feat: the former beautician flew the 2,042 miles from Los Angeles to Cleveland in an amazing 8 hours, 10 minutes, and 31 seconds. She was the first person to finish the course nonstop. More than once, she was awarded the women's Harmon Trophy, the highest honor given then to American women aviators. She also broke the women's altitude record and several speed records. "I might have been born in a hovel," Jacqueline said, "but I was determined to travel with the wind and the stars."

In 1943, during World War II, Jacqueline became the leader of the Women's Airforce Service Pilots, or WASPs. These pilots did jobs such as ferrying planes, training B-17 turret gunners, testing planes at repair depots, and teaching staff pilots at navigator schools. By the end of 1944, however, Congress unfairly refused to admit the WASPs into the military and ended the program. Despite her disappointment, Jacqueline continued to fly and set records until the 1970s, when health problems forced her to stop flying. She died in 1980.

Name _____

Focus on Facts continued

Answer these questions about the passage on page 82.

Answer these questions about the passage on page 82.

1. What opinion about Jacqueline Cochran does the author give in the first paragraph?

   <u>She deserves to be as famous as</u>
   <u>Charles Lindbergh or Amelia Earheart.</u>

2. The author includes several facts and one opinion in the second paragraph. Write them here.

   Facts: <u>Jacqueline was born in the early 1900s in Pensacola, Florida.</u>

   _____

   _____

   _____

   Opinion: <u>This was a courageous and</u>
   <u>admirable achievment.</u>

3. What opinion about Jacqueline's victory in the transcontinental Bendix Race does the author give in the third paragraph?

   _____

4. The author uses facts to support an opinion about Jacqueline's victory in the Bendix Race. What are they?

   _____

   _____

5. What opinion does the author give in the fourth paragraph?

   _____

   _____

6. Rewrite the following sentence so it states a fact and not an opinion:
   Jacqueline Cochran was an amazing female aviator.

   _____

   _____

Name _____

Be a Searcher!

Amelia Earhart's plane has words on it. Circle each word that has a suffix meaning "someone who." Then use those words to complete the sentences.

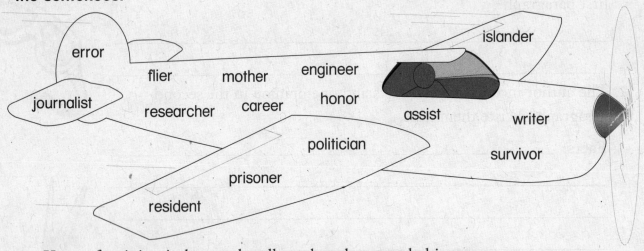

1. Years of training in how to handle a plane have made him an excellent _____.

2. The _____ thanked everyone who voted for her.

3. When the war was over, each _____ was set free.

4. Every _____ in the town had lived there at least five years.

5. The _____ took a boat to school every day.

6. The _____ had always liked to make up stories when she was a child.

7. The _____ is experimenting to find out how trees make oxygen.

8. The _____ reported on the record-breaking blizzard.

9. My grandfather was the only _____ of a house fire when he was young.

10. The _____ designed a new plan for the factory.

Vowel + /r/ Sounds

Remember the following spelling patterns for these vowel + /r/ sounds:

/ûr/	ear, ur, ir	**ear**th, **ur**ge, sk**ir**t
/ôr/	or, our	sc**or**n, m**our**n
/är/	ar	sn**ar**l
/îr/	ier	f**ier**ce

Write each Spelling Word under its vowel + /r/ sounds.

1. fierce
2. sword
3. court
4. snarl
5. thorn
6. earth
7. skirt
8. chart
9. urge
10. yarn
11. whirl
12. mourn
13. rehearse
14. curb
15. earnest
16. starch
17. purse
18. birch
19. pierce
20. scorn

/ûr/ Sounds

earth
urge
rehearse
earnest
purse
curb
_____
_____
_____

/ôr/ Sounds

sword
court
thorn
mourn
scorn

/är/ Sounds

snarl
chart
yarn
starch

/îr/ Sounds

fierce
skirt
whirl
birch
pierce

Name _____

Spelling Spree

Clues Write a Spelling Word for each clue.

1. You do this to prepare for a performance.
2. A judge presides there.
3. You step off this to cross a street.
4. A woman may wear one with a blouse.
5. A unfriendly dog may do this.
6. Some people ask the cleaner to add it to their laundry.
7. Its bark may be white and papery.
8. Kittens get tangled up in it.
9. You might find change in this.

1. <u>rehearse</u>
2. <u>court</u>
3. <u>curb</u>
4. <u>skirt</u>
5. <u>snarl</u>

6. <u>starch</u>
7. <u>birch</u>
8. <u>yarn</u>
9. <u>purse</u>

Spelling Words
1. fierce
2. sword
3. court
4. snarl
5. thorn
6. earth
7. skirt
8. chart
9. urge
10. yarn
11. whirl
12. mourn
13. rehearse
14. curb
15. earnest
16. starch
17. purse
18. birch
19. pierce
20. scorn

Word Search Write the Spelling Word that is hidden in each sentence.

Example: How is a <u>pear</u> <u>l</u>ike an apple? *pearl*

10. Everybody loves corn on the cob!
11. Did you hear that moaning sound?
12. The people at the pier celebrated the yacht's victory.
13. He gave me his word of honor.
14. The gardener will trim our new rosebushes.

10. _____
11. <u>mourn</u>
12. <u>pierce</u>
13. _____
14. _____

Proofreading and Writing

Proofreading Circle the six misspelled Spelling Words in this message. Then write each word correctly.

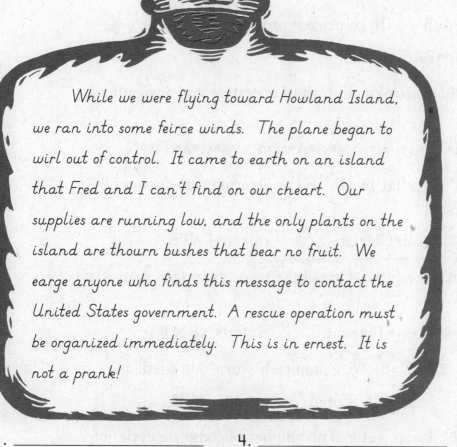

While we were flying toward Howland Island, we ran into some feirce winds. The plane began to wirl out of control. It came to earth on an island that Fred and I can't find on our cheart. Our supplies are running low, and the only plants on the island are thourn bushes that bear no fruit. We earge anyone who finds this message to contact the United States government. A rescue operation must be organized immediately. This is in ernest. It is not a prank!

Spelling Words

1. fierce
2. sword
3. court
4. snarl
5. thorn
6. earth
7. skirt
8. chart
9. urge
10. yarn
11. whirl
12. mourn
13. rehearse
14. curb
15. earnest
16. starch
17. purse
18. birch
19. pierce
20. scorn

1. _____   4. _____

2. _____   5. _____

3. _____   6. _____

✏️ **Write a Journal Entry** Amelia was a unique individual who attempted a daring feat. Have you ever tried something that may have had some element of risk to it? Did anyone try to discourage you? Did you have doubts? How did you resolve the doubts? Use your own or someone else's experience to think about the idea of taking risks.

On a separate sheet of paper, write a journal entry about taking risks. Use Spelling Words from the list.

Name _____

Stress on Syllables

Read each dictionary entry. Sound out the word several times, placing stress on a different syllable each time. Circle the choice with the correct stress.

1. **ap•proach** (ə prōch′) *v.* To come near or nearer in place or time.

   (AP•proach)   ap•PROACH

2. **a•vi•a•tion** (ā′ vē ā′ shən) *n.* The art of operating and navigating aircraft.

   A•vi•a•tion   (a•VI•a•tion)   a•vi•A•tion   a•vi•a•TION

3. **cal•cu•late** (kăl′ kyə lāt′) *v.* To find or determine an answer by using mathematics.

   (CAL•cu•late)   cal•CU•late   cal•cu•LATE

4. **con•ti•nent** (kŏn′ tə nənt) *n.* One of the seven great land masses of the earth.

   (CON•ti•nent)   con•TI•nent   con•ti•NENT

5. **ex•haust•ed** (ĭg zôst′ əd) *adj.* Completely worn-out; tired.

   EX•haust•ed   (ex•HAUST•ed)   ex•haust•ED

6. **fre•quen•cy** (frē′ kwən sē) *n.* The number of complete cycles of a wave, such as a radio wave, that occur per second.

   (FRE•quen•cy)   fre•QUEN•cy   fre•quen•CY

7. **re•fu•el** (rē fyōō′ əl) *v.* To provide with fuel again.

   (RE•fu•el)   re•FU•el   re•fu•EL

8. **re•verse** (rĭ vûrs′) *v.* To turn around to the opposite direction.

   RE•verse   (re•VERSE)

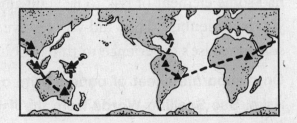

Amelia's Plane

Singular and Plural Possessive Nouns Possessive nouns show ownership or possession. To form the possessive of a singular noun, add an apostrophe and an -*s* (*'s*). To form the possessive of a plural noun that ends in -*s*, add only an apostrophe (*'*). To form the possessive of a plural noun that does not end in -*s*, add an apostrophe and an -*s* (*'s*).

> **singular noun**: dog   **singular noun**: James
> **possessive**: dog's   **possessive**: James's
> **plural noun**: boys   **plural noun**: deer
> **possessive**: boys'   **possessive**: deer's

Write the possessive form of each noun in parentheses.

1. the (plane) _plane's_ cockpit

2. the (women) _womens'_ plane

3. the (planes) _planes'_ hangar

4. the (man) _man's_ binoculars

5. our (country) _country's_ flag

Amelia Earhart's Disappearance

More Possessive Nouns Remember how to form **possessive nouns**:

1. Add an apostrophe and an -*s* (*'s*) to a singular noun.
2. Add an apostrophe and an -*s* (*'s*) to a plural noun that does not end in -*s*.
3. Add an apostrophe (*'*) to a plural noun that ends in -*s*.

The following sentences use phrases that show possession or ownership. Revise each underlined phrase to use a possessive noun.

> **Example:** Lynette visited the home of Amelia Earhart.
> Lynette visited **Amelia Earhart's home**.

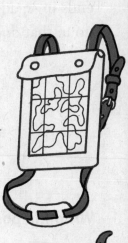

1. No one knows the fate of Amelia Earhart.

   _____Amelia Earhart's fate_____

2. Her fate has aroused the interest of many people.

   _____many people's interest_____

3. The theories of researchers are interesting to read.

   _____researchers' theories_____

4. The fascination of Ross with Earhart's disappearance has led him to read many books.

   _____Ross's fascination_____

   _____

5. The planes of early pilots seem primitive today.

   _____early pilots' planes_____

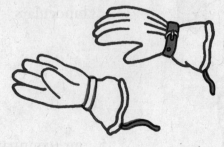
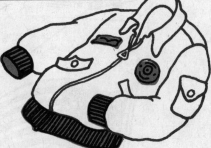

Write to My Friend

Using Apostrophes Writers use apostrophes in possessives and in contractions. If you leave an apostrophe out, you can confuse your reader. Likewise, if you use an apostrophe incorrectly, you can also confuse your reader. Look at how apostrophes change the meaning in the examples below.

We'll see you.   Well see you.   the dog's food   the dogs' food

Proofread the following draft of a letter Lynette wrote to her friend in Kansas. Underline each error in the use of apostrophes in possessives and contractions. Then rewrite each underlined word correctly above the error.

Dear Carolyn,

    I̲m̲ so glad that I had the chance to visit you

in Kansas last month. You ca̲n̲'t imagine how much

I miss seeing you in school every day, but the town

you now live in is beautiful. It is interesting that

your town is also Amelia Earharts hometown. I

enjoyed visiting her family̲'s̲' house. Her story

inspired me, and I have̲n̲t stopped thinking about

the mystery. What do you think really happened?

       Your friend,

       Lynette

Name _____

Writing a News Article

Amelia Earhart's disappearance over the Pacific Ocean during her 1937 flight around the world was front-page news. Imagine you are a reporter for the *World News and Recorder*. Use the chart below to gather facts and details for a *news article* about the disappearance of Earhart's plane or about another historic event. Answer these questions: Who was involved? What happened? When, where, and why did this event occur? How did it happen?

Who?	
What?	
When?	
Where?	
Why?	
How?	

Now use the details and facts you gathered to write your news article on a separate sheet of paper. Write a beginning that gives the facts, yet captures the reader's attention. Present the facts you recorded in the chart in the order of most to least important. Use quotations where possible to bring this news event to life, and include a headline that will grab your reader's attention.

Adding Details

A good reporter uses details to hold the interest of readers and satisfy their curiosity, to clearly explain what happened, and to make the people who were involved in the event come alive.

Read the following draft of a news article. Then rewrite it on the lines below, adding details from the list to improve it.

Aviator Mysteriously Vanishes

American aviator Amelia Earhart and her navigator mysteriously vanished in the skies on July 2, 1937. Earhart and Noonan were attempting a west-to-east flight. Their airplane, which departed from Lae, New Guinea, was headed northeast when it disappeared.

The last radio communication with Earhart occurred in the morning with William Galten, who serves aboard the United States Coast Guard cutter.

_____

_____

_____

_____

_____

_____

_____

Details

Lockheed Electra	Frederick Noonan
over the Pacific Ocean	toward tiny Howland Island
Itasca	at 8:47 A.M.
around the world	Radioman Third Class

Name _____

Revising Your Story

Reread your story. What do you need to make it better? Use this page to help you decide. Put a checkmark in the box for each sentence that describes your story.

Loud and Clear!

☐ My setting, characters, and plot are well developed.

☐ The beginning catches the reader's attention.

☐ The dialogue is realistic and effective.

☐ I use exact nouns to make the story's action clear to the reader.

☐ The conflict is resolved in a satisfying way.

☐ There are very few mistakes.

Sounding Stronger

☐ My setting, characters, and plot are described in a vague way.

☐ The beginning could be more interesting.

☐ I need more dialogue and details.

☐ I could use more exact nouns to bring the story to life.

☐ The conflict isn't resolved well.

☐ Errors make parts of the story hard to follow.

Turn Up Volume

☐ The plot is disconnected and confusing.

☐ My beginning does not hook the reader.

☐ It's hard to tell what the characters look and sound like.

☐ The story doesn't have a clear conflict.

☐ Too many grammatical mistakes make the story hard to read.

Name _____

Using Exact Nouns

Replace each underlined noun. In exercises 1–4, circle the letter of the noun that best completes each sentence. In exercises 5–8, write in a noun of your own choice.

1. A lion held a mouse in its <u>hands</u> and said, "Tell me why I should not eat you, little one."

   a. legs   b. fingers   (c. paws)   d. jaws

2. "Because one day I may save you from a great <u>situation</u>," said the mouse.

   a. peril   b. happiness   (c. accident)   d. elephants

3. The lion laughed. "How could a tiny mouse such as you ever help a great <u>animal</u> such as myself?" the lion asked.

   a. mammal   (b. beast)   c. critter   d. freak

4. The lion let the mouse go and it escaped into the <u>beyond</u>.

   a. unknown   b. trail   c. cave   (d. jungle)

5. Weeks later, the mouse heard a <u>sound</u> and found a lion caught in a net.

   roar

6. "Help me, little mouse," the lion cried. "I am in deep <u>adversity</u>."

   trouble

7. With teeth as sharp as <u>pins</u>, the mouse ate through the net and freed the lion. "How can I ever repay you?" said the lion.

   Knives

8. "You already have," said the mouse. "For I am the same mouse that you caught weeks ago. You let me make an <u>exit</u> then, so I helped you now."

   escape

Name _____

Spelling Words

Look for familiar spelling patterns to help you remember how to spell the Spelling Words on this page. Think carefully about the parts that you find hard to spell in each word.

Write the missing letters in the Spelling Words below.

Spelling Words

1. tonight
2. everywhere
3. everybody
4. another
5. because
6. whole
7. people
8. cousin
9. clothes
10. height
11. always
12. right
13. might
14. really
15. everything

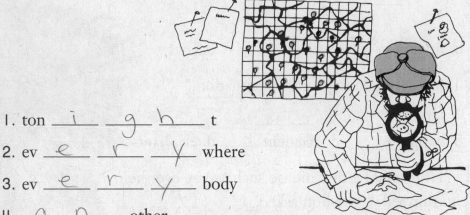

1. ton __i__ __g__ __h__ __t__
2. ev __e__ __r__ __y__ where
3. ev __e__ __r__ __y__ body
4. __a__ __n__ other
5. bec __a__ __u__ __s__ e
6. __w__ __h__ ole
7. p __e__ __o__ ple
8. c __o__ __u__ __s__ __i__ n
9. clo __t__ __h__ __e__ s
10. h __e__ __i__ __g__ __h__ t
11. a __l__ __w__ __a__ ys
12. r __i__ __g__ __h__ t
13. m __i__ __g__ __h__ t
14. re __a__ __l__ __l__ y
15. ev __e__ __r__ __y__ thing

Study List On a separate sheet of paper, write each Spelling Word. Check your spelling against the words on the list.

Name _____

Spelling Spree

Syllable Scramble **Rearrange the syllables in each item to write a Spelling Word. There is one extra syllable in each item.**

1. ways al all
2. oth un an er
3. cause be coz
4. ry were eve where
5. nite night to
6. ple pe peo
7. ev thing ry eve
8. bo eve ry in dy

1. _always_
2. _another_
3. _because_
4. _everywhere_
5. _tonight_
6. _people_
7. _everything_
8. _everybody_

> **Spelling Words**
>
> 1. tonight
> 2. everywhere
> 3. everybody
> 4. another
> 5. because
> 6. whole
> 7. people
> 8. cousin
> 9. clothes
> 10. height
> 11. always
> 12. right
> 13. might
> 14. really
> 15. everything

Find a Rhyme **Write a Spelling Word that rhymes with the underlined word and makes sense in the sentence.**

9. It looks like we _____ have to find <u>another</u> <u>site</u> for the building.
10. <u>Somebody</u> <u>stole</u> the _____ eight thousand dollars!
11. There's only a <u>slight</u> difference between your _____ and mine.
12. When she gets _____ mad, she gets a <u>steely</u> look in her eyes.
13. My brother really <u>loathes</u> buying new _____.
14. Turn the screw to the _____ until it gets really <u>tight</u>.
15. I'm going to pick up a <u>dozen</u> donuts for my _____.

9. _might_
10. _whole_
11. _height_
12. _really_
13. _clothes_
14. _right_
15. _cousin_

Reading-Writing Workshop

Frequently Misspelled Words

Proofreading and Writing

Proofreading Circle the five misspelled Spelling Words in this advertisement. Then write each word correctly.

Read all about it!

You mite think you've heard the whole story behind last winter's plane crashes, but if you do, you're wrong. Do you want to know what realy happened? Then read the book that everyone everwhere is talking about! This book tells you evrything that you could want to know about why those flights went down. It just goes to show that you can't allways believe what you see on television!

1. tonight
2. everywhere
3. everybody
4. another
5. because
6. whole
7. people
8. cousin
9. clothes
10. height
11. always
12. right
13. might
14. really
15. everything

1. _____might_____   4. _____everything_____
2. _____really_____   5. _____always_____
3. _____everywhere_____

✏️ **Write a Tag-Team Mystery** Team up with a classmate. Then, taking turns writing sentences, write a mystery story. Use Spelling Words from the list.

Name _____

Fishing for the Right Word

Fill in each blank with a word from the box.

Vocabulary

mainland
suspicious
common room
sod
hearth
phases
kayak
sparkling
village

1. If you are in a light, one-person boat traditionally used in the Arctic, you are in a _____.

2. If you watch the moon each night for a month, you will observe all its _____.

3. If you live in a very small settlement, you live in a _____.

4. If you had been alive hundreds of years ago, you might have cooked on a _____.

5. If you do not trust someone, you are _____ of that person.

6. If your roof is made of squares of soil held together with the roots of grasses, it is made of _____.

7. If you are on an island, you are not on the _____.

8. If you are looking at waves on which the sun is shining, you are seeing _____ waters.

9. If you are in the part of a traditional dwelling where family members gather, you are in the _____.

Name _____

Inferences Chart

Question	Evidence from the Story	Own Knowledge	Inference
Pages 172–173 What does nature mean to the cousins and their culture?			
Pages 175–176 Why do you think Moon wants the most patient cousin for his wife?			
Page 176 What is the work Moon must do?			
Pages 178–179 Why are the star people lying facedown?			
Page 180 Why does Moon's wife cover her head with a blanket and say she has a pain on her face?			

Name _____

Questioning the Answers

Write an answer for each question below.

1. When did the cousins fall in love with the Moon?

   _____

   _____

2. What did the cousins have to do in order to become the Moon's wife?

   _____

   _____

3. What happened to the cousin who opened her eye?

   _____

4. What did the Moon tell his wife not to do?

   _____

5. Who were the one-eyed people whom the Moon's wife met?

   _____

6. What did the Moon's wife find in the storeroom?

   _____

7. What happened to Moon's wife when she tried on one of his masks?

   _____

8. What job did the Moon give his wife?

   _____

   _____

Name _____

Putting Clues Together

Read the passage. Then complete the activity on page 103.

Eos and Tithonus, A Greek Myth

It was still dark when Eos, the dawn, awoke. She rose from her pink pillows and pushed her yellow bedcover aside. Pale light glowed from her hair. Eos dipped her rosy fingers into a glass and sprinkled dewdrops over the world. Then she ran outside and threw open the palace gates. She shaded her eyes as four fiery stallions pulled a golden chariot with her brother Helios, the sun, through the gates into the early morning sky. After latching the gates, Eos yawned and strolled back into the palace.

From the bedroom she heard a tiny cough. Tithonus, her husband, must be awake. "Poor dear," Eos thought, hurrying to the bedside. She caught sight of herself in the mirror and couldn't help smiling. She didn't look a day over twenty, although she was far, far older than her husband.

Eos looked everywhere for Tithonus, but she couldn't find him. At last she spied him crouching in a corner, a shriveled, tiny man about the size of a grasshopper. In fact, his wheezing sounded a little like chirping. Eos sighed sadly. "He is quite old — almost 350," she thought. It seemed only yesterday that she had glimpsed him on Earth, the handsomest young man imaginable. She had begged Zeus to make him immortal so she could marry him. Zeus had done his best, but he'd warned her that something like this might happen.

After serving Tithonus a very small breakfast, she had an idea. Why not keep him in her little handkerchief basket? A basket might keep him safe, and it was certainly a better size for him than furniture in the palace. Tithonus did not object to his new home, and Eos set the basket on the windowsill so he could enjoy the sun. That night his sad chirping lulled her to sleep. When Eos peered into the basket next morning, she thought he looked greener than he did the day before.

Name _____

Putting Clues Together   continued

Answer these questions about the story on page 102.

1. How does Eos feel about Tithonus?

   She thinks he is handsome.

2. What clues in the story tell you that Eos loves and pities her husband?

   He is 350 years old.

   _____

3. What has happened to Tithonus that has not happened to Eos?

   He became shriveled and as tiny as a

   grasshopper.

4. What seems to be happening to Tithonus? How can you tell?

   He's turning into a ^grasshopper^. It says he was as

   small and green as a grasshopper.

5. What do you think Tithonus might become? Why?

   A grasshopper. He turned greener the next

   day.

6. Myths and folktales often do more than entertain. What purpose do you think this story has? Circle one answer.

   A. to teach a lesson about what is right

   B. to explain how grasshoppers came to be

   C. to explain the movement of the sun and moon

Name _____

What's the Ending?

Read the letter. Circle the ten words with the endings -s or -es. Write each word in the first column, and then write the base word and the ending.

> Dear cousin,
>
> We have different lives now, and I won't see you again. But there are many possible husbands in the villages all around you. Do you still walk on the beaches in the evenings to glimpse the moon? If you look up, you will see me in the heavens. My husband and I share the cycles of the moon. He enjoys his work, and so do I. He carries the moon for the first half of each cycle, and I carry it for the second half. So, whenever the moon glimmers down on you, think of me.
>
> Your loving cousin

Word	Base word	Ending
1. _____	_____	_____
2. _____	_____	_____
3. _____	_____	_____
4. _____	_____	_____
5. _____	_____	_____
6. _____	_____	_____
7. _____	_____	_____
8. _____	_____	_____
9. _____	_____	_____
10. _____	_____	_____

Name _____

Homophones

Words that sound alike but have different spellings and meanings
are called **homophones**. When you use a homophone, be sure
to spell the word that has the meaning you want.

v**ai**n	(vān)	unsuccessful, fruitless
v**ei**n	(vān)	a blood vessel

Write the homophone pairs among the Spelling Words.

Spelling Words

1. fir
2. fur
3. scent
4. sent
5. scene
6. seen
7. vain
8. vein
9. principal
10. principle
11. manor
12. manner
13. who's
14. whose
15. tacks
16. tax
17. hangar
18. hanger
19. died
20. dyed

Homophones

_____   _____

_____   _____

_____   _____

_____   _____

_____   _____

_____   _____

_____   _____

_____   _____

_____   _____

_____   _____

Name _____

Spelling Spree

Homophone Riddles Write a pair of Spelling Words to complete each statement.

1–2. A hook to hang your coat on in an airport storage building is a _____ _____.

3–4. A dog might call the needles of a pine tree _____ _____.

5–6. The most important one in a set of rules or standards is the _____ _____.

7–8. A gift of perfume mailed to a friend is a _____ _____.

1. _____   5. _____

2. _____   6. _____

3. _____   7. _____

4. _____   8. _____

Familiar Phrases Write the Spelling Word that completes each phrase or sentence. Remember to capitalize the first word in a sentence.

9. as _____ as a peacock

10. a tie-_____ shirt

11. the _____ of the crime

12. not pushpins, but _____

13. draw blood from a _____

14. federal income _____

15. Knock, knock. _____ there?

9. _____   13. _____

10. _____   14. _____

11. _____   15. _____

12. _____

Name _____

Proofreading and Writing

Proofreading Circle the five misspelled Spelling Words in this e-mail message. Then write each word correctly.

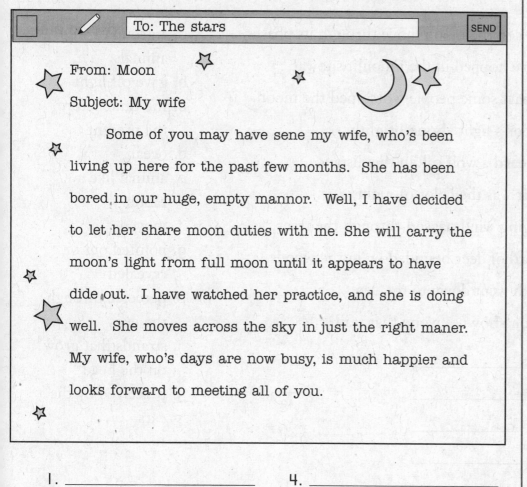

To: The stars   SEND

From: Moon

Subject: My wife

   Some of you may have sene my wife, who's been living up here for the past few months. She has been bored in our huge, empty mannor. Well, I have decided to let her share moon duties with me. She will carry the moon's light from full moon until it appears to have dide out. I have watched her practice, and she is doing well. She moves across the sky in just the right maner. My wife, who's days are now busy, is much happier and looks forward to meeting all of you.

1. fir
2. fur
3. scent
4. sent
5. scene
6. seen
7. vain
8. vein
9. principal
10. principle
11. manor
12. manner
13. who's
14. whose
15. tacks
16. tax
17. hangar
18. hanger
19. died
20. dyed

1. _____   4. _____

2. _____   5. _____

3. _____

━━━ **Write a Job Description** Moon decided to give his wife half of his work to do, but suppose he had wanted to hire someone he didn't know. How would he have described the job in a Help Wanted ad?

On a separate sheet of paper, write a job description for Moon's work. Use Spelling Words from the list.

Name _____

Match the Sounds

Match the correct definition to the boldface word. Then complete the homophone pairs below.

_h._ 1. We can **see** the moon move through its phases.

_e._ 2. The **hare** hopped in the moonlit snow.

_c._ 3. In the **past** some people worshiped the moon.

_b._ 4. The moon's light **shone** brightly.

_j._ 5. They **heard** a wolf call in the distance.

_i._ 6. Her **hair** was the color of night.

_f._ 7. The raging wind **passed** through the trees.

_a._ 8. The **herd** of deer bounded by in the woods.

_d._ 9. The path went down to the **sea**.

_g._ 10. Have you **shown** anyone that trail?

a. a group of wild animals

b. gave off light

c. the time before the present

d. ocean

e. animal like a rabbit

f. moved

g. pointed out or revealed

h. perceive through the eyes

i. strands that grow on the head

j. perceived by the ears

11. see _____ sea _____

12. hare _____ hair _____

13. past _____ passed _____

14. shone _____ shown _____

15. heard _____ herd _____

Name _____

We Collect Shells

Action Verbs and Direct Objects An **action verb** tells what the subject does. A **direct object** receives the action of the verb. To find the direct object in a sentence, first find the verb. Then ask who or what receives the action of the verb:

> **Jeff found a shell on the beach.** The action verb is *found*. Jeff found *what* on the beach? He found a shell. *Shell* is the direct object.

The following sentence has a **compound direct object**.

> **Karen wore her jacket and scarf to the beach.** The action verb is *wore*. Karen wore *what* to the beach? She wore her *jacket* and her *scarf*. The compound direct object is *jacket and scarf*.

Find the action verb and the direct object in each sentence below. Circle the verb and underline the direct object.

1. The older girls (collect) shells on the beach.

2. Grandfather (builds) a blazing fire.

3. Earlier, little Anna and Michael (chased) a flock of sandpipers.

4. Grandmother (tells) stories in the moonlight.

5. Father (wraps) Anna and Michael in a blanket.

Name _____

Auxiliary Verbs Will Help Us

Main Verbs and Auxiliaries A **verb phrase** is made up of a main verb and an auxiliary. The **main verb** usually shows action. The **auxiliary** works with the main verb.

Common Auxiliary Verbs					
am	were	do	has	must	might
is	be	does	had	will	would
are	being	did	can	shall	should
was	been	have	may	could	

What is the main verb in each sentence below? Is there an auxiliary verb? Fill in the chart below the sentences. If there is no auxiliary verb write _none_.

1. Peggy will tell us fascinating stories.
2. She has told two stories about her life.
3. Joan and Margaret have laughed harder than ever before.
4. Should Peggy repeat that story?
5. Peggy is a great storyteller!

	Main Verb	**Auxiliary Verb**
1.	tell	will
2.	told	has
3.	laughed	have
4.	repeat	none
5.	is	is

Name _____

Look at the Moon and Stars

Sentence Combining with Compound Direct Objects A good writer avoids writing too many short sentences, which can sound choppy. You can combine two sentences that have the same verb and different direct objects to make one sentence with a **compound direct object**.

Nora has **binoculars**. She has a **telescope** too.

Nora has **binoculars and a telescope**.

Here is the draft of an essay Nora is writing. Revise the draft by changing short, choppy sentences into sentences with compound direct objects. Write your version below.

Ancient people told stories about the moon. They told stories about the stars too. Today we have seen people on the moon. We have seen robots on Mars. Giant telescopes in the sky take pictures of Saturn. The telescopes take pictures of other planets too. Every night, I look at the moon through a telescope. I look at stars and planets too. Someday, I'll study Mars at an observatory. I'll also study Venus. I'll be a scientist. I'll be an astronaut. I'm shooting for the stars!

_____

_____

_____

_____

_____

_____

_____

Name _____

Writing a Journal Entry

A **journal** is a notebook, diary, folder, or file in which you can record and save notes, lists, questions, ideas, thoughts, and feelings. For example, imagine that one of the two cousins in *The Girl Who Married the Moon* keeps a journal. She might write an entry to express her feelings about the Moon, to describe what happened when she received her chin tattoo, or to tell about such activities as weaving a basket from spruce roots or taking a sweat bath.

On the lines below, write your own journal entry for one day's events. Follow these guidelines:

► Write the date at the beginning. You may also want to note the location.

► Write in the first person, using the pronouns *I, me, my, mine, we,* and *our.*

► Describe the day's events or experiences.

► Include personal thoughts, feelings, reactions, questions, and ideas.

► Use sequence words when you narrate events.

_____

_____

_____

_____

_____

_____

_____

_____

_____

When you finish your journal entry, you may want to share it with a friend or a classmate.

Name _____

Using Exact Verbs

Good writers use exact verbs to bring their experiences to life. For example, exact verbs like *glow* or *sparkle* describe actions more precisely than does a common verb such as *shine*. When you write a journal entry, you can use exact verbs to create a more vivid picture of what happened.

Suppose this journal entry was written by the cousin who became the Moon's wife in *The Girl Who Married the Moon*. Read it and then rewrite it on the lines below, replacing the general verbs that have been underlined with more exact verbs from the list.

May 25, Moon's House

Today I felt incredibly bored, so I <u>looked</u> into Moon's storeroom and then <u>went</u> inside. What a surprise! Moon's storeroom is <u>filled</u> with sparkling pieces of light. I <u>found</u> all the moon phases except for the full moon. Now I know where my husband <u>hides</u> his phases.

The phases <u>shined</u> so temptingly! I <u>took</u> a piece of moon from a shelf and <u>put</u> it on my own face. Now the piece will not come off. What if Moon becomes angry?

_____

_____

_____

_____

_____

_____

_____

	Exact Verbs	
conceals		peeked
placed		glittered
sneaked		discovered
plucked		crammed

Name _____

Categorizing Vocabulary

Write each word from the box under the correct category.

Vocabulary

two kinds of scientists

_____

_____

two kinds of artifacts

_____

_____

**two names for beliefs based
on facts and observations**

_____

_____

a word for proof or support

_____

**two ways soil can be
removed**

_____

_____

**a word for a vanished
species of animals or plants**

_____

Vocabulary

theory

erosion

paleontologist

extinct

specimens

geologists

fossils

hypotheses

evidence

excavation

**Now choose at least five words from the box. Use them to write a
short paragraph about searching for the remains of ancient plants
and animals.**

_____

_____

_____

_____

_____

_____

_____

Name _____

Text Organization Chart

Organization: Main Ideas and Details

A Big Find of Small Dinosaurs
What did Dr. Ned Colbert find in 1947 at Ghost Ranch,
New Mexico?

_____

What question did Dr. Colbert's discovery make scientists ask
themselves?

_____

What Happened Here?
List two details about the dinosaur bones scientists found.

_____

_____

_____

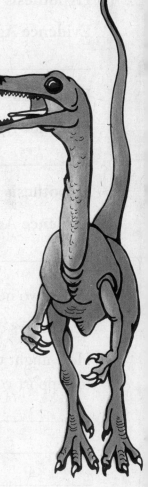

Organization: Hypothesis and Evidence

Stuck in the Mud? Hypothesis 1:
_____

Support *For* or *Against*:
_____

_____

Volcanic Violence? Hypothesis 2:
_____

Support *For* or *Against*:
_____

_____

_____

Name _____

What Happened to Coelophysis?

Scientists decided that the hypotheses below were *not* the best explanations for *Coelophysis*'s death. List the evidence *against* each one. Then answer the questions below.

Hypothesis Notes: *Why Coelophysis might have died*
Hypothesis 1: *Stuck in mud*

Evidence Against: _____

_____

Hypothesis 2: *Volcanic eruption*

Evidence Against: _____

_____

Hypothesis 3: *Asteroid fallout caused starvation*

Evidence Against: _____

_____

What two new hypotheses did scientists decide best explain

Coelophysis's death? _____ and _____

How might these two hypotheses have worked together? Give evidence
to support your explanation.

_____

_____

_____

Name _____

Taking Text Apart

Read the article. Then answer the questions on page 118.

Trapped in Amber

A clear golden lump sells for $27,000 at an auction. This lump of *amber*, as the material is called, started out as sap from a tree. What makes it so valuable now? Look closely — inside the amber is a small thirty-million-year-old lizard.

What Is Amber?

Amber is hardened sap from ancient trees. Over millions of years the sap has changed into a rock-hard material. Because it is beautiful and lasts many years, amber is often used in jewelry. Some amber pieces give scientists a rare opportunity to study prehistoric *inclusions* such as leaves, insects, and reptiles preserved in the once-sticky sap.

How Does Amber Form?

Picture this process. Long ago (perhaps as long ago as the age of dinosaurs), sap oozes from a tree. It hardens on the tree trunk and is covered by more sap. After many years, the tree dies and decays. It is swept into a stream and eventually ends up under the sea or beneath layers of rock. If the sap had been left out in the air, it would have rotted. Because the sap is not exposed to oxygen, however, its molecules change, forming stronger and stronger bonds. Eventually, all its oils evaporate, and it becomes hard and shiny, a beautiful golden brown. It becomes amber.

How Is Something Trapped in Amber?

It is possible today to see plants, insects, and even small reptiles from long ago preserved in amber. How did they get there? Here is one way this might have happened: an unlucky insect lands on a tree trunk that is sticky with sap. It gets stuck. More sap flows down the tree, entirely covering the bug. Over the centuries the sap slowly turns to amber. The insect dries out but otherwise stays perfectly preserved.

Name _____

Taking Text Apart continued

Answer these questions about the passage on page 117.

1. How many sections does the article have? (Don't count the introductory paragraph.)

   _____

2. What feature of the text helps you identify the different sections?

   _____

3. Reread the section under the heading *What Is Amber?* Is it organized by main idea and details, or by sequence of events?

   _____

4. Reread the section under the heading *How Does Amber Form?* Is this section organized by main idea and details, or by sequence?

   _____

5. What sequence words or phrases can you find in the second section? Write them here.

   _____

Name _____

Sorting Out Suffixes

Read this field diary page. Underline each word with the suffix -al, -ive, or -ous.

> Beginning today, we will use our best investigative methods to figure out why so many dinosaurs died here. The area is one massive burial ground. There are so many skeletons, it looks almost comical, as though the dinosaurs were gathering to watch a famous celebrity when they died. We know that this animal was carnivorous because of the bones of other animals in the skeletons' bellies. Our theories may be experimental, but only if we are creative and inventive can we solve the mystery. Really, it is marvelous work.

Now write the words you underlined. Use the paragraph above to help you find the meaning of each word.

1. _____

2. _____

3. _____

4. _____

5. _____

6. _____

7. _____

8. _____

9. _____

10. _____

Name _____

Final /ər/, /ən/, and /əl/

The **schwa sound,** shown as /ə/, is a weak vowel sound often found in an unstressed syllable. Remember the following spelling patterns for the /ə/ sound:

final /ər/	er, or, ar	messeng**er**, direct**or**, simil**ar**
final /n/ or /ən/	on, en	weap**on**, fright**en**
final /l/ or /əl/	le, el, al	strugg**le**, chann**el**, ment**al**

► The spelling of the final /ər/ sound in *acre* differs from the usual patterns. The final /ər/ sound in *acre* is spelled *re*.

Write each Spelling Word under its final sound.

1. struggle
2. director
3. weapon
4. similar
5. mental
6. frighten
7. channel
8. messenger
9. familiar
10. acre*
11. error
12. gallon
13. rural
14. calendar
15. elevator
16. stumble
17. youngster
18. kitchen
19. passenger
20. quarrel

Final /ər/ Sound

_____

_____

_____

_____

_____

_____

_____

Final /n/ or /ən/ Sound

_____

_____

_____

_____

Final /l/ or /əl/ Sound

_____

_____

_____

_____

_____

Name _____

Spelling Spree

Match Game Match each word beginning below to an ending to form a Spelling Word. Then write each word correctly.

Word Beginnings

1. ac
2. quarr
3. weap
4. elevat
5. stumb
6. ment
7. messeng
8. kitch

Word Endings

on
er
le
en
al
re
or
el

1. _____
2. _____
3. _____
4. _____

5. _____
6. _____
7. _____
8. _____

Syllable Spot Write the Spelling Word that includes one of the syllables in each word below.

Example: format *matter*

9. frightfully _____
10. gallery _____
11. passage _____
12. correction _____
13. tunnel _____
14. calculate _____
15. fanatic _____

Spelling Words

1. struggle
2. director
3. weapon
4. similar
5. mental
6. frighten
7. channel
8. messenger
9. familiar
10. acre*
11. error
12. gallon
13. rural
14. calendar
15. elevator
16. stumble
17. youngster
18. kitchen
19. passenger
20. quarrel

Proofreading and Writing

Proofreading Circle the five misspelled Spelling Words in this journal entry. Then write each word correctly.

Spelling Words

July 25

After weeks in this rurel area searching for dinosaur skeletons, I have finally had some success. Today, I found several skeletons similiar to *Coelophysis*. However, unless I made an errer in my measurements, these are larger and have a sturdier bone structure. The smallest, probably a yongster, is the most curious. It seems to have died in some sort of strugle. The rest of the skeletons are spread over an acre of land, and I have not had time to analyze them in detail. It looks like my work is cut out for me.

1. struggle
2. director
3. weapon
4. similar
5. mental
6. frighten
7. channel
8. messenger
9. familiar
10. acre*
11. error
12. gallon
13. rural
14. calendar
15. elevator
16. stumble
17. youngster
18. kitchen
19. passenger
20. quarrel

1. _____ 4. _____

2. _____ 5. _____

3. _____

✎ **Write an Explanation** What do you think about the answer put forward in the selection for why so many dinosaur skeletons have been found at Ghost Ranch? Do you think the conclusions match the evidence? What about the possibility of new evidence suggesting another explanation?

On a separate piece of paper, write a short description of how you think the dinosaur skeletons wound up at Ghost Ranch. Use Spelling Words from the list.

Name _____

Discovering the Key

Use the spelling table/pronunciation key below to figure out
how to pronounce each underlined vowel sound. Find a
word in the vocabulary box with a similar vowel sound, and
write that word after the sentence.

Vocabulary

blow
late
nut
reel
sail
ton

Spellings	Sample Words
a, ai, ei, ey	made, plait, vein, they
e, ee, ie, y	these, fleet, chief, bumpy
o, oe, ou, ow	fold, toe, boulder, slow
o, u, ou, oo	stomach, cut, rough, flood

1. Sh<u>ou</u>lder bones were found among the fossils.

_____ blow _____

2. The scientists found d<u>o</u>zens of skeletons of the little
dinosaur.

_____ ton _____

3. Each specimen was carefully w<u>ei</u>ghed and recorded.

_____ sail _____

4. The dinosaurs hunted for pr<u>ey</u> along rivers and lakes.

_____ late _____

5. Red bl<u>oo</u>d cells were made in the marrow cavity.

_____ ton _____

6. These dinosaurs had no armor to sh<u>ie</u>ld themselves from
predators.

_____ reel _____

Name _____

Dinosaurs Eat . . .

Transitive and Intransitive Verbs A **transitive verb** is an action verb with a **direct object**, which receives the action. An **intransitive verb** has no direct object. See the examples below.

Verb	Transitive	Intransitive
read	I **read** the book.	I **read** quickly.
sit	(none)	They **sit** on the bus.
visit	He **visits** the ranch.	He **visits** often.

Underline the verb or verb phrase in each sentence below.
Then write *transitive* or *intransitive* after the sentence.

1. Maurice saw a movie about dinosaurs. _____

2. I researched prehistoric times. _____

3. My friend went to the La Brea Tar Pits. _____

4. Some dinosaurs ate meat. _____

5. We will see dinosaur bones at the museum. _____

6. Dinosaurs lived during the Mesozoic era. _____

7. Some dinosaurs hunted other animals. _____

8. Still other dinosaurs munched plants. _____

9. Birds may have evolved from dinosaurs. _____

10. Not all dinosaurs grew to become giants. _____

Name _____

Dinosaurs Are Extinct

Being Verbs and Linking Verbs A **being verb** shows a state of being, not action. A **being verb** is called a **linking verb** when it links the subject to a predicate noun or a predicate adjective. A **predicate noun** identifies or renames the subject. A **predicate adjective** describes the subject.

Common Being and Linking Verbs				
am	was	be	become	feel
is	were	being	look	taste
are	seem	been	appear	smell

Underline the linking verb in each sentence below. After each sentence, write whether the verb links to a predicate noun or predicate adjective.

Example: Some dinosaurs <u>were</u> giants. _____predicate noun_____

1. The paleontologist <u>seems</u> excited by that stone. *predicate adjective*

2. That stone <u>is</u> a fossil of a dinosaur. *predicate noun*

3. The work of a paleontologist <u>looks</u> interesting to me. *predicate adjective*

4. Fossils of ferns <u>are</u> common here. *predicate noun*

5. A paleontologist <u>is</u> a scientist. *predicate noun*

Name _____

Dinosaurs Was/Were . . .

Using Forms of the Verb *be* A good writer uses the correct form of the verb *be*, especially when writing sentences with linking verbs. Study the present and past tense forms of the verb *be* in the chart below.

	Present Tense	**Past Tense**
Singular	I am	I was
	You are	You were
	She/he/it is	She/he/it was
Plural	We are	We were
	You are	You were
	They are	They were

Below is the beginning of a report written by a student who found a fossil. Write the correct form of the verb *be* above any incorrect verbs.

                  was
Example: I were tired.
              ^

                          are

My brother and I is interested in dinosaurs. Yesterday,
                   ^
were
we was at the creek looking for fossils. My brother showed
 ^
                       was
me a good place to look. It were a place with a lot of slate.
               ^
                                 are
I didn't think we'd find anything because fossils is hard
                               ^
        am
to find. I are happy to tell you that I was wrong. I found
      ^

a fossil impression of a tiny snail in a piece of slate.

Writing a Business Letter

When Ned Colbert in *Dinosaur Ghosts* began to study *Coelophysis* skeletons in 1947, he probably wrote business letters to ask paleontologists at other museums and universities around the United States for help. You write a **business letter** to request or persuade someone to do something, to apply for a job, to order a product from ads or catalogs, to ask for information, to complain about a product or service, or to express an opinion to a newspaper, radio, or TV station.

Use this page to plan and organize a business letter in which you write to either a company or a government agency requesting information. Follow these steps:

1. Write a **heading** (your own address and the date) in the upper right corner.
2. Write the **inside address** (the address of the person or business you are writing to) at the left margin.
3. Write a **greeting** (*Dear Sir or Madam:* or *Dear [business name]:)* at the left margin below the inside address.
4. Write the **body** of your letter below the greeting. Be brief and direct, but present all of the necessary details. If you state an opinion, support it with details. Make sure to use a formal and polite tone.
5. Write a formal **closing** such as *Sincerely, Cordially,* or *Yours truly* in the lower right corner.
6. Sign your full name under the closing. Then print or type your name below your **signature**.

When you finish your business letter, copy it onto a clean sheet of paper. Then share it with a classmate.

Name _____

Using the Right Tone

The attitude that a writer has toward a subject is called the **tone**. A writer's choice of words and details conveys his or her tone. When you write a business letter, you want to create a good impression by using the right tone. Here are some tips to follow: Use polite language. Use a more formal tone than you would use in a friendly letter. Use correct grammar, complete sentences, and well-formed paragraphs. Avoid the use of slang. Do not include personal information.

Read the following business letter from a college student to Ned Colbert. Fill in the chart below with examples of language and details that are *not* businesslike.

Dear Ned,

    Wow! I seen the cool photographs of your project in <u>Life</u> magazine. I do not have anything better to do, so I am interested in coming to New Mexico this summer to help with the <u>Coelophysis</u> excavation at Ghost Ranch. Would you tell me how to join your field crew?

    I am fascinated by the Ghost Ranch skeletons. Since I will be studying history and geology next semester, this job would give me some excellent firsthand knowledge. I am a hard worker. Ask anyone at the Ribs Palace on Route 120 where I used to work. Keep in touch.

      Sincerely,
      Dennis Sauer

Slang	
Impolite Language	
Informal Tone	
Personal Information	
Incorrect Grammar	

Name _____

Filling in the Blank

Use the test-taking strategies and tips you have learned to help you answer this type of multiple-choice question. This practice will help you when you take this kind of test.

Read each item. Fill in the circle in the answer row for the answer that best completes the sentence.

1 It is a fact that the first place Amelia Earhart and Fred Noonan took off from on June 1, 1937, was —

A Karachi, India.   C Miami, Florida.

B San Juan, Puerto Rico. D Lae, New Guinea.

2 Many people believe that taking the telegraph key and antenna would not have helped Amelia and Fred because —

F they would be too far away for the communications to be heard.

G neither one of them knew Morse code.

H they did not know how to connect the equipment.

J there was no one on the ground who could understand their signals.

3 Newspaper reporters shared the opinion that Amelia's fans were —

A anxious to read about her trip.

B concerned about Amelia taking the survival equipment off the plane.

C tired of hearing about long-distance flights.

D afraid that it was too dangerous for Amelia and Fred to fly in bad weather.

4 It is documented that in one month of flying Amelia and Fred had gone —

F 7,000 miles (11,300 km).   H 29,000 miles (46,700 km).

G 200 miles (320 km).   J 22,000 miles (35,400 km).

ANSWER ROWS 1 Ⓐ Ⓑ Ⓒ Ⓓ   3 Ⓐ Ⓑ Ⓒ Ⓓ
             2 Ⓕ Ⓖ Ⓗ Ⓙ   4 Ⓕ Ⓖ Ⓗ Ⓙ

Name _____

Filling in the Blank continued

5 The trip from Lae, New Guinea, to Howland Island was considered the most dangerous because —

    A the plane radio would not work in this area.

    B the airspace had never been mapped.

    C there was no runway to land on Howland Island.

    D the journey would take about 18 hours.

6 The reason Amelia and Fred did not see the smoke signals sent up by the crew of the *Itasca* might have been that —

    F no one knew that the U.S. Coast Guard had a ship in the area.

    G there was a problem with the Electra's radio.

    H thick cloud banks blocked the view of Howland Island.

    J the Electra was running out of gas.

7 Some people think that Amelia and Fred —

    A were spies for the U.S. government.

    B never really took the plane trip.

    C returned home without any problems.

    D decided to get married and live on an island in the Pacific.

8 A fact from the story is that the search for Amelia and Fred —

    F was the largest in the history of the world.

    G included a battleship, four destroyers, a minesweeper, and a seaplane.

    H went on for many months.

    J was cancelled due to bad weather around Howland Island.

ANSWER ROWS   **5** Ⓐ Ⓑ Ⓒ Ⓓ   **7** Ⓐ Ⓑ Ⓒ Ⓓ
                  6 Ⓕ Ⓖ Ⓗ Ⓙ   **8** Ⓕ Ⓖ Ⓗ Ⓙ

Name _____

Spelling Review

Write Spelling Words from the list to answer the questions.

1–24. Which twenty-four words contain the /ûr/, /ôr/, /är/, or /îr/ sounds, or have the final /ər/, /ən/, or /əl/ sounds?

1. _____   13. _____
2. _____   14. _____
3. _____   15. _____
4. _____   16. _____
5. _____   17. _____
6. _____   18. _____
7. _____   19. _____
8. _____   20. _____
9. _____   21. _____
10. _____   22. _____
11. _____   23. _____
12. _____   24. _____

25–30. Which six one-syllable words are homophones?

25. _____   28. _____
26. _____   29. _____
27. _____   30. _____

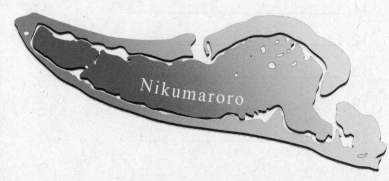
Nikumaroro

Spelling Words

1. channel
2. familiar
3. hanger
4. who's
5. chart
6. calendar
7. rehearse
8. starch
9. purse
10. whose
11. hangar
12. curb
13. mourn
14. director
15. frighten
16. manor
17. thorn
18. vain
19. messenger
20. pierce
21. struggle
22. sent
23. vein
24. manner
25. sword
26. similar
27. scent
28. whirl
29. gallon
30. rural

Name _____

Spelling Spree

Syllable Scramble **Rearrange the syllables in each item to
write a Spelling Word. There is one extra syllable in each
item.**

    Example: er for sid con   *consider*

1. sen ger mes ize   *messenger*

2. en cal men dar   *calendar*

3. ger iar mil fa   *familiar*

4. hearse in re   *rehearse*

5. rec na tor di   *director*

Word Maze **Begin at the arrow and follow the Word Maze
to find ten Spelling Words. Write the words in
the order you find them.**

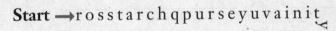

Start → r o s s t a r c h q p u r s e y u v a i n i t

q u p o m o u r n w a t

6. _____

7. _____

8. _____

9. _____

10. _____

11. _____

12. _____

13. _____

14. _____

15. _____

Spelling Words

1. familiar
2. calendar
3. mourn
4. frighten
5. gallon
6. rehearse
7. starch
8. purse
9. director
10. vain
11. messenger
12. scent
13. curb
14. vein
15. manner

Name _____

Proofreading and Writing

Proofreading Circle the six misspelled Spelling Words in this detective's journal. Then write each word correctly.

The case of Mrs. Van Cash's jewels has put me into a whurl. At first I didn't know how to chaurt a course. It's been a real struggel for me, Sherlock McGillicuddy, to find the truth. The mystery was truly a thorne in my side! When the maid swore the jewels were hers, I wondered whos they really were. Then I solved the mystery! The maid was telling the truth. Her jewels were simalar to the stolen ones, but hers were fakes.

1. channel
2. hanger
3. who's
4. chart
5. whose
6. hangar
7. thorn
8. pierce
9. struggle
10. sword
11. similar
12. sent
13. whirl
14. manor
15. rural

1. _____   4. _____

2. _____   5. _____

3. _____   6. _____

Reporting the Facts Write the Spelling Words that best complete this television news report.

An ancient, long-bladed 7. _____ has been found in a

8. _____ area outside town. The weapon was found in an old

airplane 9. _____. A worker picked it up, thinking it was a coat

10. _____. Experts believe this may be the blade used centuries

ago to 11. _____ a stone near the 12. _____ house

of Sir Percy. The blade will be 13. _____ to a lab for testing.

Now the question is, 14. _____ going to claim this treasure?

Stay tuned to this 15. _____!

✏➤ Write a Plot Outline On a separate sheet of paper, write a plot outline for a story about an unsolved mystery.

Name _____

Compare and Contrast

Two of the characters in these plays learn more about themselves.
Complete the chart to compare and contrast their searches and what
they find out.

	The Diary of Anne Frank	A Better Mousetrap
What challenges do Anne Frank in *The Diary of Anne Frank* and the Woman in *A Better Mousetrap* face?		
How do Anne and the Woman change?		

Name _____

Critic's Corner

Think of a movie, play, or television show you have read or seen recently. (It can be one of the plays you have read in the *Focus on Plays* section.) Think about the characters, the setting, the plot, and other details. Write a critical review of the play, telling what you liked and didn't like about the production. Be specific. Use examples from the piece to support your points.

Name _____

Growing Up

How do the characters in this theme grow? Add to this chart
and the one on the next page after you read each story.

	Where the Red Fern Grows	Last Summer with Maizon
Who is the main character or characters?		
What problem does the main character have?		

Name _____

Growing Up

	The Challenge	The View from Saturday
Who is the main character or characters?		
What problem does the main character have?		
What does the main character learn about himself or herself in the story?		

Sometimes struggle leads to growth. How do the stories in this theme support this statement?

_____

_____

Name _____

Going to Market

Use the words in the box to complete the paragraph below.

Vocabulary

~~provisions~~
~~determination~~
~~depot~~
~~urgency~~
~~wares~~
~~cheap~~

Several times a year, people who live in the mountains load up their wagons and travel to town to sell homemade pies, jars of jam, and other ___wares___. It takes ___determination___ to rise before dawn and ride such a long distance. Restaurants in town are not ___cheap___, so the mountain people usually bring their own food. They carry strips of dried meat and other ___provisions___ in their packs. The travelers feel a sense of ___urgency___ as they approach the town because they must hurry to set up their displays before shoppers from the city begin arriving at the train ___depot___.

Name _____

Generalization Chart

Generalizations	Information from the Story	Information from My Own Life
Page 242	Page 242	
Pages 243–245	Pages 243–245	
Pages 247–248	Pages 247–248	
Page 249	Page 249	
Pages 249–254	Pages 249–254	
Pages 255–258	Pages 255–258	

A Conversation with Papa

Suppose that Billy returns from Tahlequah, and must tell his parents where he's been and why. Below is a conversation he might have with his father. Use details from the story to help you fill in the words Billy might say.

Papa: Billy, where've you been? Your mother and I have been worried about you.

Billy: _____

Papa: Why did you go there?

Billy: *(showing the bag with the hound pups)* _____

Papa: Hound pups! Who'd you buy them from?

Billy: _____

_____

Papa: Those pups must be worth 30 dollars apiece! How'd you pay for them?

Billy: _____

_____

Papa: Where'd you get that much money?

Billy: _____

_____

_____

Papa: Now wait a minute. How'd you order the puppies?

Billy: _____

Papa: Why did you walk to Tahlequah by yourself? Did Grandpa tell you to?

Billy: _____

_____

Broadly Speaking . . .

Read the passage. Then complete the activity on page 143.

Dot and the Turkeys

All families were poor during the Great Depression. Dot's family was no exception. Even after selling milk and butter from the dairy farm, Ma and Pa struggled to keep food on the table for themselves and their seven children. The family's meals usually consisted of cornbread and buttermilk. Only on holidays did the children get treats such as nuts or a piece of fresh fruit. For children during the Depression, oranges were a particularly special treat. In general, families had little money for clothes, and often made their clothes by hand. Dot had no shoes and only owned one dress to wear to school, a homemade dress her older sister outgrew.

For a while Pa tried to make ends meet by raising turkeys. Ma had warned six-year-old Dot to stay away from the turkey pen. "Most turkeys are just plain mean," she said. Dot, however, was fascinated with the big birds and their drooping red wattles. She listened for hours to their clucking and gobbling and watched them strut about proudly. One day she slipped inside the pen to pet the huge, soft-looking birds. The turkeys, however, were not amused by the small girl inside their pen. The flock rushed at her and nearly smothered her. Dot's terrified screaming brought Ma and her brothers to her rescue. She never went near the turkeys again.

Name _____

Broadly Speaking . . . continued

Answer these questions about the passage on page 142.

1. The underlined sentence in the first paragraph states a generalization. Do you think it is valid or invalid? Why?

   invalid

   It barely talks about the great depression.

2. How could you rewrite this sentence so that it states a valid generalization?

   Dot's family raised turkeys during the
   Great Depression

3. What two generalizations about food are made in the first paragraph?

   A. _Selling milk and butter_

   B. _Eating cornbread and buttermilk._

4. What two generalizations about clothes are made in the first paragraph?

   A. _____

   B. _____

5. How do the details about Dot's clothes support these generalizations?

   _____

6. What other generalization could you make about life during the Depression?

   _____

   _____

   _____

Name _____

Word Patterns in Writing

Add slashes between the syllables of each underlined word.
Then write another sentence using the word correctly.

1. My hands were <u>calloused</u> after raking leaves all day.

_____

_____

_____

2. The girl was <u>dumbfounded</u> by the sight of the vast prairie.

_____

_____

_____

3. My sister and I like to tease our <u>grandfather</u> about his beard.

_____

_____

_____

4. At the first light of dusk, the <u>mosquitoes</u> begin biting.

_____

_____

_____

5. The boys saw a <u>shadowy</u> figure move in the window of the house.

_____

_____

Name _____

VCV, VCCV, and VCCCV Patterns

To spell a two-syllable word, divide the word into syllables. Look for spelling patterns, and spell the word by syllables.

Divide a VCV word after the consonant if the first syllable has the short vowel pattern. Divide the word before the consonant if the first syllable ends with a vowel sound.

VC/V **bal / ance**   V/CV **mi / nus**

VCCV words are usually divided between the consonants. They can be divided before or after two consonants that together spell one sound.

VC/CV **law / yer**   V/CCV **au / thor**   VCC/V **meth / od**

VCCCV words are often divided after the first of the three successive consonants.

When *y* spells a vowel sound, it is considered a vowel.

VC/CCV **sup / ply**

Write each Spelling Word under its syllable pattern.

VCV	**VCCV**
_____	_____
_____	_____
_____	_____
_____	_____
_____	_____
_____	_____
_____	**VCCCV**
_____	_____
_____	_____
	_____

1. balance
2. lawyer
3. sheriff
4. author
5. minus
6. method
7. item
8. require
9. supply
10. whisper
11. spirit
12. tennis
13. adopt
14. instant
15. poison
16. deserve
17. rescue
18. journey
19. relief
20. laundry

Theme 3: **Growing Up**   145

Spelling Spree

The Third Word Write the Spelling Word that belongs with each group of words.

Name _____

1. police chief, marshal, _____

2. save, recover, _____

3. demand, insist, _____

4. editor, publisher, _____

5. venom, toxin, _____

6. earn, merit, _____

7. liveliness, energy, _____

8. ping pong, badminton, _____

9. way, technique, _____

10. object, article, _____

Syllable Scramble Rearrange the syllables in each item to write a Spelling Word. An extra syllable is in each item.

11. jour di ney _____

12. nus mi less _____

13. yer pre law _____

14. dol ance bal _____

15. lief re ant _____

16. a com dopt _____

17. ex ply sup _____

18. dry im laun _____

19. per whis un _____

20. in port stant _____

mer   chant

Name _____

Proofreading and Writing

Proofreading Circle the five misspelled Spelling Words in this advertisement. Then write each word correctly.

> NEEDED: People needed to addopt one or more puppies. They are playful and full of spirrit, and they require lots of love and attention. They have been living in our londry room, but they still need to be housebroken. We will suply the first two weeks of food. These are great dogs, and they desserve a good home. Call 555-3647.

1. _____

2. _____

3. _____

4. _____

5. _____

Spelling Words

1. balance
2. lawyer
3. sheriff
4. author
5. minus
6. method
7. item
8. require
9. supply
10. whisper
11. spirit
12. tennis
13. adopt
14. instant
15. poison
16. deserve
17. rescue
18. journey
19. relief
20. laundry

➤ **Write Guidelines for Pet Care** Dogs, cats, and other pets need a great deal of care. What kinds of guidelines would a new pet owner need?

Choose a type of pet. Then, on a separate sheet of paper, write a list of guidelines for caring for that pet. Use Spelling Words from the list.

Name _____

Synonym Sampler

Read each entry word, its definition, and its synonyms on the thesaurus page below. Then rewrite the numbered sentences using synonyms to replace the words in bold print.

happiness *n.* The state or quality of feeling joy or pleasure.

> **joy** A feeling of great happiness or delight.
> **gladness** The state or quality of feeling joy or pleasure.
> **bliss** Extreme happiness; joy.

courage *n.* The quality of spirit that enables one to face danger or hardship; bravery.

> **spirit** A mood marked by vigor, courage, or liveliness.
> **mettle** Spirit; daring; courage.
> **bravery** The quality or condition of showing courage.

1. Billy's **courage** helped him to reach his goal.

   _bravery_____

2. As he touched the pups, **happiness** welled up in Billy's heart.

   _____bliss_____

3. Billy's **happiness** was hardly contained when he knew that the pups were about to come.

   _____joy_____

   _____

4. Billy needed extra **courage** to carry out his plan.

   _____spirit_____

5. Billy's **courage** as he hiked through the hills was matched by his **happiness** when he arrived.

   _____mettle_____gladness_____

   _____

Name _____

Summer Days

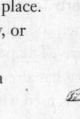

Verb Tenses The **tense** of a verb tells when the action takes place. The **present tense** is used when something is happening now, or happens regularly over time. The **past tense** is used when something has already happened. Here is how the verb *walk*, a regular verb, looks in these two tenses:

Present Tense	Past Tense
I **walk**.	I **walked**.
You **walk**.	You **walked**.
She/He/It **walks**.	She/He/It **walked**.
We **walk**.	We **walked**.
You **walk**.	You **walked**.
They **walk**.	They **walked**.

Circle the verb in each of the following sentences. Decide whether the verb is in the past tense or the present tense, and write *past* or *present* on the line.

1. He (lived) in the Ozark Mountains. ___past___

2. Celia (fishes) in the river. ___present___

3. I (strolled) through the grass in my bare feet. ___past___

4. They (played) with Kelly's new puppy. ___past___

5. You (like) the outdoors. ___present___

Now rewrite the five sentences above. If the original verb was in the past tense, change it to the present tense. If the original verb was in the present tense, change it to the past tense.

1. ___He lives in the Ozark Mountains.___

2. ___Celia fished in the river.___

3. ___I stroll through the grass in my bare feet.___

4. ___They play with Kelly's new puppy.___

5. ___You liked the outdoors.___

Name _____

Money!

More About Verb Tenses The **present tense** of a verb is used when something is happening now or happens regularly. The **past tense** of a verb is used when something has already happened. The **future tense** of a verb is used when something is going to happen. To form the future tense, use the helping verb *will* or *shall* with the main verb.

Circle the verb in each sentence. Then write its tense on the line.

1. We (saved) our allowance for a month. __past__

2. The package (will arrive) on time. __future__

3. William (ordered) new track shoes. __past__

4. We (will earn) money for our vacation. __future__

5. Pat (saves) for the future. __present__

Now rewrite each sentence using the verb tense shown.

1. **Future** We will save our allowance for a month.

2. **Present** The package arrives on time.

3. **Present** William orders new track shoes.

4. **Past** We earned money for our vacation.

5. **Future** Pat will save for the future.

Name _____

When Did That Happen?

Choosing the Correct Verb Tense Switch tenses when you write only to tell about different times.

Dorinda wrote the following paragraph. Rewrite her paragraph using correct verb tenses. The first sentence will not change.

Every summer I visit my aunt and uncle. They ~~lived~~ live in a mountain valley. I ~~will~~ like to walk there in my bare feet and ~~waded~~ wade in the creek behind their house. Last summer, I ~~help~~ helped my aunt and uncle with their vegetable garden. It ~~is~~ was hard work, but we all ~~will enjoy~~ enjoyed the vegetables. Vegetables fresh from a garden ~~will taste~~ tasted so much better than vegetables from a store! Now I ~~wanted~~ want to grow vegetables at home. When spring arrives, my parents ~~helped~~ will help me plant tomatoes and green beans. Then we ~~enjoy~~ will enjoy eating vegetables from our garden.

Every summer I visit my aunt and uncle. They live in a mountain valley. I like to walk there in my bare feet and wade in the creek behind their house. Last summer I helped my aunt and uncle with their vegetable garden. It was hard work, but we all enjoyed the vegetables. Vegetables fresh from a garden tasted so much better than vegetables from a store! Now I want to grow vegetables at home. When spring arrives, my parents will help me plant tomatoes and green beans. Then we will enjoy eating vegetables from our garden.

Name _____

Writing a Problem-Solution Composition

Writing about a character's problems in a **problem-solution composition** can help you better understand characters and events in a story. In *Where the Red Fern Grows*, for example, Billy Colman faces a problem. How Billy solves his problem reveals the kind of person he is.

Brainstorm problems that Billy solves in this story as well as problems that characters solve in other stories you have read. Write three of these problems and solutions on the graphic organizer below.

Problem	Solution(s)
Billy wants to buy two hound pups but does not have enough money.	He works hard for two years until he has saved fifty dollars.

Now pick one problem and its solution. On a separate sheet of paper, write your problem-solution composition. Begin with an introductory sentence that tells who or what you are writing about. Then state the problem in the first paragraph. In the second paragraph, describe how Billy or another character solves the problem. Include details that lead to the solution. Finally, end with a strong concluding sentence.

Organization

Good writers organize their ideas by sequence of events, by causes and effects, or by main ideas and details.

Help to unscramble this composition. Write students' ideas in a logical order in the organization outline below.

> In the winter, he traps opossums and sells their hides to fur buyers.
> Through hard work and determination, Billy finally realizes his dream.
> Billy desperately wants to buy two hound pups.
> Billy Colman is growing up during the Great Depression.
> Also, he catches crawfish and minnows and sells them to fishermen.
> To earn what he needs, Billy decides to work hard and save the money.
> However, each dog costs twenty-five dollars.
> During the summer, he picks berries and sells them.
> After two years, Billy has saved fifty dollars.
> Neither Billy nor his parents have fifty dollars to spend.

Paragraph 1: Introductory sentence

_____

Problem

_____

_____

Paragraph 2: Solution

_____

_____

_____

_____

Concluding sentence

_____

Name _____

Revising Your Description

Reread your description. What do you need to make it better? Use this page to help you decide. Put a checkmark in the box for each sentence that describes what you've written.

Loud and Clear!

- [ ] My description is well organized and clearly written.
- [ ] My beginning pulls the reader into the story.
- [ ] I combine sentences to make my writing more compact.
- [ ] The events are in a sequence that is easy to follow.
- [ ] The description has a satisfying ending.
- [ ] There are a few mistakes.

Sounding Stronger

- [ ] My description could be better organized.
- [ ] The beginning could be more interesting.
- [ ] I could combine more sentences to vary my writing.
- [ ] The sequence of events is confusing in parts.
- [ ] My ending could be more exciting.
- [ ] Errors make parts of the story hard to follow.

Turn Up Volume

- [ ] My description is disconnected and unorganized.
- [ ] The beginning is boring.
- [ ] I need to combine sentences to vary my writing.
- [ ] The description doesn't have an interesting ending.
- [ ] Too many mistakes make the story hard to read.

Name _____

Sentence Combining

**Combine each pair of sentences to make them
flow more easily. Use the joining word in parentheses. Add commas
where needed.**

1. Tom was born in Minnesota. (AND) Tom grew up there.

    Tom was born and grew up in Minnesota.

2. Toby was also born in Minnesota. (BUT) He grew up in Chicago.

    Toby was also born in Minnesota but he grew up in Chicago.

3. Tom and Toby were twins. (AND) They had been separated at birth.

    Tom and Toby were twins and they had been separated at bi

4. The twins had different last names. (BUT) They shared many traits.

    The twins had different last names but they shared many
    traits.

5. Tom owned a beagle named Willie. (OR) Toby owned a beagle named Willie.

    Tom or Toby owned a beagle named Willie.

6. The other owned a cat named Billy. (OR) The other owned a cat name Millie.

    The other owned a cat named Billy or Millie

7. Both twins loved baseball. (AND) Both twins hated fishing.

    Both twins loved baseball and hated fishing

8. Both twins owned the same kind of truck.(BUT) Tom's was blue and Toby's was red.

    Both twins owned the same kind of truck but tom's
    was blue and Toby's was red.

9. They both liked the same movie. (OR) They both hated the same movie.

    They both liked or hated the same movie.

10. Once the twins were together, they were happy. (AND)
    Once the twins were together, they would never part.

    Once the twins were together, they wer happy and
    would never part.

Name _____

Words Often Confused

Do cows graze in a pastor or a pasture? Is a glass ring a bauble or a bubble? It is easy to confuse words that have similar spellings and pronunciations even though the meanings are different. The Spelling Words in each pair on the list are often confused. Pay careful attention to their pronunciations, spellings, and meanings.

Write the missing letters in the Spelling Words below.

Spelling Words

1. bland
2. blend
3. below
4. bellow
5. pastor
6. pasture
7. moral
8. mortal
9. bauble
10. bubble
11. bisect
12. dissect
13. assent
14. ascent

1. bl _a_ nd
2. bl _e_ nd
3. be _l_ _o_ _w_
4. be _l_ _l_ ow
5. past _o_ _r_
6. pas _t_ _u_ _r_ _e_
7. mor _a_ _l_
8. mor _t_ _a_ _l_
9. b _a_ _u_ _b_ le
10. b _u_ _b_ _b_ le
11. b _i_ _s_ ect
12. d _i_ _s_ _s_ ect
13. a _s_ _s_ ent
14. a _s_ _c_ ent

Study List On a separate piece of paper, write each Spelling Word pair. Check your spelling against the words on the list.

Name _____

Spelling Spree

Contrast Clues The second part of each clue contrasts with the first part. Write a Spelling Word to fit each clue.

1. not a descent, but an _____
2. not spicy, but _____
3. not real jewelry, but a _____
4. not a whisper, but a _____
5. not living forever, but _____
6. not a forest, but a _____
7. not to cut into unequal pieces, but to _____

1. _ascent_
2. _bland_
3. _bauble_
4. _bellow_
5. _mortal_
6. _pasture_
7. _dissect_

Spelling Words

1. bland
2. blend
3. below
4. bellow
5. pastor
6. pasture
7. moral
8. mortal
9. bauble
10. bubble
11. bisect
12. dissect
13. assent
14. ascent

Word Switch For each item below, replace the underlined definition or synonym with a Spelling Word.

8. Next week in my sister's biology class, they're going to <u>cut apart in order to study</u> frogs.
9. We were halfway up the mountain when we heard a cry for help from a <u>lower position</u>.
10. If you <u>combine completely</u> these red and yellow paints, you should get the right shade of orange.
11. Did your mom give her <u>approval</u> to our plan to go hiking?
12. The <u>minister</u> greeted the new couple the first time they walked into the church.
13. Each of Aesop's fables has a <u>lesson</u>.
14. There was a soap <u>ball of air surrounded by a thin film of liquid</u> on the surface of the dishwater.

8. _dissect_
9. _below_
10. _____
11. _____
12. _____
13. _____
14. _____

Name _____

Proofreading and Writing

Proofreading Circle the five misspelled Spelling Words in this movie description. Then write each word correctly.

1. bland
2. blend
3. below
4. bellow
5. pastor
6. pasture
7. moral
8. mortal
9. bauble
10. bubble
11. bisect
12. dissect
13. assent
14. ascent

Growing Up ★★★✦ is a welcome change from the typical, blend children's movie. The director manages to bland four stories into one film. Together, they give a picture of the often difficult assent from childhood to the teenage years. Each story has its own morral, but teaches it quietly instead of trying to bellow it from the rooftops. Movie times are listed balow.

1. _____   4. _____

2. _____   5. _____

3. _____

✏️━━━▶ **Two for One** Pick four word pairs from the Spelling Word list. Then, for each pair, write a sentence using both words.

Name _____

City Similars

Read the word in each box from *Last Summer with Maizon*.
Then write two words from the list that are related to it in
meaning. Use a dictionary if necessary.

Vocabulary

earlier
lifeless
porch
imagining
empty
past
say
platform
thinking
communicate

express
_____
_____

desolate
_____
_____

daydreaming
_____
_____

previous
_____
_____

stoop
_____
_____

Name _____

Inferences Chart

	Evidence from the Story	Own Experiences	Inference
How does Margaret feel about Maizon moving away? (page 279)			
How does Margaret feel about her friendship with Maizon once Maizon has left? (pages 280–281)			
How does Margaret feel about being in Ms. Peazle's class? (page 283)			
How do you think Margaret's classmates feel about her poem? (page 286)			

Name _____

Story Frames

Think about what happened in *Last Summer with Maizon.* **Write what happened in each part of the story by completing the story frames.**

1. On the M train:	**Best Friends or Old Friends?**
	_____
	_____
	_____
	_____

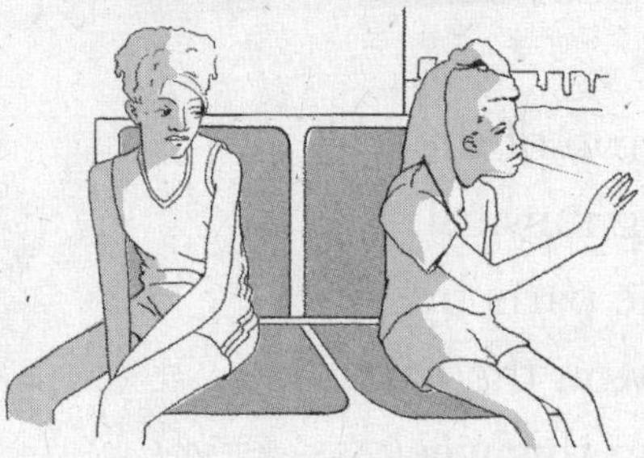

2. First Day in 6–1:	**The Essay**
	_____
	_____
	_____
	_____

3. Next Day in 6–1:	**The Poem**
	_____
	_____
	_____
	_____

4. On the Front Stoop:	**What's Changed? What Hasn't?**
	_____
	_____
	_____
	_____

Theme 3: **Growing Up**   161

Name _____

Reading Between the Lines

Read the passage. Then complete the activity on page 163.

The Audition

Serena ran into the girls' dressing room and locked the door behind her. "It's not fair! It's just not fair!" she cried, breaking into uncontrollable sobs. Just one week before, she had been on top of the world. She had been picked for the leading role in the spring musical. Mr. O'Toole, the choir director, had had the choir choose the parts by show of hands, after hearing the auditions for each part. "I won the part fair and square!" Serena wailed. "How dare Rebecca show up this week and ask to audition for my part! How could Mr. O'Toole have let her to do it? He's never done anything like that before! Rebecca should have been here last week if she wanted the part!"

The audition had been short, with only Serena and Rebecca performing. At first Serena hadn't been concerned. She'd won the part once, and she had figured that everyone would love her singing again. Mr. O'Toole had had everyone close their eyes again and raise their hands to vote. "The winner is Rebecca," Mr. O'Toole had announced. At that moment, the color had drained out of Serena's face as the choir applauded for Rebecca. Ashen-faced, she had bolted for the dressing room.

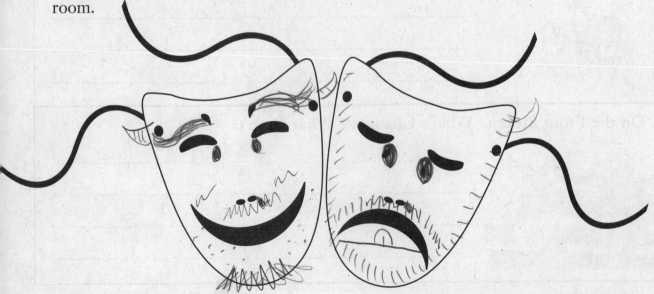

Name _____

Reading Between the Lines

continued

Answer the following questions about the passage on page 162.

1. How does Serena feel when the choir votes for Rebecca?

   Serena felt mad.

2. What story clues help you figure out how she feels?

   She was ashen-faced. She broke out into uncontrollable sobs.

3. Why do you think Mr. O'Toole allows Rebecca to audition for the role even though the choir already picked Serena? (To answer, think about what is probably important to Mr. O'Toole as the choir director.)

   He probably wants the best person for the musical.

4. How do you think Serena feels toward Rebecca at this moment in the story?

   I think she doesn't like Rebecca

5. What do you know from real life that can help you figure out how Serena feels toward Rebecca?

   Whenever someone takes something from you you feel mad

Name _____

Words, Inc.

For each word in column 1, write the base word in column 2 and the
ending in column 3. Check a dictionary if you are unsure about the
spelling of a base word.

	Base word	Ending
1. whispered	_____	_____
2. stumbled	_____	_____
3. exaggerated	_____	_____
4. sweating	_____	_____
5. smiling	_____	_____

Write the word from the chart that best completes each sentence.

6. When Margaret was unexpectedly asked to read her poem,

   she began _____.

7. Her classmates _____ among themselves.

8. They _____ their reactions as she got
   ready to read.

9. Margaret _____ over her feet on her
   way back to her desk.

10. When Margaret looked up, her teacher was _____.

Name _____

Words with *-ed* or *-ing*

Remember that when a one-syllable word ends with one vowel and one consonant, the final consonant is usually doubled before *-ed* or *-ing* is added. When a two-syllable word ends with a stressed syllable, double the final consonant before adding *-ed* or *-ing*.

      map**ped**   fit**ting**   pilot**ing**   begin**ning**

Write each Spelling Word under the heading that tells how the word is changed when *-ed* or *-ing* is added.

Spelling Words

1. mapped
2. piloting
3. permitting
4. beginning
5. bothered
6. limited
7. forgetting
8. reasoning
9. preferred
10. equaled
11. wondering
12. slipped
13. listening
14. fitting
15. pardoned
16. shoveled
17. favored
18. knitting
19. answered
20. modeling

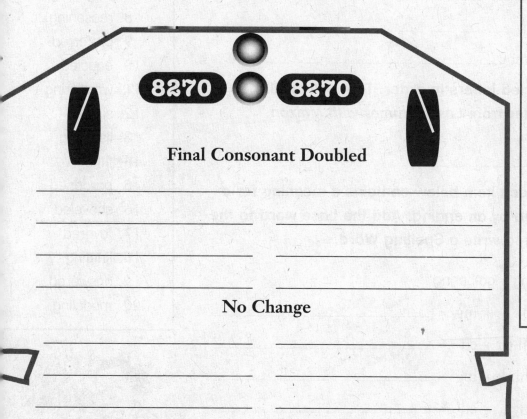

Final Consonant Doubled

_____   _____
_____   _____
_____   _____

No Change

_____   _____
_____   _____
_____   _____
_____   _____
_____   _____

Name _____

Last Summer with Maizon

Spelling Words with *-ed* or *-ing*

Spelling Spree

Puzzle Play **Write a Spelling Word to fit each clue.**

1. posing for a photographer ⚪ __ __ __ __ __ __ __

2. forgiven __ ⚪ __ __ __ __ __ __

3. allowing __ __ ⚪ __ __ __ __ __

4. flying a plane __ __ __ __ __ ⚪ __ __

5. replied ⚪ __ __ __ __ __ __ __

6. liked better __ ⚪ __ __ __ __ __ __ __

7. was the same as __ __ __ __ __ ⚪ __

8. making a sweater __ __ __ ⚪ __ __ __ __

Now write the circled letters in order. They will spell the name of a character from *Last Summer with Maizon*.

__ __ __ __ __ __ __ __ __

Meaning Match **Each item below contains a meaning for a base word followed by an ending. Add the base word to the underlined ending to write a Spelling Word.**

Example: collect + ing = gathering

9. be suitable for   + ing = _____

10. be for or partial to + ed = _____

11. the ability to think + ing = _____

12. disturb or annoy   + ed = _____

13. fail to remember   + ing = _____

14. start   + ing = _____

15. plan in detail   + ed = _____

Spelling Words

1. mapped
2. piloting
3. permitting
4. beginning
5. bothered
6. limited
7. forgetting
8. reasoning
9. preferred
10. equaled
11. wondering
12. slipped
13. listening
14. fitting
15. pardoned
16. shoveled
17. favored
18. knitting
19. answered
20. modeling

166   Theme 3: **Growing Up**

Name _____

Proofreading and Writing

Proofreading Circle the five misspelled Spelling Words in this letter. Then write each word correctly.

> **C**
>
> Dear Leslie,
>   How's it going? I've been lisening to the tape you sent with your last letter. It's great! I really like the song you sang at the beginning. I'm sorry it's taken me so long to write. My mom sliped on our sidewalk last week. She was shovelling snow. Since then, I've been doing a lot of things around the house. I guess my time is pretty limeted right now. Actually, I should get going. Mom must be wondring why the laundry hasn't been done. I 'll write again soon!
>   Your friend,
>   Carmen

1. mapped
2. piloting
3. permitting
4. beginning
5. bothered
6. limited
7. forgetting
8. reasoning
9. preferred
10. equaled
11. wondering
12. slipped
13. listening
14. fitting
15. pardoned
16. shoveled
17. favored
18. knitting
19. answered
20. modeling

1. _____
2. _____
3. _____
4. _____
5. _____

✏ **Write a Poem** Margaret wrote a poem to express her feelings about her father's death. Has there been an event in your life that caused you to feel great joy or sadness?

On a separate sheet of paper, write a poem about that event and the feelings you experienced then. Use Spelling Words from the list.

Name _____

Finding Word Forms

**Read each entry word, its inflected forms, and its definition. Write the
form of the word that best completes each sentence.**

> **choose** (chōōz) *v.* **chose, chosen, choosing, chooses.** To decide.
>
> **close** (klōs) *adj.* **closer, closest.** Near in space or time.
>
> **exchange** (ĭks chānj′) *v.* **exchanged, exchanging, exchanges.** To give
> and receive mutually; interchange.
>
> **smart** (smärt) *adj.* **smarter, smartest.** Intelligent, clever, or bright.
>
> **worry** (wûr′ ē) *v.* **worried, worrying, worries.** To feel uneasy or
> concerned about something.

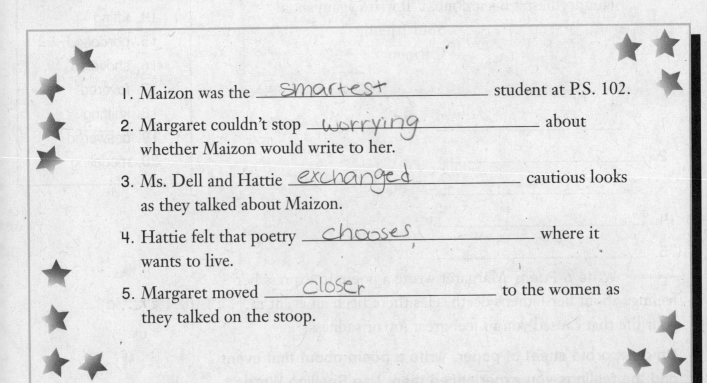

1. Maizon was the ___*smartest*___ student at P.S. 102.

2. Margaret couldn't stop ___*worrying*___ about
   whether Maizon would write to her.

3. Ms. Dell and Hattie ___*exchanged*___ cautious looks
   as they talked about Maizon.

4. Hattie felt that poetry ___*chooses*___ where it
   wants to live.

5. Margaret moved ___*closer*___ to the women as
   they talked on the stoop.

168   Theme 3: **Growing Up**

Name _____

Verb Trouble

Principal Parts of Regular and Irregular Verbs The **principal parts**, or basic forms, of a verb are the present form of the verb, the present participle, the past, and the past participle. All verb tenses are formed with these basic parts.

When the past and the past participle of a verb are formed by adding *-d* or *-ed*, the verb is **regular**. When the past and the past participle of a verb are formed in some other way, the verb is **irregular**.

	Present	Present Participle	Past	Past Participle
Regular	walk	(is) walking	walked	(has) walked
Irregular	ride	(is) riding	rode	(has) ridden

Margaret is having trouble with some verbs in a poem. The troublesome verbs are listed below. Complete the verb chart by writing the missing principal parts. Use a dictionary if needed. The first one is done for you.

Present	Present Participle	Past	Past Participle
sing	(is) singing	sang	(has) sung
write	(is) writing	wrote	(has) written
search	(is) searching	searched	(has) searched
feel	(is) feeling	felt	(has) felt
become	(is) becoming	became	(has) become
shout	(is) shouting	shouted	(has) shouted

Score with Perfect Tenses

► There are three **perfect tenses**: **present perfect**, **past perfect**, and **future perfect**. Form the present perfect tense with *have* or *has* and a past participle.

► Form the past perfect tense with *had* and a past participle.

► Form the future perfect tense with *will have* and a past participle.

Complete the chart below with the verb in the proper tense. The first one has been done for you.

Verb	Present Perfect	Past Perfect	Future Perfect
work	have worked	had worked	will have worked
move	have moved	had moved	will have moved
play	have played	had played	will have played
write	have written	had written	will have written
feel	have felt	had felt	will have felt
take	have taken	had taken	will have taken

Write the correct form of the verb in parentheses ( ) in each sentence below. Use the verb forms from the chart.

1. Maria ___moved___ away before school started. (move)
   past perfect

2. At the beginning of the year, my teacher ___worked___ with me after school. (work)
   past perfect

3. We ___have played___ together all day. (play)
   present perfect

4. I ___have felt___ this way before. (feel)
   present perfect

5. In two weeks, she ___will have written___ her report. (write)
   future perfect

Name _____

Letter Perfect Tenses

Choosing the Correct Verb Form To correctly form a perfect tense, use the **past participle** form of the verb with *have*, *has*, and *had*.

Proofread the following letter that Margaret might have written to a friend who moved away. Insert the proper verb forms where needed.

Example: I had ~~took~~ ^{taken} the long route.

> Hi!
>
> It has been a long time since I have heared from you. Since you left,
>
> John K. has ~~ask~~ ^{asked} me about you six times! Sarita says, "Hi." Even Ms.
>
> Whitney has ~~says~~ ^{said} she wonders how you are. J.D. has ~~wrote~~ ^{written} you a letter, but
>
> he has not mailed it yet.
>
> In the past month, I have went to the movies twice. Yesterday, I saw a
>
> TV movie called My Friend Flicka. I ~~had~~ ^{have seen} ~~seed~~ it before but I still liked it.
>
> Tomorrow I will have ~~taked~~ ^{taken} my fifth math quiz. We have one each week.
>
> I plan to rake leaves and shovel snow to make money this year. By
>
> summertime, I will have ~~save~~ ^{saved} enough to visit you. Remember last summer
>
> when we ~~goed~~ ^{went} to the beach? I had ran errands for months to earn that
>
> money.
>
>   Your friend,
>
>   Margaret

Responding to a Prompt

In *Last Summer with Maizon*, Ms. Peazle gives her sixth-grade class a writing prompt. She asks them to write an essay about their summer vacations. A **writing prompt** is a direction that asks for a written response of one or more paragraphs.

Read the following prompts and choose one you would like to respond to.

Prompt 1
Describe a time when you had to adjust to a change.

Prompt 2
Write about a person who is important to you. Describe the person and tell why he or she is important.

Prompt 3
Describe what you look for in a friend.

Use the chart below to help you plan your response. First, list key words in the prompt such as *compare, explain, describe,* or *discuss*. Next, jot down main ideas and details you might include. Finally, number your main ideas, beginning from most to least important.

Key Words	Main Ideas	Details

Write your response on a separate sheet of paper. Start by restating the prompt. Then write your main ideas and supporting details in order of importance from most to least important. Finally, check your response to make sure it answers the prompt.

Name _____

Correcting Sentence Fragments and Run-on Sentences

Good writers check to make sure that their sentences are complete. **Rewrite the body of the letter on the lines below. Correct run-on sentences and sentence fragments so that the reader can understand them.**

> 1234 Winding Drive Lane
> Greenfield, Connecticut 06606
> September 15
> Dear Bethany,
>   How are you? Boarding school is okay. I miss our old class. Teachers are pretty strict and they give tons of homework and they teach hard subjects. My tiny room at the end of the hall. Is already crammed with books and papers. Yesterday I met some other scholarship students. In my class. Unfortunately, none of them can jump rope.
>   I can't wait to come home on vacation. Boston seems so far away. I miss you! Write soon.
>   Your friend,
>   Allison

_____

_____

_____

_____

_____

_____

_____

_____

Name _____

What a Racquet!

Answer each of the following questions by writing a vocabulary word.

1. Which word tells what a show-off tries to attract?

   _____

2. Which word means "claimed to be great"?

   _____

3. Which word tells what friends do when they want you to do

   well? _____

4. Which word describes how you might feel if you accidentally walked into the wrong classroom?

   _____

5. Which word means the same as *swiftly* and *rapidly*?

   _____

6. Which word could replace *was able* in the sentence "Willa finally was able to return a serve"?

   _____

7. Which word means "become aware of"?

   _____

8. Which word means "to have a discussion"?

   _____

Write two new questions of your own that use at least one vocabulary word each.

9. _____

10. _____

Name _____

Story Map

Setting	Characters
_____	_____
_____	_____
_____	
_____	

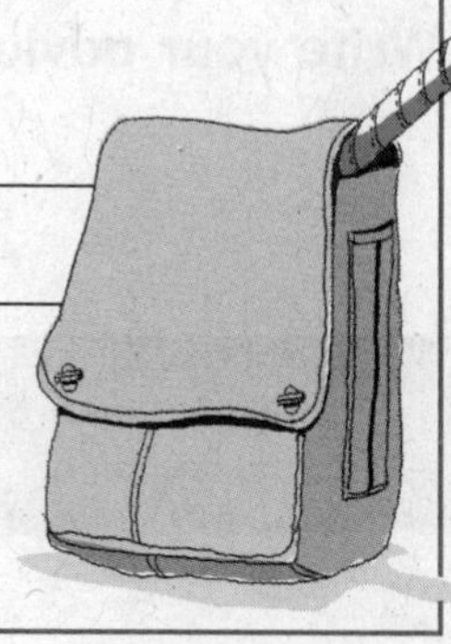

Plot

Story problem: _____

_____

Events:

1: _____

_____

2: _____

_____

3: _____

_____

4: _____

_____

Resolution: _____

_____

_____

_____

Name _____

Give Advice

What would you tell a friend who was thinking of lying to impress someone? Write your advice using José's experience as an example.

Lying to impress someone won't work. I know of a boy named José

who wanted to impress _____.

He tried studying harder to _____.

He even tried to show her _____

Nothing worked.

Then he saw that Estela had a _____.

That gave him the idea to _____.

Telling her that he could play racquetball was a lie, though, because

_____!

As soon as she said yes, José knew _____.

He went to his uncle Freddy's house to _____.

Uncle Freddy was sure _____

When José met Estela at the courts, he saw right away that

_____. Estela beat him

_____ Instead of

impressing her, José just felt _____.

So don't lie! Just be yourself.

Name _____

Story Building Blocks

Read the story. Then complete the story map on page 178.

The Spelling Bee

Marty had been nervous all morning. The Lincoln Middle
School Spelling Bee was about to begin, and he was the
representative from Ms. Higgins's sixth-grade class. Ms. Higgins
had asked Marty to compete earlier in the week. He'd said yes
because he was a good speller and he thought it might be fun.
However, now that he was up on the stage, he wondered what he
could have been thinking. "What if I make a mistake and
everyone laughs at me?" he worried.

The spelling bee began. Marty's first word was *nervous*.
"What a perfect word for me," he thought. He spelled the word
correctly, and his classmates applauded and cheered. Marty
smiled gratefully. "This isn't so bad after all," he decided.

After three rounds, only Marty and an eighth-grade girl
were left. Marty's next word was *enthusiastically*. "Wow. Long
word!" he thought. He started spelling the word, and then
stopped. He was trying to picture the word in his mind, but he
couldn't remember the last letter he had spoken! Marty made a
guess and continued at the *u*. When he finished, the judge said,
"I'm sorry, Marty. The word has only one *u*." The spelling bee
was over. Marty had lost.

As he was packing up his books, Marty saw Ms. Higgins.
He was about to apologize when she said, "Marty, what a great
job! You did better than all the seventh graders and most
of the eighth graders!" Marty smiled. He hadn't thought about
it that way. He hadn't lost. He'd finished near the top!

Name _____

Story Building Blocks continued

Complete the story map with details from "The Spelling Bee."

Story Map

Setting	Characters
When: _____	Who: _____
_____	_____
Where: _____	_____

Plot

Problem: _____

Events:

1. _____

2. _____

3. _____

4. _____

5. _____

Resolution: _____

Name _____

Suffix Chart

**Read each sentence. For each underlined word, write the base and
the suffix of the word in the chart. Then use sentence clues and
what you know about the meaning of each suffix to write the meaning
of each word. An example is provided.**

1. José's class learned how the Egyptians would <u>mummify</u> their dead.
2. Estela's racket was <u>blackened</u> by her frequent playing.
3. She <u>flattened</u> her milk carton as she finished her lunch.
4. He tried to keep his face from <u>reddening</u> with shame.
5. José didn't want to <u>dramatize</u> his feelings, even though Estela
   could <u>terrify</u> him on the court.

Base word	Suffix	Meaning
mummy	-ify	make into a mummy

Name _____

Endings and Suffixes

Remember that if a word ends with *e*, the *e* is usually dropped when a suffix or an ending beginning with a vowel is added. The *e* is usually not dropped when a suffix beginning with a consonant is added.

divide + ed = divid**ed**   grace + ful = grace**ful**

► In the starred words *mileage* and *manageable*, the final *e* of the base word is kept when a suffix beginning with a vowel is added.

Write each Spelling Word under the heading that tells what happens to its base word when a suffix or ending is added.

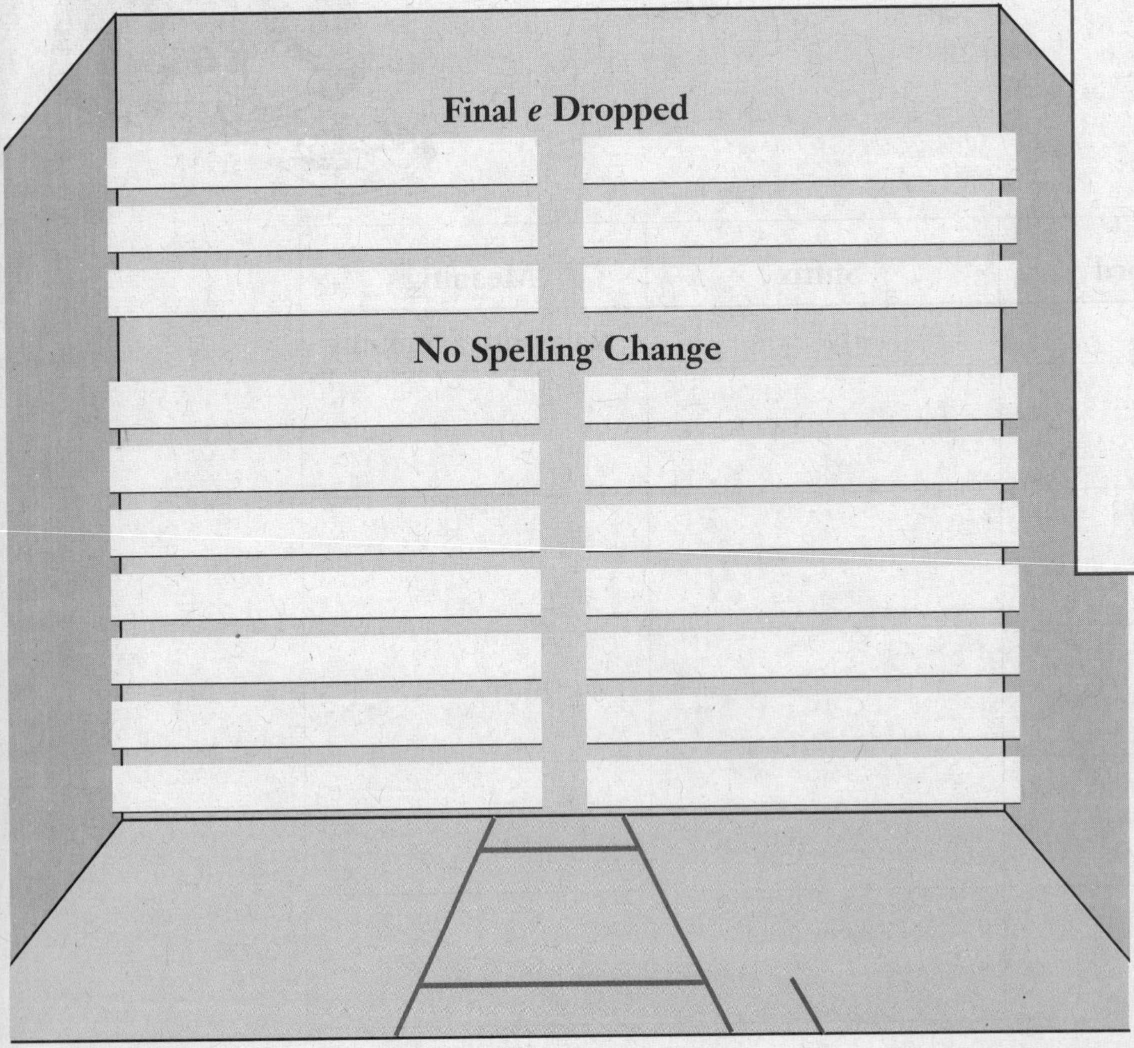

Final *e* Dropped

No Spelling Change

Name _____

Spelling Spree

Adding Suffixes or Endings Write the Spelling Word that has each base word below. The spelling of a base word may change.

1. use   _____

2. forgive   _____

3. grace   _____

4. adore   _____

5. sincere   _____

6. heave   _____

7. mile   _____

8. life   _____

9. replace   _____

10. scarce   _____

1. graceful
2. divided
3. advanced
4. privately
5. replacement
6. excitement
7. adorable
8. heaving
9. forgiveness
10. mileage*
11. barely
12. forceful
13. scarcely
14. blaming
15. entirely
16. usable
17. sincerely
18. amusement
19. lifeless
20. manageable*

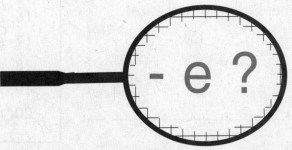

Contrast Clues The second part of each clue contrasts with the first part. Write a Spelling Word to fit each clue.

11. not united, but   _____

12. not partly, but   _____

13. not basic, but   _____

14. not publicly, but   _____

15. not impossible, but _____

Theme 3: **Growing Up**   181

Name _____

Proofreading and Writing

Proofreading Circle the five misspelled Spelling Words in this script for a scene from a movie. Then write each word correctly.

Spelling Words

Setting: A basketball court, with a boy and girl playing.

LUCY: *(She makes a forcefull move to the basket and scores. Her face lights up with exitement.)* Yes!

DANIEL: *(His chest is heaving.)* That was a lucky lay-up. You barly got past me. If it wasn't for these old, worn-out shoes . . .

LUCY: *(She looks at Daniel with amusment.)* Quit blamming your shoes. It's my ball. The score's ten to ten. Next point wins.

DANIEL: Hold on! Let me catch my breath. . . . Okay, let's go.

LUCY: *(She gets the ball and shoots a graceful jump shot, which goes in.)* That's game, little brother!

Spelling Words

1. graceful
2. divided
3. advanced
4. privately
5. replacement
6. excitement
7. adorable
8. heaving
9. forgiveness
10. mileage*
11. barely
12. forceful
13. scarcely
14. blaming
15. entirely
16. usable
17. sincerely
18. amusement
19. lifeless
20. manageable*

1. _____   4. _____

2. _____   5. _____

3. _____

✎▶ **Write a Challenging Invitation** Are you especially good at a sport or game? Is there someone whom you'd like to challenge to be your competitor?

On a separate sheet of paper, write an invitation challenging a friend to compete against you in your chosen sport or game. Use Spelling Words from the list.

Name _____

Using Parts of Speech

Read the dictionary entries. For each word, write two sentences, using the word as a different part of speech in each sentence.

▶ **palm** (päm) *n.* The inside surface of the hand. *–tr.v.* **palmed, palming, palms.** To conceal an object in the palm of the hand.

▶ **quiz** (kwĭz) *tr.v.* **quizzed, quizzing, quizzes.** To test the knowledge of by asking questions. *–n., pl.* **quizzes.** A short oral or written examination.

▶ **strain** (strān) *v.* **strained, straining, strains.** *–tr.* To exert or tax to the utmost. *–n.* An injury resulting from excessive effort or twisting.

▶ **whip** (wĭp) *v.* **whipped, whipping, whips.** *Informal.* To defeat; outdo. *–n.* A flexible rod or thong attached to a handle, used for driving animals.

1. _____
   _____
   _____

2. _____
   _____
   _____

3. _____
   _____
   _____

4. _____
   _____

Name _____

The Irregular Verb Challenge

Irregular verbs have the past or past participle formed, not by adding -*ed* or -*d*, but in some other way. You must memorize the forms of irregular verbs. Here are five irregular verbs to study.

Present	Past	Past Participle
become	became	become
feel	felt	felt
go	went	gone
see	saw	seen
take	took	taken

Now cover the chart above, and complete the exercise below. Fill in the blank in each sentence with either the past or the past participle form of the verb in parentheses. Remember that there must be a helping verb in order to use the past participle form.

1. Bob had ____become____ a skilled tennis player. (become)

2. He ____taken____ his racket to the court. (take)

3. He ____felt____ confident. (feel)

4. Bob's friends had ____seen____ him play many times. (see)

5. Last week they ____went____ to a big tournament with him. (go)

Name _____

In Agreement

The verb in a sentence must agree in number with its subject. In the
present tense, if the subject is singular, add -*s* or -*es* to the verb. Do not
add -*s* or -*es* if the subject is *I* or *you* or if the subject is plural.

**Kyle has started a conversation with Rosa,
the new girl in his class. To find out what
they are saying, choose from among these
verbs to fill in the blanks. Make each verb
agree with its subject.**

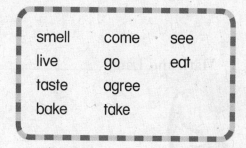

smell	come	see
live	go	eat
taste	agree	
bake	take	

Kyle: This tomato soup _____tastes_____ salty.

Rosa: You _____come_____ from Ohio, don't you?

Kyle: Yes. My cousin still _____lives_____ in Ohio.

Rosa: My cousin does too! He _____goes_____ to college
there.

Kyle: I _____see_____ my cousin during the holidays.

Rosa: Our cafeteria chef _____bakes_____ cookies every Friday.

Kyle: They _____taste_____ terrific!

Rosa: Chris and Kelly always _____eat_____ six cookies each.

Kyle: Our homework _____takes_____ a long time to do.

Rosa: I _____agree_____ with you!

Name _____

Writing Challenge

Verbs That Agree The people below are facing challenges.
Complete each sentence by writing an appropriate verb to
describe each scene. Be sure that subjects and verbs agree.

1. Mark and Laura _____.

2. A girl with three rings _____.

3. Mary _____.

4. Latasha and Bill _____.

5. Roberto _____.

Name _____

Writing a Character Sketch

A **character sketch** is a written profile that tells how either a real person or a character like Estela or José looks, acts, thinks, and feels.

Think about a real person or a story character from a selection you have read whom you would like to write about. Then use the web below to help you brainstorm details about this character's physical appearance and personality traits.

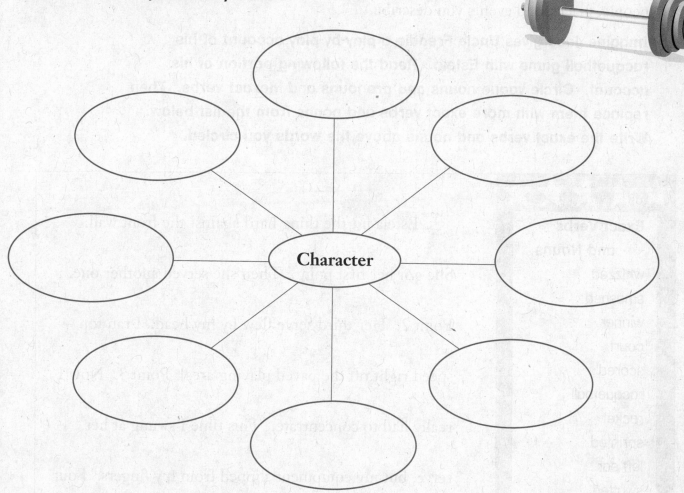

On a separate sheet of paper, write your character sketch. Begin with an anecdote or quote about the character. Then write a sentence that summarizes the character's most significant traits. Next, give two or three details from the web that support your summary. Conclude by restating the traits that are most significant.

Name _____

Using Exact Nouns and Verbs

Which noun, *sport* or *racquetball*, is more exact? Which verb, *held* or *gripped*, is more exact? A good writer avoids using vague nouns and verbs. Exact nouns and verbs like *racquetball* and *gripped* will make your writing clearer and help readers get a more vivid mental picture of the people, places, and events you describe.

Imagine José gives Uncle Freddie a play-by-play account of his racquetball game with Estela. Read the following portion of his account. Circle vague nouns and pronouns and inexact verbs. Then replace them with more exact verbs and nouns from the list below. Write the exact verbs and nouns above the words you circled.

Exact Verbs and Nouns
whizzed
smashed
winner
court
scored
racquetball
racket
sprinted
left ear
swatted

Estela hit the thing hard against the front wall.

She got her first point. Then she served another one.

Point 2. Her third serve flew by my head. I ran top

speed right off the paved playing area! Point 3. Now I

really had to concentrate. This time I swung at her

serve, but my equipment slipped from my fingers. Four

to zip.

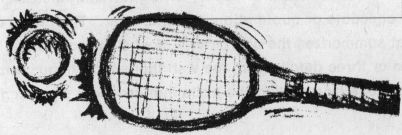

Name _____

Turtle Patrol Puzzle

Words are missing in the sentences. Fill each blank with a vocabulary word. Then follow the directions to help you find the letters that need to be unscrambled to answer the question below.

1. If you go back and forth between two places, you

    _____.

    Directions: Circle the fifth letter.

2. If you are moving to a new place, you are

    _____.

    Directions: Circle the first and seventh letters.

3. If something is not very obvious, it is

    _____.

    Directions: Circle the first and second letters.

4. If you remain in one place in the sky, you

    _____.

    Directions: Circle the third and fourth letters.

5. If something is allowed, it is _____.
    Directions: Circle the fifth and eighth letters.

6. If you and your friends offer to do something, you are

    _____.

    Directions: Circle the third and ninth letters.

7. If you are too curious about other people's business, you are

    _____.

    Directions: Circle the seventh letter.

What do turtle patrols try to do during big storms?

h ◯ ◯ p t ◯ ◯ t ◯ ◯ ◯

s ◯ ◯ v ◯ ◯ ◯

Name _____

Problem-Solution Chart

Problem	Solution
If tall buildings hide the horizon's light, baby turtles head toward the city lights instead of the sea, and many die.	Turtle volunteers _____ _____ _____
Nadia is jealous when she learns that Dad wants to be listed on Margaret's permit. She feels left out.	Nadia decides that, from now on, _____ _____
Dad knows that Nadia is upset and jealous of the time he spends with Margaret and the turtles.	Dad invites Nadia _____ _____ _____
A storm hits the Florida Coast, and the turtles are in danger.	Nadia decides to _____ _____
Dad and Nadia realize that, like the turtles, they too need help settling into their new lives.	They agree that there will be times when they need a _____ _____

Name _____

How Does Nadia Feel?

The following questions ask about how Nadia feels about her
new family situation in *The View from Saturday*. Answer
each one.

**Why does it upset Nadia to learn that Margaret set up her
mother's job interview?**

_____

_____

_____

Why does Nadia's father decide to take her to Disney World?

_____

_____

_____

**How does Nadia feel about her grandfather's remarriage and her
new family at first?**

_____

_____

_____

Why does Nadia decide not to go to Disney World?

_____

_____

_____

**What connection does Nadia discover between her life and the lives
of the sea turtles?**

_____

_____

_____

_____

Name _____

What Would You Do?

Read the story. Then complete page 193.

The Tag-Along

Ben whooped with joy as he rode down the hill on his mountain bike. He heard Ann shout with glee as she started down the same trail. When he glanced over his shoulder, however, Ben noticed that someone else was following them. It was Joyce. Ben felt annoyed.

Joyce had arrived in their class a few months ago. She was new to town and didn't know anyone. That became a problem for Ben when Joyce decided she wanted to become Ann's friend. For the past few weeks, no matter where Ben and Ann went, Joyce always seemed to show up a few minutes later.

Last week, Joyce came across Ben and Ann as they read comic books in Ben's tree house. She watched them for a while, but Ben did not invite her to join them. Yesterday, when Ann and Ben went swimming at the local pool, Joyce showed up and put her towel down right next to theirs.

Ben wanted to resolve the situation one way or another. He stopped his bike and waited for Joyce to catch up. He decided he was going to tell Joyce to stop following Ann around.

Name _____

What Would You Do? continued

**Complete the chart and answer the questions based on
"The Tag-Along."**

Character	Problem	Solution
Joyce		
Ben		

1. Is Joyce's way of dealing with her problem a good one?
   Why or why not?

   _____

   _____

   _____

2. How else can Joyce handle her problem?

   _____

   _____

   _____

3. Do you think Ben handles his problem in the best way possible?
   Explain your answer.

   _____

   _____

   _____

Name _____

Prefix Puzzle

**Each of the words in the eggs begins with the prefix *in-*, *im-*, or *con-*.
Find the word that matches each clue and write it in the letter spaces.**

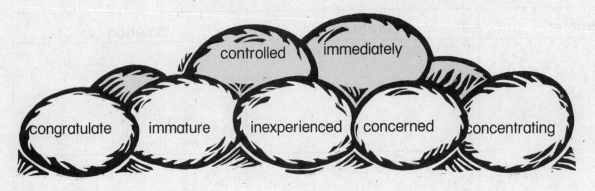

controlled immediately

congratulate immature inexperienced concerned concentrating

1. worried; anxious; troubled

   __ __ __ __ __ __ __ __ __

2. held in check; restrained

   __ __ __ __ __ __ __ __ __ __

3. not fully grown or developed

   __ __ __ __ __ __ __ __

4. taking place at once; happening without delay

   __ __ __ __ __ __ __ __ __ __ __

5. to express joy or good wishes to someone for an achievement

   __ __ __ __ __ __ __ __ __ __ __ __

6. thinking very hard; focusing attention on something

   __ __ __ __ __ __ __ __ __ __ __ __ __

7. not having knowledge or experience

   __ __ __ __ __ __ __ __ __ __ __ __ __

**Read the tinted letters down. Write the word, which means "to travel
regularly between one place and another."**

_____

194 Theme 3: **Growing Up**

Name _____

Prefixes: *in-* and *con-*

A **prefix** is a word part added to the beginning of a base word or a word root to add meaning. A **word root** is a word part that has meaning but cannot stand alone.

The prefix *in-* is spelled *im* before a base word or a word root beginning with *m* or *p*. The prefix *con-* is often spelled *com* before the consonant *m* or *p*.

Prefix + Base Word	**Prefix + Word Root**
incomplete, **im**polite	**in**volve, **im**mense
contest	**con**trol, **com**ment, **com**pete

To spell words with these prefixes, find the prefix, the base word or word root, and any ending. Spell the word by parts.

Write each Spelling Word under the spelling of its prefix.

Spelling Words

1. computer
2. impolite
3. control
4. include
5. immigrant
6. compete
7. consumer
8. involve
9. immediate
10. comment
11. infection
12. concert
13. import
14. conversation
15. community
16. incomplete
17. immense
18. contest
19. inactive
20. complicate

in-

_____

_____

_____

_____

con-

_____

_____

_____

_____

im-

_____

_____

_____

_____

com-

_____

_____

_____

_____

Name _____

Spelling Spree

Alphabetizing Write the Spelling Word that fits alphabetically between the two words in each group.

1. indoors, _____, inform

2. contract, _____, convene

3. compromise, _____, comrade

4. income, _____, increase

5. compass, _____, complain

6. inability, _____, incentive

7. consonant, _____, contain

8. concern, _____, conduct

Base Word/Word Root Match Write the Spelling Word that has the same base word or word root as each word below.

9. detest _____

10. export _____

11. exclude _____

12. duplicate _____

13. emigrant _____

14. politeness _____

15. immunity _____

Spelling Words

1. computer
2. impolite
3. control
4. include
5. immigrant
6. compete
7. consumer
8. involve
9. immediate
10. comment
11. infection
12. concert
13. import
14. conversation
15. community
16. incomplete
17. immense
18. contest
19. inactive
20. complicate

Name _____

Proofreading and Writing

Proofreading Circle the five misspelled Spelling Words in these instructions. Then write each word correctly.

Instructions for Permitted Volunteers

1. Watch the hatching quietly. Keep conversasion to a minimum.

2. Don't involv yourself in the hatching process. Let the turtles do it!

3. The turtles' inmediate goal is to reach the water. Don't get in their way.

4. You will seem immence to the hatchlings. Don't stand too close to them.

5. Take notes about the results of the hatching. Include figures for all the eggs as well as for any dead or half-pipped turtles. Add a coment about anything unusual.

1. computer
2. impolite
3. control
4. include
5. immigrant
6. compete
7. consumer
8. involve
9. immediate
10. comment
11. infection
12. concert
13. import
14. conversation
15. community
16. incomplete
17. immense
18. contest
19. inactive
20. complicate

1. _____   4. _____

2. _____   5. _____

3. _____

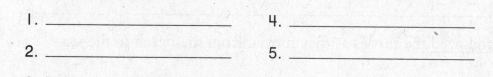 **Write a Personal Narrative** Have you ever taken part in a project or program as a volunteer? What was the experience like?

On a separate piece of paper, write a personal narrative about a time when you served as a volunteer. Use Spelling Words from the list.

Theme 3: **Growing Up**   197

Name _____

Connotation Correction

You are writing a screenplay for the selection, and the director would like to see some changes. Rewrite each sentence replacing the underlined word with a word from the box that has a negative connotation. Then rewrite it again using a word with a positive connotation. If you don't know the meanings of the words, use a dictionary to find them.

beamed   interrogated
chaperoned   invited
enthusiastic smirked
fanatic   stalked

1. People who volunteer to help turtles can be <u>excited</u> about their work.

_____

_____

2. Nadia <u>asked</u> Ethan about the comments he had heard.

_____

_____

3. The volunteers <u>followed</u> the turtles as they moved from the beach to the sea.

_____

_____

4. Ethan <u>smiled</u> during the performance of *Phantom of the Opera*.

_____

_____

Name _____

Up in the Sky

sit, set; lie, lay; rise, raise Some verb pairs can be confusing. Below are the definitions of three such pairs of words.

> **sit**—to rest in an upright position
> **set**—to put or place an object
>
> **lie**—to rest or recline
> **lay**—to put or place an object
>
> **rise**—to get up or go up
> **raise**—to move something up

Complete the sentences below by filling in the blanks with the correct verb in parentheses ( ) .

1. (sits/sets) A robin _____ on its nest.

2. (lie/lay) I _____ on my back to watch geese fly overhead.

3. (rises/raises) Mario _____ from his chair when the flock flies over.

4. (sits/sets) That bird watcher _____ down his binoculars.

5. (rise/raise) I _____ at dawn when I go bird watching.

6. (lie/lay) I will _____ my backpack on the grass.

7. (sit/set) We _____ out food for the migrating birds.

8. (lies/lays) She _____ under the tree listening to the chirping birds.

9. (sit/set) I _____ the fallen baby bird back in its nest.

10. (rise/raise) I _____ my binoculars to my eyes.

Theme 3: **Growing Up**   199

Name _____

Dog Days

lend, borrow; let, leave; teach, learn Here are the definitions of three
more easily confused word pairs:

lend—to give
borrow—to take

let—to permit
leave—to go away

teach—to give instruction
learn—to receive instruction

**Complete the sentences below by filling in the blanks with the correct
verb in parentheses ( ).**

1. Sadie _____ from Mr. Karol a book on dog
training. (lends/borrows)

2. She _____ from the book how to train puppies.
(teaches/learns)

3. Sadie and her puppy, Kipper, _____ for dog
obedience school. (let/leave)

4. The instructor _____ Sadie how to handle
her dog. (teaches/learns)

5. Sadie _____ me take Kipper to obedience school
one day. (lets/leaves)

6. The instructor _____ me a better leash. (lends/borrows)

7. Kipper _____ to sit on command. (teaches/learns)

8. We _____ for home. (let/leave)

9. My parents _____ me have a puppy. (let/leave)

10. I _____ to be responsible for her well-being. (teach/learn)

Name _____

Autumn in New England

Choosing the Correct Verb **Proofread the following passage written by a girl on her way to New England in the fall. Correct each incorrect verb form.**

        lent

Example: The libarian bor~~row~~ed me a book.

    Please leave me explain something. I like setting on Florida

beaches, but when it is autumn, I'd rather head to New England.

Teachers learn me better and I rise my hand more often when it is cool

outside. I look forward to seeing the trees turn red and gold. I set in

newly raked leaves and watch the sky. Sometimes my mother leaves me

make hot chocolate with marshmallows, and I wonder who learns

squirrels to gather nuts. When I come home, I sit my books on my desk

and lie my good school clothes over a chair. By February I will want to

lend a little warmth from Florida, and by June I will be ready to fly south

again, but in autumn, I am a New England girl.

Name _____

Writing a Speech

In *The View from Saturday*, Nadia gives an informal speech to persuade her father to let her help Grandpa with the sea turtles. Now you will write your own speech. Choose a topic listed below or come up with an idea of your own.

► Write a speech in which the mayor of the Florida town where Nadia lives thanks the turtle volunteers for their efforts.

► Write a speech to persuade local residents to clean up a beach or park.

► Write a speech to inform a group of children about what the turtle patrol's job is and why it is important.

Use the chart below to help you get started. First, identify the purpose of your speech—to entertain, to persuade, to inform, or to thank—and the audience to whom you will speak. Then jot down facts about the situation and reasons why you feel a certain way about it. Before you begin to write, number your ideas, in the order you in which you will present them.

Purpose	Audience	Facts and Reasons

Write your speech on a separate sheet of paper. At the beginning, mention whom you are addressing and the purpose of your speech. Then present your facts and reasons in a logical order. Finally, end with a conclusion that sums up or restates the purpose.

Name _____

Audience

Speech writers not only keep in mind their purpose for writing but also the **audience** they are addressing. Their audience affects what they say and how they say it. When you write a speech, you need to use language and examples that will best reach your audience.

Read each of the following excerpts from different speeches. What audience do you think the speech writer most likely had in mind when writing the speech? Choose a possible audience from the list and write it on the lines.

1. The Plum Beach condominium will offer lucky owners wonderful views from each unit, including a close look at this area's marine life.

   _____

2. Although small turtles used to be commonly available, stores no longer sell them. If you want to observe sea life at home and up close, you might consider buying tropical fish.

   _____

3. Thank you so much for a job well done! You greatly contributed to this year's successful turtle patrol. Most importantly, you have helped Florida's sea turtles.

   _____

4. Sea turtles face extinction. Some are hunted for their meat, and turtle eggs are sold as a delicacy. Tragically, beach-front development has also destroyed the traditional breeding grounds of some species.

   _____

Name _____

Writing a Personal Response

Use the test-taking strategies and tips you have learned to help you answer this kind of question. Then read your response and see how you may improve it. This practice will help you when you take this kind of test.

Write one or two paragraphs about one of the following topics.

a. In *Where the Red Fern Grows*, the narrator saved the money he earned over a two-year period to buy some hunting dogs. Tell about a time when you had to work for a long time to reach a goal. What was the goal? How did you reach it? How long did it take? How did you feel while you were working toward the goal and after you reached it?

b. The narrator of *Where the Red Fern Grows* shared his happiness with his little sisters by giving them some of the candy he brought home. Write about a time when you have shared your happiness with someone. What were you happy about? Who did you share your happiness with? What did you do to share your happiness?

_____

_____

_____

_____

_____

_____

_____

_____

_____

_____

_____

Name _____

Writing a Personal
Response continued

Read your answer. Check to be sure that it

- focuses on the topic
- is well organized
- has supporting details
- includes vivid and exact words
- has few mistakes in capitalization, punctuation, grammar, or spelling

Now pick one way to improve your response. Make your changes below.

_____

_____

_____

_____

_____

_____

_____

_____

_____

_____

_____

_____

_____

_____

_____

_____

Name _____

Spelling Review

1–30. **Write each Spelling Word.**

1. conversation
2. supply
3. minus
4. impolite
5. graceful
6. author
7. beginning
8. forgiveness
9. immediate
10. forgetting
11. slipped
12. method
13. answered
14. relief
15. consumer
16. heaving
17. amusement
18. include
19. advanced
20. listening
21. adorable
22. scarcely
23. excitement
24. control
25. balance
26. complicate
27. preferred
28. involve
29. community
30. lawyer

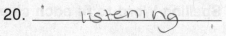

Spelling Words

1. conversation
2. supply
3. minus
4. impolite
5. graceful
6. author
7. beginning
8. forgiveness
9. immediate
10. forgetting
11. slipped
12. method
13. answered
14. relief
15. consumer
16. heaving
17. amusement
18. include
19. advanced
20. listening
21. adorable
22. scarcely
23. excitement
24. control
25. balance
26. complicate
27. preferred
28. involve
29. community
30. lawyer

Name _____

Spelling Spree

Contrast Clues The second part of each clue contrasts with
the first part. Write a Spelling Word to fit each clue.

1. not remembering, but ___forgetting___

2. not boredom, but ___excitement___

3. not plus, but ___minus___

4. not simplify, but ___advanced___

5. not asked, but ___answered___

6. not distress, but ___relief___

7. not retreated, but ___slipped___

Code Breaker Parts of some Spelling Words have been
written in code. Use the code below to figure out each word.
Then write the words correctly.

@ = con	¤ = or	$ = ed	# = ing	* = ate
% = ance	+ = im	Ø = er	& = ation	¶ = ly

8. + medi * ___immediate___

9. slipp $ ___slipped___

10. bal % ___balance___

11. @ sum Ø ___consumer___

12. heav # ___heaving___

13. scarce ¶ ___scarcely___

14. @ vers & ___conversation___

15. auth ¤ ___author___

1. relief
2. author
3. forgetting
4. consumer
5. slipped
6. conversation
7. minus
8. immediate
9. advanced
10. complicate
11. scarcely
12. heaving
13. answered
14. balance
15. excitement

Proofreading and Writing

Proofreading Circle the five misspelled Spelling Words in these rules. Then write each word correctly.

Rules for Growing Up

You can learn a lot by (lissening) to what older people say. Never be (impalite) to anyone. Keep your temper under (controal). This might (invollve) biting your tongue once in a while, but it's worth doing. If you hurt someone's feelings, ask for (forgivness).

1. _____listening_____   4. _____involve_____

2. _____impolite_____   5. _____

3. _____control_____

Write the Spelling Words that best complete this discussion.

Question: All of you must be 6. _____ to think about your futures. What kinds of jobs do you

7. _____ in your thinking?

Amy: I'd like to be a comedian! I love to see the 8. _____ on people's faces when I tell jokes.

Jaime: I'm 9. _____, so I might be a dancer.

Later, if I 10. _____ to, I could teach dance.

Laura: As a vet, I'd have a steady 11. _____ of

12. _____ animals in my life!

Dion: I would like to be a 13. _____, like my mom. She helps people in the 14. _____ fight for their rights.

Bart: I'll invent a fast 15. _____ for growing up!

➜ **Write a Song** On a separate sheet of paper, write a song about growing up. Use Spelling Review Words.

Spelling Words

1. method
2. listening
3. lawyer
4. include
5. amusement
6. adorable
7. graceful
8. forgiveness
9. supply
10. control
11. impolite
12. preferred
13. beginning
14. community
15. involve

Name ______________________________

Discovering Ancient Cultures

The selections in this theme will take you on a journey to the world of long ago. After reading each selection, complete the chart below to show what you learned.

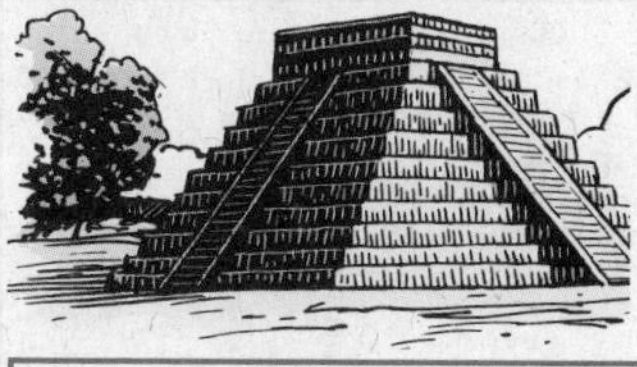

	What is the location of the culture described in the selection?	When did the events described in the selection take place?
Lost Temple of the Aztecs		
The Great Wall		
The Royal Kingdoms of Ghana, Mali, and Songhay		

Name _____

Discovering Ancient Cultures

	What was remarkable about the culture described in the selection?
Lost Temple of the Aztecs	
The Great Wall	
The Royal Kingdoms of Ghana, Mali, and Songhay	

What have you learned about ancient cultures in this theme?

_____

_____

Name _____

In the Time of the Aztecs

Words are missing in the sentences. Fill each blank with a word from the box.

1. If you rule over many lands, you rule over an
   ___empire___.

2. If you live in a very large city, you live in a
   ___metropolis___.

3. If you travel on raised pathways across marshlands,
   you travel on ___Sites___.

4. If you have defeated another nation in a war and won
   control over it, you have ___conquered___ that nation.

5. If a building has carvings that are carefully done and show great
   detail, it has ___intricate___ carvings.

6. If you have decorated an emperor or empress with jewelry, you have
   ___adorned___ that person.

7. If you deliver valuable goods to a foreign ruler who holds control of
   your nation, you give ___tributes___ to that ruler.

8. If you visit several places where archaeologists have found relics, you
   have visited archaeological ___causeways___.

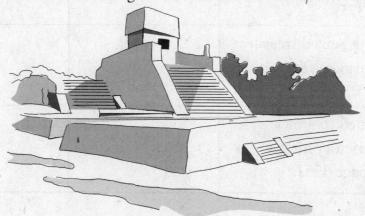

Name _____

Author's Viewpoint Chart

Passage from Selection	Whom It Tells About	Viewpoint
"one of the most famous and tragic rulers in history" (page 365)	Moctezuma	positive
Should they be destroyed or treated as guests? Moctezuma decided to welcome the strangers. (page 365)		
Moctezuma was filled with fear and confusion at these unnatural happenings. (page 370)		
Cortés looked at everything they had given him. "Are these your gifts of welcome?" he asked. "Is this all you have brought?" (page 374)		
Cortés ordered his men to fasten irons around the messengers' ankles and necks. (page 374)		
"You will do as I say," said Cortés. (page 374)		
A few months later Moctezuma, against the advice of his chiefs, welcomed Cortés and his army as friends. (page 375)		
The next year the Spaniards seized treasure and attacked the Aztecs during a festival. (page 375)		
In May 1521 Cortés returned to attack Tenochtitlán and claimed victory after leaving the city in ruins. (page 375)		

Name _____

Anniversary Speech

The year is 2019. It is the 500th anniversary of the arrival of Cortés at Veracruz. You have been chosen to give a speech honoring all who played a part in the momentous events of that year and the following two. Plan your speech by completing these statements:

1. We remember the Aztecs for (name at least two things): _____
_____

2. We remember Tenochtitlán for (name at least two things): _____
_____
_____

3. We remember Moctezuma II for _____

4. We remember Hernán Cortés for _____
_____

5. We wonder if the Aztec society would have survived, if only Moctezuma hadn't
   mistaken Cortés for _____

6. We are glad that the Great Temple of the Aztecs was rediscovered because
_____
_____

Name _____

To Be Fair . . .

Read the passage. Then complete the activity on page 217.

Cadenza Laurance

~~Cabeza~~ de Vaca's Journey

Álvar Núñez Cabeza de Vaca ranks among the greatest explorers who ever lived. In 1528, he joined a Spanish expedition headed to the New World to look for cities filled with gold and other riches.

When the expedition's five ships arrived on the coast of Florida, their leader proposed that they begin an overland exploration. Cabeza de Vaca disagreed with this dangerous and foolish plan but was too proud to stay behind. The landing party never found any cities of gold. Instead, the men lost contact with their ships and became stuck in the Florida swamps. In an effort to find their ships, they built crude boats and set sail. A hurricane separated Cabeza de Vaca's boat from the others and blew it to Texas, where it was destroyed. One by one, his companions died, leaving him alone.

Over the next four years, Cabeza de Vaca survived on his own, a superhuman achievement. He learned to live off the land and helped different native groups trade with each other. Then one day he miraculously came across three other members of the original expedition, who were now enslaved by a native group. He helped these men to escape, and together they wandered through what today is Mexico and the American Southwest. At one point, he healed a Native American man shot by an arrow. News of this feat traveled quickly, and soon many people came to him to be healed. Everywhere he and his companions went, they were welcomed and greeted with gifts.

Finally, the men crossed paths with four Spanish soldiers, who took them to a Spanish city on the Pacific Coast. Cabeza de Vaca returned to Spain to a hero's welcome. He told the king that he would like to go back to the New World. The king asked him to return as an aide to the new governor of Florida, but he refused because he had vowed never again to follow anyone else's orders. By sticking to his principles, he once again showed himself to be a truly great man.

Name _____

To Be Fair . . . continued

Answer the questions below about the passage on page 216.

1. What is the author's view of Cabeza de Vaca? He was a
   adventorous and brave man?

2. Would you say the author is biased toward Cabeza de Vaca? Why or
   why not? Yes, because the author is telling
   everything good about him.

3. Do you think the facts in the article support the author's statement
   that Cabeza de Vaca "showed himself to be a truly great man"? Why or
   why not? Yes, because

4. In his writings, Cabeza de Vaca describes native peoples in an unfavorable
   way. Why do you think the author does not include this information
   in the article? It doesn't show

Name _____

Aztec Artifacts

Circle the suffixes *-ic, -al*, and *-ure* in the underlined words in the sentences below.

1. The museum had <u>original</u> Aztec artifacts on display for the <u>public</u>.

2. These <u>national</u> treasures of Mexico would only be in the United States for a short time.

3. The <u>arrival</u> of many visitors made the museum crowded by ten o'clock.

4. Visitors could not touch the stone artifacts because they were protected by a rope <u>enclosure</u>.

5. A plaque told of the <u>historic</u> importance of the Aztecs' <u>tragic</u> defeat by Cortés in the year 1521.

6. A letter that showed Cortés's <u>authentic</u> <u>signature</u> was on display in a glass case.

7. A <u>professional</u> archaeologist was also there to answer questions about her work.

Now, choose five underlined words and use them correctly in sentences of your own.

1. _____

2. _____

3. _____

4. _____

5. _____

Name _____

The /sh/ Sound

The /sh/ sound is usually spelled with two letters. When you
hear the /sh/ sound, think of the patterns *sh*, *ti*, *ci*, and *ss*.

/sh/   poli**sh**   mo**ti**on   offi**ci**al   mi**ss**ion

**Write each Spelling Word under its spelling of the
/sh/ sound.**

Spelling Words

1. glacier
2. motion
3. pressure
4. direction
5. caution
6. partial
7. ancient
8. polish
9. station
10. shallow
11. official
12. edition
13. musician
14. mention
15. mission
16. portion
17. session
18. selfish
19. establish
20. cushion

sh   **ci**

_____   _____

_____   _____

_____   _____

_____   **ss**

ti   _____

_____   _____

_____   _____

_____

_____

_____

_____

Theme 4: **Discovering Ancient Cultures**   219

Name _____

Spelling Spree

Adding the /sh/ Sound Write a Spelling Word by adding
the correct spelling of the /sh/ sound to the incomplete
word in each phrase below.

1. the second edi_____on of a book

2. a drop in air pre_____ure

3. the _____allow end of the pool

4. a large por_____on of food

5. a par_____al eclipse of the sun

6. a comfortable seat cu_____ion

7. a musi_____an in a band

Word Detective Write a Spelling Word for each clue.

8. a "river" of ice

9. inconsiderate of others

10. a meeting

11. very old

12. where you board a train or bus

13. a synonym for *movement*

14. to found or set up

15. the state of being careful

8. _____   12. _____

9. _____   13. _____

10. _____   14. _____

11. _____   15. _____

Spelling Words

1. glacier
2. motion
3. pressure
4. direction
5. caution
6. partial
7. ancient
8. polish
9. station
10. shallow
11. official
12. edition
13. musician
14. mention
15. mission
16. portion
17. session
18. selfish
19. establish
20. cushion

Name _____

Proofreading and Writing

Proofreading **Circle the five misspelled Spelling Words in this letter. Then write each word correctly.**

To the Royal Governor:

You will be pleased to know that our mishun has been successful so far. After leaving Cuba, we sailed in a westerly direccion until making landfall. We were quickly able to astablish that a great empire lay farther inland. Later, we received some offical visitors from this empire. Among their gifts to us were gold and precious stones, which were shined to a very high polish. In return, we demonstrated the power of our guns to them. This they will no doubt mension to their lord back in the capital. We believe this country possesses great riches, and we are confident of success.

Your servant,
Hernán Cortés

Spelling Words

1. glacier
2. motion
3. pressure
4. direction
5. caution
6. partial
7. ancient
8. polish
9. station
10. shallow
11. official
12. edition
13. musician
14. mention
15. mission
16. portion
17. session
18. selfish
19. establish
20. cushion

1. _____   4. _____

2. _____   5. _____

3. _____

✏ **Write an Explanation** The Aztecs had a calendar just for keeping track of special religious days. Have you ever crossed off on a calendar the days leading up to a holiday? What is your favorite holiday?

On a separate piece of paper, write about your favorite holiday. Remember to name the holiday and tell why it is your favorite. Use Spelling Words from the list.

Name _____

Expand the Meaning

Read the news article and the clues below it. Find the word that answers each of the ten clues. Be careful! The meaning of the word in the article is different from the meaning in the clue. Circle each word in the article and write it on the line next to the clue.

Amazing Recent Events

Lots of news should interest readers this week. Our ruler, Moctezuma, received word that an important stranger with light skin has appeared near the city wall. For years Moctezuma visited the Great Temple hoping that Quetzalcoatl would return there, even though no one knows the spot where this will happen. Strange stories of recent events in our rich country also signal that a change is near.

1. more unusual _Strange_

2. the flat area at the side of the head _Temple_

3. a stain _spot_

4. a tool for drawing lines and measuring length _ruler_

5. the floors of a building _stories_

6. empty pieces of land _spot_

7. seemed _signal_

8. heavy and sweet _rich_

9. not heavy _light_

10. a charge for borrowing money _change_

Name _____

Many Ways to Describe

Descriptive adjectives:	what kind, how many, which one	Visitors, **old** and **young**, are awed by **ancient** ruins.
Demonstrative adjectives:	which one	**These** postcards show **those** sites. **This** photograph was taken at **that** place.
Articles:		**The** people built a temple. It was uncovered in **an** excavation.

Adjectives **Identify the adjectives in each sentence. Write each adjective on the correct line under each sentence. Hint: Every sentence does not contain every kind of adjective, and some sentences may contain more than one of a kind.**

1. The Aztecs used a circular stone calendar.

   descriptive adjectives: _Circular, stone_

   articles: _the, a_ **demonstrative adjectives:** _____

2. They created a great empire.

   descriptive adjectives: _great_

   articles: _a_ **demonstrative adjectives:** _they_

3. Those workers found that temple and made an important discovery.

   descriptive adjectives: _important_

   articles: _an_ **demonstrative adjectives:** _those, that_

4. It was a magnificent building.

   descriptive adjectives: _magnificent_

   articles: _it, a_ **demonstrative adjectives:** _____

5. That temple was in the capital city.

   descriptive adjectives: _capital_

   articles: _the_ **demonstrative adjectives:** _than_

Name _____

It's Only Proper!

A **proper adjective** is formed from a proper noun and always begins with
a capital letter.

Proper noun	Ending	Proper adjective
Germany	-an	German poetry
Chile	-an	Chilean fruit
China	-ese	Chinese art
Japan	-ese	Japanese language
Sweden	-ish	Swedish bread
Ireland	-ish	Irish music

Proper Adjectives Complete each sentence. Write the proper
adjective formed from the proper noun in parentheses. Use a
dictionary if you need to.

1. Nancy read about an _____Alaskan_____ sled race.
   (Alaska)

2. Tim prepared an _____Italian_____ meal for us. (Italy)

3. A trifle is an _____English_____ dessert. (England)

4. Our class saw _____African_____ art at the museum.
   (Africa)

5. This _____Chinese_____ vase is extremely old. (China)

6. The design on that _____Portugese_____ dish is lovely.
   (Portugal)

Name _____

First or Last?

A good writer can change the position of adjectives to make
sentences more effective. Here is an example:

Awkward: The letter was long and interesting, and he read it twice.
Improved: He read the long, interesting letter twice.

**Below are some of the postcard messages Keesha has sent from
Europe. Rewrite the second sentence of each one, changing
the position of adjectives to make the sentence more effective.**

1. Greetings from France! The paintings in the Louvre are beautiful, and
   I want to see them all!

   _____

   _____

2. Greetings from Germany! Here is the place where the Berlin Wall
   once stood, and it is lively and interesting.

   _____

   _____

3. Greetings from Ireland! The countryside is green, and I am enjoying
   hiking in it.

   _____

   _____

4. Greetings from Spain! The days are sunny and warm, and I swim.

   _____

   _____

5. Greetings from Italy! The ruins are ancient, and I am learning about them.

   _____

   _____

Name _____

Writing an Explanation

Lost Temple of the Aztecs explains who the Aztecs were and why they were
conquered by Spanish explorers in 1519. The purpose of a written
explanation is to explain

► who or what something is
► what is or was important about something or someone
► how something works or worked
► the steps of a process
► why something happens or happened

**Fill in the graphic organizer to help you plan and organize an
explanation that answers this question:** *Why did Moctezuma decide
to welcome the strangers as friends rather than treat them as
enemies?* **Write this topic in the center box of the graphic organizer.
Then list reasons and supporting details from the selection that
explain why this event happened.**

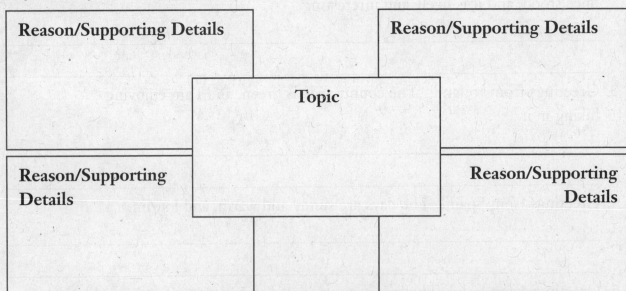

Reason/Supporting Details

Reason/Supporting Details

Topic

**Reason/Supporting
Details**

**Reason/Supporting
Details**

**Now write a two- to three-paragraph explanation on a separate sheet
of paper, using the information you recorded. In the first sentence
or paragraph, clearly state the topic. Provide enough reasons to
help readers understand the subject, and give details to clarify each
reason. Be sure to define any unfamiliar terms the first time you use
them. End with a conclusion.**

Name _____

Eliminating Unnecessary Words

Good writers revise their writing to eliminate unnecessary words and
repeated ideas that can make their writing seem awkward.

Unnecessary Word: The two of them were **both** running track.
Revised: The two of them were running track.

**Read the following paragraph. Cross out unnecessary words and
repeated phrases. Then write the revised paragraph on the lines
below. You may want to revise and combine sentences to make the
paragraph read more smoothly.**

> My mother, Mom, is an anthropologist. She studies ancient
> civilizations. She also teaches on the subject too. Both my sister and I,
> the two of us want to be anthropologists when we're grown-up adults.
> I'm taking a course at the Natural History Museum after school. The
> course at the Natural History Museum is on ancient Egyptian
> civilizations. I'm learning about Egypt. In addition to learning about
> Egypt, I'm reading some books right now on the Inca culture of Peru.
> Peru is in South America.

_____

_____

_____

_____

_____

_____

Name _____

Revising Your Research Report

Reread your research report. What do you need to make it better? Use this page to help you decide. Put a checkmark in the box for each sentence that describes your research report.

Loud and Clear!

☐ I chose an interesting topic to research.

☐ I used different sources to find information on the topic.

☐ I used an outline to help organize my information.

☐ I used adjectives to help make my writing more interesting.

☐ There are very few mistakes.

Sounding Stronger

☐ I could make the topic sound more interesting to the reader.

☐ More sources might help me make sure I have the facts right.

☐ I need to follow my outline more closely.

☐ I could add more adjectives to describe what I'm writing about.

☐ Errors make the report hard to read.

Turn Up Volume

☐ My topic isn't very interesting.

☐ I didn't use enough sources to find my facts.

☐ I didn't use an outline to plan my report.

☐ Too many mistakes make the report hard to read.

Name _____

Using Adjectives

Adjectives are words that modify nouns or pronouns. Choose the best adjective to complete each sentence.

1. The _____ Mayan civilization flourished long ago in Central America.
   a. humorous   b. popular   c. ancient   d. youthful

2. The Maya built _____ temples and pyramids.
   a. gleaming   b. roasting   c. rotting   d. grinding

3. The Maya were one of the _____ cultures in the western hemisphere to develop a writing system.
   a. biggest   b. first   c. heaviest   d. second

4. The Mayan writing system included symbols for sounds as well as _____ symbols.
   a. baseball   b. murky   c. heavy   d. picture

5. The Maya also invented the zero in their _____ system.
   a. geology   b. number   c. religious   d. government

6. _____ crowds came to see the Maya play a ball game called pokta-pok.
   a. Careless   b. Rippled   c. Microscopic   d. Immense

7. The game seems to have been an _____ combination of basketball, soccer, and volleyball.
   a. exciting   b. inner   c. outer   d. empty

8. At their peak, _____ cities of the Maya had populations of 50,000 or more.
   a. tall   b. fruitless   c. major   d. empty

9. In the year 909 the Mayan civilization suffered a _____ defeat from which it never recovered.
   a. popular   b. clever   c. colorful   d. devastating

Name _____

Spelling Words

Is ice slick or sleek? Is a friend an alley or an ally? It is easy to confuse words that have similar spellings and pronunciations even though the meanings are different. The pairs of Spelling Words in the box are often confused. Pay careful attention to their pronunciations, spellings, and meanings.

Write the missing letters in the Spelling Words below.

1. de _____ ent

2. de _____ _____ ent

3. _____ ffect

4. _____ ffect

5. de _____ ert

6. de _____ _____ ert

7. sl _____ ck

8. sl _____ _____ k

9. all _____ _____

10. all _____

11. confid _____ nt

12. confid _____ nt

13. hur _____ le

14. hur _____ le

Study List On a separate piece of paper, write each Spelling Word. Check your spelling against the words on the list.

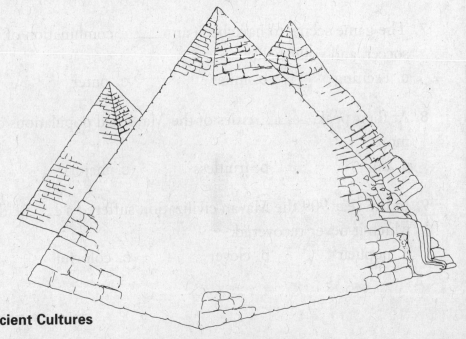

Spelling Spree

Word Switch Write a Spelling Word to replace each underlined definition in the sentences below.

Spelling Words

1. decent
2. descent
3. affect
4. effect
5. desert
6. dessert
7. slick
8. sleek
9. alley
10. ally
11. confident
12. confidant
13. hurdle
14. hurtle

1. For the <u>part of the meal that comes after the main course</u>, we had a choice of chocolate cake or blackberry pie.
2. The speech the governor gave was <u>reasonably good</u>, although it went on a little too long.
3. The cold weather will <u>cause a change in</u> the garden.
4. When I need someone to talk to, I'm glad I have a <u>person entrusted with secrets</u> like Anna.
5. If you get involved in a conflict, it's helpful to have a <u>person who joins with another to achieve a goal</u>.
6. After a day of traveling through <u>the area that gets little rainfall</u>, the caravan reached an oasis.
7. The horse was groomed until its coat was <u>smooth and glossy</u>.

1. _____
2. _____
3. _____
4. _____

5. _____
6. _____
7. _____

The Third Word Write a Spelling Word that belongs with each group of words.

8. slippery, icy, _____
9. sure, certain, _____
10. result, outcome, _____
11. fall, plunge, _____
12. rush, speed, _____
13. lane, passageway, _____
14. obstacle, difficulty, _____

8. _____
9. _____
10. _____
11. _____

12. _____
13. _____
14. _____

Proofreading and Writing

Proofreading Circle the five misspelled Spelling Words in this archaeologist's diary entry. Then write each word correctly.

September 16th.

The ruins we've found out here in the dessert appear to be part of a lost city. Dr. Boxer is confidint that this city was part of a previously undiscovered ancient culture. I try not to let his opinion afect me too much as I investigate. The past few days have been spent excavating what appears to be an aley off one of the main streets. The building stones that we have found are still in descent shape. It looks as though the climate has had surprisingly little effect on them. I remain extremely curious about this place's past.

Spelling Words

1. decent
2. descent
3. affect
4. effect
5. desert
6. dessert
7. slick
8. sleek
9. alley
10. ally
11. confident
12. confidant
13. hurdle
14. hurtle

1. _____
2. _____
3. _____
4. _____
5. _____

✏ **Write Context Sentences** Choose three word pairs from the Spelling List. Then write three pairs of sentences, one for each word.

Name _____

Words on the Wall

Vocabulary

~~domain~~
~~massive~~
~~craftsmen~~
~~terrain~~
extravagance
~~laborers~~
~~dynasty~~
durable
steppe
nomadic
~~excluding~~

Read each description. Then write one or two words from the box that match that description.

terms for land

_____ domain _____

_____ terrain _____

term for territory ruled over

_____

descriptive terms for objects

_____

_____

term for reign of one group

_____ dynasty _____

terms for workers

_____

_____ laborers _____

action word for "keeping out"

_____ excluding _____

descriptive term for people

_____ craftsmen _____

term for lavishness and excess

_____

Cause and Effect Chart

Cause		Effect
Cause		**Effect**
Mongol warriors threatened to overpower the Chinese.	→	
	→	Laborers built the western part of the Great Wall from packed dirt.
The Great Wall had to be guarded against the Mongols.	→	
The Great Wall demanded great sacrifices of the Chinese people, yet their leaders lived extravagant lives.	→	
The Ming dynasty had been disliked by its own people.	→	
	→	The Great Wall was no longer needed for defense.

Name _____

The People Behind the Great Wall

Each entry below names a group of people who were important in the history of the Great Wall. Next to each entry write a sentence or two telling about that group and its role.

Ming Leaders _____

_____

Mongols _____

_____

Laborers and Craftsmen _____

_____

_____

Chinese Soldiers _____

_____

Chinese People _____

_____

_____

Manchus _____

_____

Name _____

How It Started

Read the following passage. Then complete the activity on page 237.

The Egyptian Pyramids

The pyramids of Egypt are among the wonders of the ancient world. Many were built as tombs for the Egyptian pharaohs, or kings. Because the pharaohs were considered to be gods living on earth, their tombs had to be very special places.

The greatest Egyptian pyramid is the Great Pyramid of Khufu, built more than 4,500 years ago. The Great Pyramid is one of three pyramids set along the Nile River at Giza. It was built to hold the remains of Khufu, a pharaoh who ruled Egypt for twenty-three years, beginning in 2589 B.C. The pyramid is around 480 feet tall with sides that measure 760 feet long at the base. It is one of the largest structures ever built.

The Egyptians built the pyramids out of giant stone blocks that weighed several tons each. This stone came from rock quarries many miles away. It had to be floated down the Nile on barges and then moved into place using logs, levers, and pulleys. This took enormous effort! As many as twenty thousand workers helped build the Great Pyramid over a period of twenty years.

The Egyptians also built temples near the pyramids. They believed that the pharaoh's spirit traveled between the earth and the heavens, and that it continued to watch over them and help them in their lives. To nourish the pharaohs' spirits, they filled the temples and tombs with food and valuable objects. This wealth attracted grave robbers, however, who looted the tombs, even in ancient times. Later Egyptian leaders built their tombs in rock cliffs, making entry more difficult.

How It Started continued

**Complete the chart below to show the missing cause or effect.
Refer to the passage on page 236.**

	Cause		Effect
Paragraph 1	Egyptians considered their pharaohs to be gods living on earth.	→	
Paragraph 3	The rock quarries from which the stones were cut were many miles away from where the pyramids were built.	→	
Paragraph 4	A.	→	They built temples for worshipping pharaohs after death and filled both the temples and tombs with food and valuable objects.
	B.	→	Later Egyptian leaders built their tombs in rock cliffs.

Suffix Search

Circle the suffixes -*ion* and -*ation* in the underlined words in
the blocks.

1. The Great Wall marked the <u>separation</u> between the Ming and
   the Mongol territories.

2. A huge gate was the place of <u>connection</u> between two <u>sections</u> of the
   Great Wall.

3. The Ming government got money to build the Great Wall through
   years of <u>taxation</u> of the Chinese people.

4. The Chinese people finally staged a <u>rebellion</u> because they were tired
   of the Ming government's lying and <u>corruption</u>.

Now, use four of the underlined words above in sentences of your own.

_____

_____

_____

_____

_____

_____

Name _____

Adding *-ion* or *-ation*

The suffixes *-ion* and *-ation* can change verbs into nouns.
If the verb being changed ends with *e*, drop the *e* before
adding *-ion* or *-ation*.

connect, connect**ion**   situate, situat**ion**

admire, admir**ation**

**Write each pair of Spelling Words under the heading that
shows the spelling change when *-ion* or *-ation* is added.**

1. construct
2. construction
3. connect
4. connection
5. combine
6. combination
7. cooperate
8. cooperation
9. attract
10. attraction
11. admire
12. admiration
13. situate
14. situation
15. examine
16. examination
17. contribute
18. contribution
19. explore
20. exploration

No Spelling Change

_____   _____

_____   _____

_____

Final *e* Dropped

_____   _____

_____   _____

_____   _____

_____   _____

_____

Spelling Spree

Questions Write a Spelling Word to answer each question.

1. What does a magnet have for iron?
2. What do people do when they want to work well together?
3. What does a teacher give you to test your knowledge of a subject?
4. What is the opposite of *repel*?
5. When you hear static during a telephone call, you have a bad what?
6. What do you have for your favorite role model?
7. What is another word for *build*?

1. attraction
2. cooperate
3. _____
4. attract
5. connection
6. admiration
7. construct

Syllable Scramble Rearrange the syllables to write a Spelling Word. There is one extra syllable in each numbered item.

Example: de tion in spec   *inspection*

8. nect ble con   connect
9. bu con ant tion tri   contribution
10. plo at ex ra tion   exploration
11. bine dent com   combine

The Third Word Write the Spelling Word that belongs with each group of words.

12. like, appreciate, _____
13. teamwork, collaboration, _____
14. investigate, examine, _____
15. place, locate, _____

12. _____
13. _____
14. _____
15. _____

Spelling Words

1. construct
2. construction
3. connect
4. connection
5. combine
6. combination
7. cooperate
8. cooperation
9. attract
10. attraction
11. admire
12. admiration
13. situate
14. situation
15. examine
16. examination
17. contribute
18. contribution
19. explore
20. exploration

Name _____

Proofreading and Writing

Proofreading **Circle the five misspelled Spelling Words in this proclamation. Then write each word correctly.**

   The imperial architect is pleased to announce that the construcktion of our Emperor's wall is going splendidly. However, much work remains to be done. The combanation of building materials must be just right. Then we must connect all the separate parts into one solid barrier. The Chinese people are now called upon to contribuet more labor to this effort. The Mongol situashun on our northern border continues to worsen. The barbarians constantly examin our defenses to find weaknesses. Therefore, we must build a wall that has none. Let all people unite in this glorious endeavor!

Spelling Words
1. construct
2. construction
3. connect
4. connection
5. combine
6. combination
7. cooperate
8. cooperation
9. attract
10. attraction
11. admire
12. admiration
13. situate
14. situation
15. examine
16. examination
17. contribute
18. contribution
19. explore
20. exploration

1. _____   4. _____

2. _____   5. _____

3. _____

 Write a Report You are on an inspection tour of the Great Wall. You must write a report to the chief architect on the conditions along the wall. How would you describe the usefulness of the wall against Mongol attacks? Are there any suggestions you would make?

On a separate sheet of paper, write a report giving an update on the state of affairs along the Great Wall. Use Spelling Words from the list.

Name _____

Sentences with Synonyms

Read each sentence below. Find a word in the box that is a *synonym*
for each underlined word. Rewrite the sentences using the synonyms.

Vocabulary

ancient	crests	distant	earth	elaborate
grueling	patrolled	plunged	survive	withdrew

1. Some walls were built with pounded <u>dirt</u>, an <u>old</u> building technique.

   _____

   _____

2. Soldiers <u>checked</u> the wall in a <u>detailed</u> defense system.

   _____

   _____

3. The wall snaked along the <u>tops</u> of hills and <u>fell</u> down into rivers.

   _____

   _____

4. Many workers did not <u>outlive</u> the <u>exhausting</u> conditions.

   _____

   _____

5. The Mongols <u>retreated</u> to <u>remote</u> parts of the steppe.

   _____

   _____

Name _____

Compare Us!

Comparing with Adjectives Use the **comparative** form (*-er* or *more*) of an adjective to compare two persons, places, ideas, or things. Use the **superlative** form (*-est* or *most*) to compare three or more. Look at this chart of spelling changes that happen when *-er* or *-est* is added to some words.

Spelling changes with *-er* and *-est*			
► Do not add another *e* to **adjectives ending in *e*.**	nice	nic**er**	nic**est**
► You usually double the final consonant of **adjectives that end in a consonant after a single vowel.**	flat	flat**ter**	flat**test**
► Change the final *y* to *i* in **adjectives ending in *y*.**	busy	bus**ier**	bus**iest**

Complete each sentence with the correct form of the adjective in parentheses. Remember to use *more* or *most* with long adjectives.

1. My family built a _____ snow fort this year than last year. (large)

2. Our neighbors tried to build a _____ one than ours. (big)

3. We made the fort on the _____ day of the year. (cold)

4. It was the _____ snow fort ever built! (fantastic)

5. I hope tomorrow is not _____ than today. (sunny)

6. If the snow melts, we'll lose the _____ snow fort we've ever made! (ambitious)

Name _____

Good News or Bad?

Comparing with *good* and *bad* The adjectives *good* and *bad* are
irregular. They do not take the endings *-er* or *-est*, and the words *more*
or *most* are not added to them. Study their special comparative forms
in this chart.

	Positive	**Negative**
Adjective:	I have **good** news.	I have **bad** news.
Comparative form:	The news is **better** today.	Today's news is **worse**.
Superlative form:	This is the **best** news I've ever heard.	This is the **worst** news I've ever heard.

**Fill in the blank with the correct form of *good* if the word in
parentheses ( ) is *positive* and the correct form of *bad*
if the word in parentheses is *negative*.**

1. Signal fires were once a _____ means of
   communication. (positive)

2. Now we have _____ ways of getting in touch
   than ever before. (positive)

3. This is the _____ telephone connection I've ever
   had! (negative)

4. Receiving a scrambled message is _____ than no
   message at all. (negative)

5. Sending electronic mail is the _____ way of all to
   keep in touch with friends who live far away. (positive)

6. No one likes to get _____ news. (negative)

Name _____

What Good Form!

Using the Correct Forms of Adjectives It is important for a good writer to use the correct form of an adjective. Here are examples of some common mistakes writers make with adjectives:

Error: As the years went by, they found a **more better** way to build the wall.
Correct: As the years went by, they found a **better** way to build the wall.

Error: Some rulers were **benevolenter** than others.
Correct: Some rulers were **more benevolent** than others.

Error: What is the **older** place you have ever seen?
Correct: What is the **oldest** place you have ever seen?

Beth has written a draft of a letter to her friend Nell about an enjoyable visit to the art museum. In her enthusiasm, she has made some mistakes with her adjectives. Find the five incorrect adjective forms in her letter, and write them correctly on the lines below.

Dear Nell,

   Yesterday I visited the greater art museum I've ever seen. It was gooder than the one we went to last month. The works from China were the impressivest ones. Many of the works are very old. A beautifuler statue of a young man with two birds was more than 2000 years old! Can you imagine seeing anything ancienter? If an American statue is 200 years old, we think that is amazing.

1. _____   4. _____

2. _____   5. _____

3. _____

Name _____

Writing a Paragraph of Information

In *The Great Wall*, you learned about the building of China's Great Wall. A **paragraph of information** like this one from the selection presents facts in a logical order.

> Tens of thousands of workers were involved in building the Great Wall. The army provided many laborers. Soldiers became construction workers, and generals became architects and engineers. Peasants were required to work on the wall. They worked for months at a time for little or no pay. Criminals served their sentences doing hard labor on the wall.

Use this graphic organizer to build your own paragraph of information about another human structure.

Topic

_____

_____

Topic Sentence

_____

_____

Supporting Sentences

_____

_____

_____

_____

Now write your paragraph of information on a separate sheet of paper. Include a topic sentence, usually the first sentence in the paragraph, that tells what the entire paragraph is about. Arrange several supporting sentences in a logical order, and make sure all of the sentences contain facts about the topic.

Name _____

Elaborating with Adjectives

Adjectives like *strong* and *difficult* describe nouns and pronouns and help readers picture people, places, ideas, and things that are being described. A good writer uses adjectives in sentences to make his or her writing clearer and more vivid.

Read these sentences about the Great Wall. Then add adjectives from the box to make each sentence more interesting.

fierce	tall	massive	incredible	long	smoky	heavy
hardworking	well-trained	costly	high	swift	skillful	curious

1. The Chinese built a _____ wall to protect their

   country from the _____ Mongols.

2. In the eastern mountains, the _____ wall was

   made of mud bricks and _____ blocks.

3. Thousands of _____ and _____

   laborers spent years and years working on the wall.

4. A million _____ soldiers defended the Great

   Wall against _____ Mongol horsemen.

5. Stationed in _____ watchtowers, guards built

   _____ fires to send a warning about an

   approaching enemy.

6. Ming emperors imposed _____ taxes to help

   pay for the _____ project.

7. Today, many _____ tourists come to view this

   _____ structure from the ancient world.

Name _____

A Desert Journey

Use these desert words to complete the journal entry below.

Vocabulary

oasis   entourage   vicinity   primary
flourishing   bartering   goods   caravans

Today is the thirty-fourth day of our journey. Having enough water
to survive is the _____ concern when crossing the Sahara.
We reached the cool waters of this _____ just before
sunset and immediately allowed our camels to drink. We are one of seven
_____ made up of people and camels here tonight. Most
of the camels are heavily laden with _____. Some of the
different traders have already begun _____ with each
other for items they want. Trade is _____ in this region,
with gold, salt, and exotic goods in high demand in so many places. We
heard that a prince stopped here with a huge _____ just
two days ago. Too bad we did not get to see that splendid group! Still, we
are told that equally wondrous sights await us in the
_____ of the city Jenne.

Name _____

Topic, Main Idea, and Details Chart

Topic: _____

Section 1

Main Idea: _____

Key Details: 1. _____

2. _____

3. _____

Section 2

Main Idea: _____

Key Details: 1. _____

2. _____

3. _____

Section 3

Main Idea: _____

Key Details: 1. _____

2. _____

3. _____

Section 4

Main Idea: _____

Key Details: 1. _____

2. _____

3. _____

Name _____

Trader's Log—
Trans-Saharan Route

**Use information from *The Royal Kingdoms of Ghana, Mali, and Songhay*
to complete the following log of a trader who is traveling in a caravan.**

Destination: Koumbi Saleh, in the empire of _____

Method of travel: _____

Reason for traveling: to trade for _____, Ghana's most

plentiful and valuable resource

Two items brought to trade : _____

_____

Length of journey: _____

Two types of traveling companions: _____

_____

Daytime schedule: _____

_____

_____

Evening activities: _____

_____

Three interesting facts about Soninke village life: _____

_____

_____

_____

Name _____

What's the Big Idea?

Read the following passage. Then complete the activity on page 252.

Civilizations of Mesoamerica

Before Europeans arrived in the Americas, Mesoamerica (which includes Mexico and Central America) was home to several advanced civilizations. Three of the main groups were the Olmecs, the Maya, and the Aztecs.

The Olmecs were the first to create an advanced civilization. Around 1200 B.C. they began to build cities and create a trade network in the jungles of southeastern Mexico, along the Gulf of Mexico. They carved giant stone heads, some weighing as much as forty-four tons. By 400 B.C. their culture was in decline, but their achievements influenced other civilizations to come.

By A.D. 250 another powerful culture, the Maya, had emerged in Mesoamerica. The Maya built great stone cities, or ceremonial centers, in the lowland jungles and mountain highlands of southern Mexico and northern Central America. Mayan cities, including Palenque, Tikal, and Copán, featured elaborate pyramids, temples, and palaces. The Maya built irrigation canals for their fields. They also developed a writing system, a calendar, and advanced knowledge of mathematics and astronomy. After A.D. 900 their culture began to decline, though Mayan peoples continue to live in the region to this day.

The third great civilization of Mesoamerica was the Aztec. It emerged in the dry highlands of central Mexico after A.D. 1200. The Aztecs built a great city, Tenochtitlán, on an island in a large lake in the Valley of Mexico. They were also great warriors. By the early 1500s they had conquered many neighboring groups and had created a large empire. When the Spanish arrived in Mexico in 1519, they were astounded by the wealth and achievements of the Aztec empire.

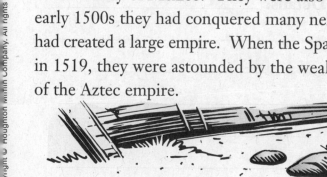

Name _____

What's the Big Idea? continued

Answer these questions about the passage on page 251.

1. What is the topic of the passage? _____

   _____

2. The topic and main idea of the second paragraph are listed below. Fill in the supporting details.

Topic: the Olmec civilization

Main Idea: The Olmecs were the first to create an advanced civilization.

Details: _____

   _____

   _____

   _____

3. On the lines below, write the topic, main idea, and details of the third and fourth paragraphs.

Third Paragraph	**Fourth Paragraph**
Topic: _____	Topic: _____
Main Idea: _____	Main Idea: _____
_____	_____
_____	_____
Details: _____	Details: _____
_____	_____
_____	_____
_____	_____
_____	_____

Recognizing Unstressed Syllables

Read each sentence. Sound out the underlined word several times, placing stress on a different syllable each time. Circle the choice with the correct unstressed and stressed syllables. Unstressed syllables are written in lowercase letters and stressed syllables are written in capital letters.

1. In bartering, the buyer and the seller reach an agreement that is satisfactory to both sides.

   SAT•is•fac•to•ry   sat•IS•fac•to•ry   sat•is•FAC•to•ry

2. In a caravan, camels are loaded with merchandise and supplies.

   MER•chan•dise   mer•CHAN•dise   mer•chan•DISE

3. Royal patrols guaranteed safe passage to all visitors to ancient Ghana.

   GUAR•an•teed   guar•AN•teed   guar•an•TEED

4. Smaller towns were surrounded by walls with moats or pits in front of them.

   SUR•round•ed   sur•ROUND•ed   sur•round•ED

5. Families in ancient Ghana worked cooperatively on the land.

   CO•op•er•a•tive•ly   co•OP•er•a•tive•ly   co•op•er•a•TIVE•ly

6. Village leaders allocated land to each family according to need.

   AL•lo•cat•ed   al•LO•cat•ed   al•lo•cat•ED

7. Farmers used dikes and earthen dams for irrigation.

   ir•RI•ga•tion   ir•ri•GA•tion   ir•ri•ga•TION

8. The women cooked, ate, worked, and entertained together.

   EN•ter•tained   en•TER•tained   en•ter•TAINED

Name _____

Unstressed Syllables

To spell a two-syllable or three-syllable word, divide the word into syllables. Look for familiar spelling patterns. Be sure to note the spelling of any unstressed syllables, and then spell the word by syllables.

prob / lem (prŏb´ ləm)   **po / si / tion** (pə zĭsh´ ən)

Write each Spelling Word under the heading that gives the number of its syllables.

Two Syllables

_____

_____

_____

_____

_____

_____

_____

_____

Three Syllables

_____

_____

_____

_____

_____

_____

_____

Spelling Words

1. company
2. success
3. position
4. problem
5. policy
6. difficult
7. document
8. quality
9. surprise
10. physical
11. crisis
12. awake
13. example
14. ignore
15. accept
16. parallel
17. admiral
18. desire
19. garage
20. ambulance

Name _____

Spelling Spree

Phrase Fillers **Write the Spelling Word that best completes each phrase.**

1. a government _____ on automobile safety

2. to set a good _____

3. a patient's _____ condition

4. to solve a _____

5. to reach the rank of _____

6. a _____ birthday party

7. a parking _____

8. rushed to the hospital in an _____

1. _____   5. _____

2. _____   6. _____

3. _____   7. _____

4. _____   8. _____

Spelling Words

1. company
2. success
3. position
4. problem
5. policy
6. difficult
7. document
8. quality
9. surprise
10. physical
11. crisis
12. awake
13. example
14. ignore
15. accept
16. parallel
17. admiral
18. desire
19. garage
20. ambulance

Code Breaker **Some Spelling Words have been written in code. Use the code below to figure out each word. Then write the words correctly.**

CODE: I S T P W A C D J R H V E L G M Y B
LETTER: a c d e f g i l m n o p q r s t u y

9. GYSSPGG _____   13. CARHLP _____

10. ISSPVM _____   14. VILIDDPD _____

11. TPGCLP _____   15. SLCGCG _____

12. VHGCMCHR _____

Theme 4: **Discovering Ancient Cultures**   255

Name _____

Proofreading and Writing

Proofreading Circle the five misspelled Spelling Words in
this travel report. Then write each word correctly.

I write these words because my employers desire
a brief documint of my recent trading expedition.
Our compeny of merchants made the desert crossing
in good time. We were all awak several hours before
sunrise each day and did most of our traveling before
the sun got too hot. It is a diffacult journey, but the
sights to be seen at the end of it make it well
worthwhile. The cities of the kingdom of Ghana are
bustling with many thousands of people. Goods of
high qualty fill the marketplaces. There are excellent
trading opportunities here.

Spelling Words

1. company
2. success
3. position
4. problem
5. policy
6. difficult
7. document
8. quality
9. surprise
10. physical
11. crisis
12. awake
13. example
14. ignore
15. accept
16. parallel
17. admiral
18. desire
19. garage
20. ambulance

1. _____ 4. _____

2. _____ 5. _____

3. _____

Write a Paragraph of Information From reading the selection,
what do you know about daily life in the medieval kingdom of Ghana?
What was it like to travel across the desert in a trade caravan?

**On a separate piece of paper, write a paragraph about one aspect of
life in the Kingdom of Ghana. Use Spelling Words from the list.**

Name _____

Prefix and Suffix Chart

**Read the journal entry. Underline each word that has a prefix or suffix
listed in Chart 1. Then fill in Chart 2 with your underlined words.**

The miners of ancient Ghana traded their gold by bartering.
Sometimes they would find the merchants' goods unacceptable, and the
merchants would reoffer more goods. Often, though, the system moved
smoothly and the bartering was successful.

Chart 1			
Suffixes	**Meanings**	**Prefixes**	**Meanings**
-er, -or -ful -ly	a person who does full of in a specified way	re- un-	again or back not

Chart 2		
Word with Suffix	**Base Word and Suffix**	**Meaning**
1. _____	_____ + _____	_____
2. _____	_____ + _____	_____
3. _____	_____ + _____	_____
Word with Prefix	**Base Word and Prefix**	**Meaning**
4. _____	_____ + _____	_____
5. _____	_____ + _____	_____

Name _____

Tell Me How!

Adverbs An **adverb** can modify, or describe, a verb or an adjective. An adverb that modifies a verb tells *how, where, when,* or *to what extent.* An adverb that modifies an adjective tells *to what extent.* Look at the example sentences. What word does each adverb in dark type modify?

How: They **carefully** guarded the secret mines.

Where: You must go **west** to reach the American deserts.

When: The people worked **daily**.

To what extent: I **really** like the book about Ghana.

To what extent: It is a **very** interesting book.

Under each sentence write the adverb, the word it modifies, and *Verb* or *Adjective* to tell what kind of word it modifies.

1. Trade was very important in ancient Ghana.

    _____

2. Merchants traveled safely in groups.

    _____

3. A full-time cameleer usually managed the camels.

    _____

4. The camels could be quite stubborn.

    _____

5. The caravans traveled south.

    _____

6. They regularly pushed their way across the desert.

    _____

7. It must have been an extremely dangerous journey.

    _____

8. Temperatures in the desert could become dangerously high.

    _____

Name _____

Time to Compare

Comparing with Adverbs Like adjectives, **adverbs** can be used to make comparisons. Use the **comparative** form (-er) to compare two things. Use the **superlative** form (-est) to compare three or more. Use *more* or *most* with adverbs that end with -*ly*.

Comparative	**Superlative**
Andrea digs **faster** than Mike.	Tony digs **fastest** of all.
Brian swims **more quickly** than you.	He swims **most quickly** of us all.

Some adverbs have completely different forms of comparison. Study the chart.

Adverb	**Comparative**	**Superlative**
well	better	best
badly	worse	worst
little	less	least
much	more	most

Write the comparative or superlative form of the adverb in parentheses ( ) to complete each sentence correctly.

1. I wonder _____ about the past than I do about the future. (frequently)

2. I'm going to work _____ on my history lesson this week than I did last week. (hard)

3. The archaeologist was the _____ interesting speaker of all at the assembly. (much)

4. I was _____ interested in the historian's speech than in hers. (little)

5. She went _____ of all into details about working in the field. (deep)

6. I may think _____ now about studying archaeology than before. (seriously)

Theme 4: **Discovering Ancient Cultures**   259

Name _____

Adverbs at Work!

Adjective or Adverb? Good writers are careful to use adverbs, not
adjectives, to tell *how much* or *to what extent* about adjectives. Review the
examples below.

Incorrect:	She plays **real** well.
Correct:	She plays **really** well.
Incorrect:	The stew was **extreme** delicious.
Correct:	The stew was **extremely** delicious.

**Brigitte has written a play about an imaginary medieval kingdom.
Here is part of the script. Proofread it to change adjectives to
adverbs where necessary. Write the correct word above
each mistake.**

King Snoof: Loyal subject, what have you brought me so eager?

Garnid the Serf: Good and kind king, I have gladly brought

this real big basket full of crops from my field.

King Snoof: You must have had a tremendous good harvest this

year, serf.

Garnid the Serf: Yes, King Snoof! Your fierce brave soldiers have

protected your kingdom and our crops.

King Snoof: Now, serf, sing me an extreme sweet tune of the land.

Garnid the Serf: But, sire, I carry no sweet tune in my

tight woven basket!

King Snoof: Then, sorry serf, sing a sour one!

Name _____

Writing a Comparison and Contrast Paragraph

In *The Royal Kingdoms of Ghana, Mali, and Songhay*, the authors compare
and contrast the roles played by men and women in Soninke village life.
For example, both men and women made baskets and pots, but men
served in the military while women harvested and processed crops. One
way to explore how things are alike and different is by writing a
comparison and contrast paragraph. Comparing shows how things are
alike, and contrasting shows how they are different.

**Use the Venn diagram to help you compare and contrast travel in the
days of the camel caravans with travel in modern times.**

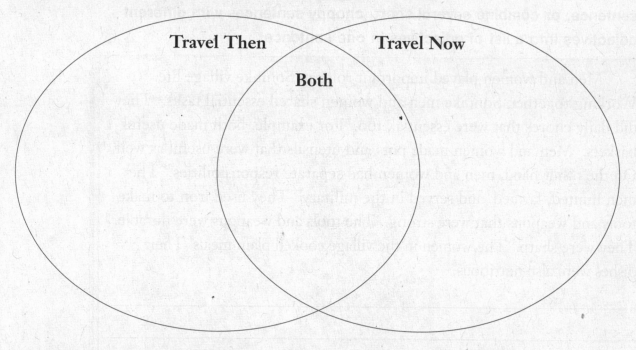

Travel Then

Travel Now

Both

**On a separate sheet of paper, write a compare-contrast paragraph
about travel today and travel in ancient North Africa. In the opening
sentence, clearly state the subject being compared and contrasted.
In the supporting sentences, group details that compare and details
that contrast in a clear manner. Use clue words such as *both* or
likewise to help readers identify likenesses, and *on the other hand* or
only to help them identify differences.**

Theme 4: **Discovering Ancient Cultures**   261

Name _____

Combining Sentences with Adjectives

Adjectives describe nouns and pronouns. You can improve your writing by combining repetitive adjectives into a single sentence.

> Ancient Ghanaians had **golden** jewelry. They also had **golden** thread.
>
> Ancient Ghanaians had **golden** jewelry and thread.

You can also combine several short, choppy sentences with different adjectives into a list of adjectives in one sentence.

> The journey was **long**. The trip was **difficult**, too. It was often **dangerous**.
>
> The journey across the Sahara was **long, difficult,** and **dangerous**.

Revise this paragraph. Combine repetitive adjectives into a single sentence, or combine several short, choppy sentences with different adjectives into a list of adjectives in one sentence.

Men and women played important roles in Soninke village life. Working together, Soninke men and women shared essential tasks. They did daily chores that were essential, too. For example, both made useful baskets. Men and women made pots and utensils that were useful as well. On the other hand, men and women had separate responsibilities. The men hunted, farmed, and served in the military. They used iron to make tools and weapons that were strong. The tools and weapons were durable. They were sharp. The women in the village cooked plain meals. Their dishes were also nutritious.

_____

_____

_____

_____

_____

Name _____

Vocabulary Items

Use the test-taking strategies and tips you have learned to help you complete each analogy with the correct answer. Take the time you need to think about each analogy and the answer choices. This practice will help you when you take this kind of test.

Read each analogy below. Then fill in the circle for the best answer at the bottom of the page.

1 Emperor was to China as _____ is to the United States.

   A China

   B United States

   C rulers of countries

   D president

2 The Great Wall was to the Chinese people as a _____ was to the early American settlers.

   F wall

   G fort

   H horse

   J sheriff

3 _____ were to the Chinese guards as telephones are to people today.

   A Swords

   B Letters

   C Smoke signals

   D Mailboxes

ANSWER ROWS **1** Ⓐ Ⓑ Ⓒ Ⓓ   **3** Ⓐ Ⓑ Ⓒ Ⓓ

                2 Ⓕ Ⓖ Ⓗ Ⓙ

Vocabulary Items continued

4 <u>Mongol</u> was to <u>threat</u> as the <u>Great Wall</u> was to _____.

   F defense

   G taxes

   H cannons

   J airplanes

5 <u>Soldier</u> was to <u>construction worker</u> as _____ was to <u>architect</u>.

   A horse

   B general

   C criminal

   D brick

6 <u>Gate</u> is to the <u>Great Wall</u> as _____ is to a <u>house</u>.

   F porch

   G window

   H door

   J roadway

ANSWER ROWS   4 Ⓕ Ⓖ Ⓗ Ⓙ   6 Ⓕ Ⓖ Ⓗ Ⓙ

                    5 Ⓐ Ⓑ Ⓒ Ⓓ

Name _____

Spelling Review

1–30. Write each Spelling Word. In words that have the /sh/ sound, underline the letters that spell that sound.

1. _____
2. _____
3. _____
4. _____
5. _____
6. _____
7. _____
8. _____
9. _____
10. _____
11. _____
12. _____
13. _____
14. _____
15. _____

16. _____
17. _____
18. _____
19. _____
20. _____
21. _____
22. _____
23. _____
24. _____
25. _____
26. _____
27. _____
28. _____
29. _____
30. _____

Spelling Words

1. establish
2. cooperate
3. edition
4. admiration
5. surprise
6. accept
7. combine
8. difficult
9. musician
10. official
11. shallow
12. ambulance
13. position
14. connection
15. partial
16. example
17. mission
18. pressure
19. crisis
20. physical
21. problem
22. construct
23. combination
24. success
25. connect
26. ancient
27. cushion
28. construction
29. admire
30. cooperation

Theme 4: **Discovering Ancient Cultures**   265

Spelling Spree

Headline Help Write the Spelling Word that means the
opposite of the underlined word in each headline. Begin
each word with a capital letter.

Spelling Words

1. <u>Solution</u> Surfaces at Archaeological Dig Site

   _____

2. Thousand-Year-Old Artifacts Found in <u>Deep</u> Pit

   _____

3. Protecting the Great Wall from Vandals Proves <u>Easy</u>

   _____

4. Experts <u>Reject</u> Award for Preserving Historic City

   _____

5. <u>Modern</u> Aztec Stone Discovered in Mexico

   _____

6. Workers Uncover <u>Total</u> Remains of Mummy

   _____

7. <u>Mental</u> Fitness Helps Dig Workers Handle Desert Heat

   _____

8. Archaeologists Meet with <u>Failure</u> on African Dig _____

Tongue Twisters Write the Spelling Word that completes each tongue twister.

9. Milly the muddled _____ made many mistakes.

10. Cousin Carl can't _____ cucumbers and carrots.

11. Adrian will always _____ Aunt Alice's albums.

12. Sarah spilled soup when startled by Sam's silly _____.

13. Ed's early _____ of the encyclopedia was expensive.

14. A calico cat is curled up on the couch _____.

15. Amber asked for an _____ after the accident.

Spelling Words

1. ambulance
2. physical
3. admire
4. difficult
5. musician
6. edition
7. surprise
8. accept
9. problem
10. ancient
11. partial
12. success
13. combine
14. cushion
15. shallow

Proofreading and Writing

Proofreading Circle the six misspelled Spelling Words in this report. Then write each word correctly.

It can be exciting to estabalish facts about an ancient culture. Often it is necessary to set up an oficial camp. The exact pesition of the camp can be based on old records. One useful activity is to construckt a model of a building that may have existed. Another is to study an exsample of the tools the people used. A combonation of study and exploration is needed.

1. _____   4. _____

2. _____   5. _____

3. _____   6. _____

Spelling Words

1. crisis
2. example
3. position
4. cooperate
5. cooperation
6. admiration
7. combination
8. connection
9. connect
10. construction
11. construct
12. mission
13. pressure
14. establish
15. official

Write the Spelling Words that best complete this log entry.

August 16

I am filled with 7. _____ for my fine crew. With their help and 8. _____, we are able to resolve each new 9. _____ quickly. We are working under some 10. _____, but we are coping.

Our goal, or 11. _____, is to study the methods of 12. _____ used to build an old temple. I hope to find a 13. _____ between the temple and the buildings in the north. If I can prove that the styles 14. _____ with one another, it will be a great discovery. Now, if the weather would only 15. _____!

━━━━▶ **Write a News Report** On a separate sheet of paper, write a news report. Use the Spelling Review Words.

Name _____

Mythical Elements

Fill in the chart below, describing the basic elements of each myth.

	Arachne the Spinner	Guitar Solo	How Music Was Fetched out of Heaven
Central Conflict			
Setting			
Superhuman Character(s)			
Human Characters (if any)			
Fantasy Elements			

Which myth did you like the most? Why?

_____

_____

Name _____

Describe Your Mythical Character

Every myth must have at least one superhuman character. Choose someone real, and imagine that person as a mythical character. Describe this character.

_____

_____

_____

_____

_____

_____

_____

Show what this character looks like.

Name _____

Doers and Dreamers

The real people profiled in this theme aimed high and reached their goals despite obstacles. After reading each selection, complete the chart below to show what you learned.

	Who is this selection about?	What kind of writing is the selection an example of?
A Kind of Grace		
Under the Royal Palms		
Chuck Close Up Close		

Name _____

Doers and Dreamers

	What examples of "dreaming" did you read about in this selection?	What examples of "doing" did you read about?
A Kind of Grace		
Under the Royal Palms		
Chuck Close Up Close		

What have you learned about being a "doer" and a "dreamer" in this theme?

_____

_____

_____

272　Theme 5: **Doers and Dreamers**

Name _____

Running Riddles

Answer each track riddle with a vocabulary word from the box.

Vocabulary

sessions
sprints
unconventional
endurance
discouraged
conditioning
squad
consoling

1. You're called this when you do the unexpected, not when you blend in with the crowd.

   _____

2. You might feel this way when you fail to meet your goals, not when you've achieved a personal best.

   _____discouraged_____

3. You do best in these races with short, quick strides, not long, graceful strides. _____sprints_____

4. You need this for running distances, but not for a short race.

   _____endurance_____

5. You hear these kinds of words from friends after a loss, but not after a win. _____

6. When you are a member of this, you are one of many people on a team, not one alone. _____squad_____

7. You do drills constantly in practice to achieve this, but you lose it quickly if you start taking it easy.

   _____

8. These are periods of practice, but they could be meetings of other kinds as well. _____sessions_____

Name _____

K-W-L Chart

What I **K**now	What I **W**ant to Know	What I **L**earned

Name _____

Interview with an Athlete

Below are questions an interviewer might ask Jackie
Joyner-Kersee. Read each question and write the
answer you think Jackie would give.

Interviewer: How old were you when you joined your first track team?

Jackie: _____

Interviewer: What made you decide to join?

Jackie: _____

_____

Interviewer: I understand that your first coach, Percy, had to end the
team because most of the girls dropped out. What did
you do then?

Jackie: _____

_____

Interviewer: Who was your new coach?

Jackie: _____

Interviewer: How did you finish in your first race?

Jackie: _____

Interviewer: What did you do to become a better runner?

Jackie: _____

_____

Interviewer: Did you participate in a track and field event besides
running? How did you train for it?

Jackie: _____

_____

Name _____

Believe It or Not

Read the ads. Then complete the activity on page 277.

1.

Do you run out of steam before the clock strikes noon?
Are you too tired to get the job done, or even to have fun?
If so . . .

Jump-start your day with PowerCrunch Cereal!
Take the PowerCrunch Challenge. Eat PowerCrunch for
breakfast every morning for just one week. We guarantee
that you'll feel healthier and more alert all day, every day!

2.

Pump up your workouts with Muscle Bound sportswear!
Are you working out or wasting time? Top athletes agree: whether you're lifting
weights, running laps, or cross training, using the right clothing gives you a better
workout. Here's what two top athletes say about Muscle Bound sportswear:

A. J. Kamada, track star: "Nothing beats
Muscle Bound for fit, price, or
performance!"

Natasha Kosko, tennis pro: "Muscle
Bound is the only gear I ever wear, both
on the courts and off. It's the best! Try it
— you'll agree."

Name _____

Believe It or Not continued

Answer these questions about the ads on page 276.

1. What is the purpose of the first ad?

   _____

   _____

2. What does the ad promise will happen if you use the product?

   _____

   _____

3. Do you think readers should believe this statement? Why or why not?

   _____

   _____

   _____

4. What is the purpose of the second ad?

   _____

5. Think about how the ads on page 276 try to convince you to buy their products.
   Write the number of each ad next to the technique it uses.

   A. Testimonial (uses celebrities to endorse a product): _____

   B. Faulty cause and effect (claims that you will be better

   or happier by simply using the product): _____

Name _____

Word Part Match-Up

**Read each definition below. Then build words with the roots *ven* and
graph to fit the definitions, and write them on the correct lines. To
build a word, try adding letters before and after it from the chart.**

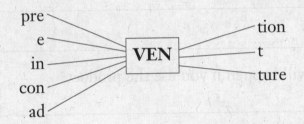

Example: an occurrence, incident, or experience: **event**

1. an opening through which vapor can escape _____

2. a newly created device or process _____

3. a memorable, exciting, or dangerous experience _____

4. a formal meeting of a group, often in a large city _____

5. to stop something from happening _____

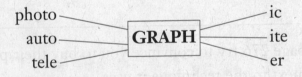

6. a signature, usually of a famous person _____

7. someone who takes pictures _____

8. an old-fashioned way to send messages using electrical impulses sent

    through wire _____

9. having to do with written or drawn representations, such as picture

    symbols on a computer or in a book _____

10. a soft form of carbon used as the writing substance in pencils

    _____

Name _____

Final /īz/, /ĭv/, /ĭj/, /ĭk/, /chər/, and /əs/ Sounds

Each of the Spelling Words ends with the final /īz/, /ĭv/, /ĭj/, /ĭk/, /chər/, or /əs/ sound. When you hear these sounds, think of the following patterns:

final /īz/	*ize, ise*	adver**tise**, rea**lize**
final /ĭv/	*ive*	act**ive**
final /ĭj/	*age*	us**age**
final /ĭk/	*ic*	scientif**ic**
final /chər/	*ture*	signa**ture**
final /əs/	*ous*	nerv**ous**

► The spelling of *college* differs from the usual spelling pattern. In this word, the final /ĭj/ sound is spelled *-ege*.

Write each Spelling Word under its final sound.

Spelling Words

1. ~~advertise~~
2. ~~serious~~
3. ~~scientific~~
4. ~~active~~
5. ~~usage~~
6. ~~signature~~
7. ~~realize~~
8. ~~nervous~~
9. ~~temperature~~
10. ~~college*~~
11. ~~tragic~~
12. ~~positive~~
13. ~~fantastic~~
14. ~~exercise~~
15. ~~jealous~~
16. ~~organize~~
17. ~~courage~~
18. ~~curious~~
19. ~~departure~~
20. ~~storage~~

Final /īz/ Sound

advertise

realize

exercise

organize

Final /ĭv/ Sound

active

positive

Final /ĭj/ Sound

usage

college

courage

storage

Final /ĭk/ Sound

scientific

tragic

fantastic

Final /chər/ Sound

signature

temperature

departure

Final /əs/ Sound

serious

nervous

jealous

curios

Name _____

Spelling Spree

Word Root Hunt Write the Spelling Word that has the same root as each word below.

1. tragedy
2. temperate
3. useable
4. signify

5. department
6. science
7. fantasy

1. advertise
2. serious
3. scientific
4. active
5. usage
6. signature
7. realize
8. nervous
9. temperature
10. college*
11. tragic
12. positive
13. fantastic
14. exercise
15. jealous
16. organize
17. courage
18. curious
19. departure
20. storage

1. _tragic_
2. _temperature_
3. _usage_
4. _signature_

5. _departure_
6. _scientific_
7. _fantastic_

Hidden Words Write the Spelling Word that is hidden in each row of letters. Don't let the other words fool you!

Example: p r e s e n s i t i v e g e   *sensitive*

8. h i s t o r a g e n t l e
9. d e p o s i t i v e r y
10. p a r t n e r v o u s i n g
11. l o a d v e r t i s e e k
12. b r o n c o l l e g e n d
13. m o r e a l i z e r o
14. o c c u r i o u s u a l
15. c o m i c o u r a g e d

8. _gentle storage_
9. _deposit positive_
10. _nervous_
11. _advertise_

12. _college_
13. _realize_
14. _curious_
15. _courage_

280   Theme 5: **Doers and Dreamers**

Name _____

Proofreading and Writing

Proofreading Circle the five misspelled Spelling Words in this poster. Then write each word correctly.

Join the team!

Are you interested in getting some (exercize)? Are you (jealus) of friends who have their summer activities all lined up already? We're trying to (organise) a track team to compete over the summer. If you're (serius) about running or just curious about the team, come to our first practice. It's this Wednesday after school at the track. Now's your chance to stay (activ) this summer instead of sitting in front of a TV!

Spelling Words

1. advertise
2. serious
3. scientific
4. active
5. usage
6. signature
7. realize
8. nervous
9. temperature
10. college*
11. tragic
12. positive
13. fantastic
14. exercise
15. jealous
16. organize
17. courage
18. curious
19. departure
20. storage

1. _exercise_ 4. _serious_

2. _jealous_ 5. _active_

3. _organize_

 Write a Play-by-Play Account Suppose that you had been present the first time that Jackie Joyner-Kersee did a long jump in front of her coach. How would you have gone about describing the action for an audience? What would you say about the jump itself? How would you describe her coach's reaction?

On a separate piece of paper, write a play-by-play account of Jackie Joyner-Kersee's jump. Use Spelling Words from the list.

Name _____

Antonym Journal

Read the following journal entry. In each blank, write an antonym of the clue word. Sample answers shown.

April 3, 1974

This ___summer___ I get to join the West Park Tornadoes track
(winter)

squad. I'm so excited! When I think ___behind___ to how I got into
(ahead)

track, I can't believe I have come so far in just two years. I remember running

around the ___wide___ track for the first time on a ___sunny___
(narrow)   (cloudy)

June afternoon when I was ten. I wasn't fast, but Coach Pierce told me that if I

just kept coming to practice, I would get ___better___. So I did. I
(worse)

would finish my homework ___quickly___ after school and then go to
(slowly)

practice. I often had to run in the ___different___ direction from the other
(same)

girls as punishment because I chatted too much, but I still loved running. I also

began _____ to practice high-jumping. Coach Pierce got excited
(openly)

when he saw me high-jump one day, and began to coach me in that too. I don't

know where my running and jumping will ___take___ me, but I'm
(follow)

hoping it will be to a world ___full___ of adventure and a few ribbons!
(empty)

Name _____

The Subject Is Pronouns!

Subject and Object Pronouns A pronoun is a word that replaces one or
more nouns. A **subject pronoun** replaces a noun used as a subject or
after a linking verb. An **object pronoun** replaces a noun used as a direct
object or after a word such as *to, of, in, for, at,* or *by.* This chart shows the
singular and plural forms of subject pronouns and object pronouns.

Subject Pronouns		Object Pronouns	
Singular	**Plural**	**Singular**	**Plural**
I	we	me	us
you	you	you	you
he/she/it	they	him/her/it	them

**Write the correct subject or object pronoun shown in parentheses ( )
for each sentence below.**

1. (We/Us) will have another race in our neighborhood this Saturday.
2. Liza will run with (we/us).
3. It is (she/her) who runs faster than anyone else in the neighborhood.
4. The prize is always awarded to (she/her).
5. When the people cheer, Liza waves at (they/them).
6. My brother Tim wants Zach to run with (he/him) this year.
7. (He/Him) thinks that maybe Zach will get the prize this year.
8. (They/Them) have been running every morning for practice.

1. _____we_____
2. _____us_____
3. _____she_____
4. _____her_____
5. _____them_____
6. _____him_____
7. _____He_____
8. _____THEY_____

Name _____

I Am Always Last!

Pronouns in Compound Subjects and Objects A **compound subject** is made up of two or more simple subjects joined by *and* or *or*. A **compound object** is made up of two or more objects of an action verb.

▶ Use a **subject pronoun** in a compound subject.

▶ Use an **object pronoun** in a compound object.

▶ If you include yourself as part of a compound subject or object, mention yourself last.

To check that the pronoun is correct in a compound subject or object, ask yourself which pronoun you would use alone. Here is an example.

Incorrect: James and **me** went to the baseball game.

You would not use *me* alone as a subject pronoun. You would use *I*.

Correct: James and **I** went to the baseball game.

Write the correct word or words from those in parentheses ( ) to complete the compound subject or compound object in each sentence. Then underline the compound subject or compound object in each sentence.

1. My friend Jenna and ___I___ dream of running in the Olympics. (I/me)

2. The spirit of the Olympics motivates Jenna and ___I___ to do our best. (I/me)

3. ___She and I___ go together to the outdoor track at our school. (She and I/Her and me)

4. Our track coach encourages Jenna and ___I___ to run for the fun of it. (I/me)

5. ___He___ and our teammates make every race fun. (He/Him)

6. ___Jenna and I___ will hold on to our dream. (I and Jenna/Jenna and I)

Name _____

What's Right?

Using the Right Pronoun Be sure to use the correct forms of subject and object pronouns in your writing.

Austin has written a story for his school paper about his dream of playing his violin in an orchestra. He has had some trouble choosing the correct pronouns. Proofread his story, crossing out the six incorrect pronouns and writing the correct ones above the errors.

In Perfect Tune

I play the violin, and my older brother Gary plays the trumpet with

the high school jazz band. Us brothers want to play in an orchestra

together, but our school doesn't have one. My brother and me decided to

audition for the community orchestra. First, we each played a solo piece

and did pretty well. Then the orchestra members came in to start

rehearsal. One player said I should sit next to she. At first, I couldn't

hear my own violin. The player next to I helped. It was her who told me

to listen closely to the other violins. And now Gary and me are junior

members of the community orchestra!

Name _____

Clarification Composition

You write a **clarification composition** to clarify a quote, proverb, or statement, using examples and other details to support your explanation.

Use this clarification map to plan and organize a composition in which you clarify the meaning of the statement by Hall of Fame football coach Vince Lombardi. First, jot down what you think the statement means. Then list examples from Jackie Joyner-Kersee's story in *A Kind of Grace* **or from your own experience to support your ideas.**

```
┌─────────────────────────────────────────────┐
│                  Statement                    │
│ It's easy to have faith in yourself and have  │
│ discipline when you're a winner. . . . What   │
│ you've got to have is faith and discipline    │
│ when you're not a winner. (Vince Lombardi)    │
└─────────────────────────────────────────────┘
                      │
┌─────────────────────────────────────────────┐
│                  Meaning                      │
│                                               │
│                                               │
└─────────────────────────────────────────────┘
```

Examples   **Examples**   **Examples**

On a separate sheet of paper, write a composition at least three paragraphs long. The first sentence should include the Vince Lombardi statement. In the first paragraph, write what you think the statement means, restating it in your own words to expand or refine its meaning. In the following paragraphs, write reasons, details, and examples from *A Kind of Grace* **or from your own experience that support your opinion. Summarize with a concluding statement.**

Name _____

Being Precise

When you write, use precise words and phrases to help your readers understand
your meaning and create clearer mental pictures. Follow these guidelines:

► Replace pronouns that are unclear with the nouns they stand for.
► Replace vague verbs with more exact verbs.
► Add precise adjectives and adverbs to nouns and verbs.

**Read this scouting report. Replace vague words with more precise words
from the chart. Add adjectives and adverbs from the chart. Then write
the revised report on the lines.**

Two girls, Gwen and Jackie, on the Franklin-Freeman team threaten our
own jumpers. One sprints down the runway but needs work on her landing.
She places her foot solidly, though, and her form is superb. Jackie also runs
down the lane. She pushes off and kicks her legs well. She soars through the
air, and lands. They are in peak condition because of their training and will
undoubtedly break many records.

Precise Words and Phrases

Nouns	Gwen	Gwen and Jackie	the girls
Verbs	plants	charges	shatter
Adjectives	powerful	track-and-field	rigorous
Adverbs	cleanly	squarely	

_____

_____

_____

_____

_____

_____

Name _____

Revising Your Personal Essay

Reread your personal essay. What do you need to make it better? Use this page to help you decide. Put a checkmark in the box for each sentence that describes your personal essay.

Loud and Clear!

☐ My essay has a strong beginning that will get my readers' attention.

☐ I keep to the focus of the topic.

☐ My voice comes through in the tone of the essay.

☐ I have an effective conclusion that sums up my point.

☐ There are almost no mistakes.

Sounding Stronger

☐ I could make the beginning more attention grabbing.

☐ I stray from the point in a couple of places.

☐ My voice isn't always clear in the writing.

☐ I need to add a stronger conclusion.

☐ There are a few mistakes, including some sentence fragments.

Turn Up the Volume

☐ I need a better beginning.

☐ There are a lot of things in here that aren't related to the topic.

☐ There is no conclusion.

☐ There are a lot of mistakes, including many sentence fragments.

Sentence Fragments

► A complete sentence expresses a complete thought. It has both a subject and a predicate.

► A fragment is an incomplete sentence. It lacks either a subject or a predicate.

Identify each group of words as a Complete Sentence or a Fragment. Change each fragment into a complete sentence on the lines provided. You may need to rearrange or add words.

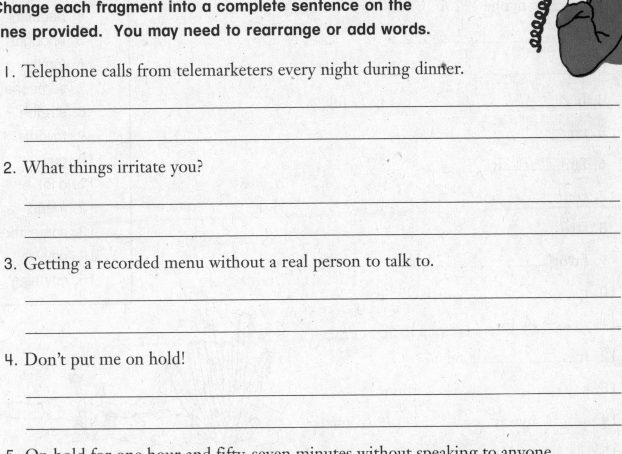

1. Telephone calls from telemarketers every night during dinner.

   _____

   _____

2. What things irritate you?

   _____

   _____

3. Getting a recorded menu without a real person to talk to.

   _____

   _____

4. Don't put me on hold!

   _____

   _____

5. On hold for one hour and fifty-seven minutes without speaking to anyone.

   _____

   _____

6. When I finally spoke to someone, I forgot what I was going to say.

   _____

   _____

Spelling Words

Look for familiar spelling patterns to help you remember how to spell the Spelling Words on this page. Think carefully about the parts that you find hard to spell in each word.

Write the missing letters in the Spelling Words below.

1. _____ nyone

2. cap _____ _____ _____ n

3. _____ _____ _____ right

4. b _____ _____ _____ t _____ ful

5. en _____ _____ _____ _____

6. fam _____ ly

7. som _____ one

8. stre _____ _____ _____

9. favor _____ _____ _____

10. g _____ _____

11. _____ lot

12. fr _____ _____ nd

13. s _____ _____ _____ times

14. _____ nyway

15. _____ nything

Study List On a separate piece of paper, write each Spelling Word. Check your spelling against the words on the list.

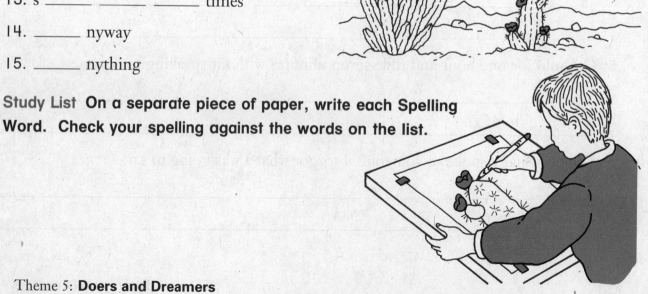

Name _____

Spelling Spree

Contrast Clues The second part of each clue contrasts with the first part. Write a Spelling Word to fit each clue.

1. not all the time, but _____
2. not a gal, but a _____
3. not fantastic, but _____
4. not to shrink, but to _____
5. not a little, but _____

1. _____
2. _____
3. _____
4. _____
5. _____

Word Maze Begin at the arrow and follow the Word Maze to find ten Spelling Words. Write the words in order.

6. _____
7. _____
8. _____
9. _____
10. _____
11. _____
12. _____
13. _____
14. _____
15. _____

Name _____

Proofreading and Writing

Proofreading Circle the five misspelled Spelling Words in this acceptance speech. Then write each word correctly.

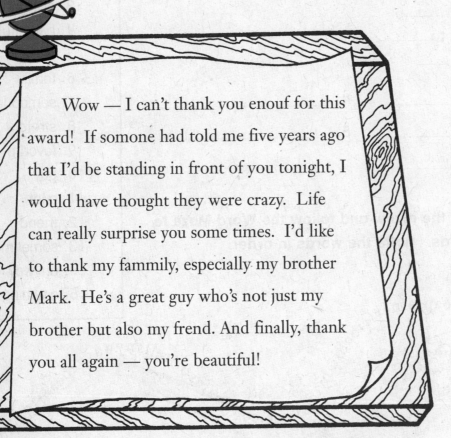

Wow — I can't thank you enouf for this award! If somone had told me five years ago that I'd be standing in front of you tonight, I would have thought they were crazy. Life can really surprise you some times. I'd like to thank my fammily, especially my brother Mark. He's a great guy who's not just my brother but also my frend. And finally, thank you all again — you're beautiful!

1. _____   4. _____

2. _____   5. _____

3. _____

➤ **Write Inspirational Sentences** Write five sentences that you could use to encourage someone to go out and achieve their dreams. Use Spelling Words from the list.

Name _____

"Account" for These Sentences

Use the words in the box to complete the sentences below.

1. Tiny statues you might place on your bookshelf for

   decoration are called ___Figurienes___ .

2. Something that is easy for people to get is

   _____ .

3. Someone who is extremely careful and exact is

   _____ .

4. Books in which numbers are recorded are called

   ___ledgers_____ .

5. Someone trained to keep financial records for businesses is an

   _____ .

6. Something used in place of something else is

   _____ .

7. If you don't try to act like you are rich or important, you are

   ___humble_____ .

8. If you are officially recognized as qualified to do something,

   you are _____ .

9. If you move your old books to make room for new ones on your

   bookshelf, you have _____ your

   old books to another shelf.

10. Small items of little value are

    called ___trinkets_____ .

Theme 5: **Doers and Dreamers**   293

Name _____

Problem–Solution Chart

Fill in the solution the characters found to each problem stated on the chart.

Problem		Solution
The author's mother wanted to complete her education, but she had to take care of a new baby.	➡	
The author's mother wanted to continue her accounting work while running her store.	➡	
The author's mother had to watch her two daughters while working at the store.	➡	
The author's family didn't have enough money to keep up the big family house.	➡	
The author's family wanted to make the jewelry store a successful business.	➡	
The author's family wanted to find affordable Nativity figurines to sell.	➡	

Name _____

What's the Order?

First, read each sentence below. Circle *Mother* or *Father* to correctly complete each sentence. Then number the sentences to show the order in which the events occur in the selection. The first item has been numbered for you.

_____ (Mother/Father) created molds for the figurines.

_____ (Mother/Father) convinced the family to take over a jewelry store in the city.

_____ (Mother/Father) searched for inexpensive figurines to sell.

___1___ (Mother/Father) studied to become an accountant.

_____ (Mother/Father) learned how to fix watches.

_____ (Mother/Father) came up with a plan for the whole family to help make figurines.

_____ (Mother/Father) opened a small store selling buttons, thread, pencils, and paper.

_____ (Mother/Father) gave the figurines their first coat of paint.

Name _____

Finding a Way

Read the passage below. Then complete the activity on page 297.

A Life of Art

Igor Koutsenko was born in the former Soviet Union. When he was six years old, his father brought him to a children's art school. It was there that he first saw a large box filled with what seemed like thousands of colored pencils. To him, that box shone with all the wonderful possibilities of art. Igor knew right then that he wanted to be an artist.

To become an artist, Igor decided to study in several art schools. After he graduated, he was required to serve in the Soviet Army for two years. Although he wanted to do his duty, he did not want to stop working as an artist. So he designed posters and slogans for the army. After leaving the army, he earned his living as an artist in Moscow.

Igor wanted to use his art to show people the difficulties in his country at that time. So he started drawing pen-and-ink miniatures with social or political themes. His drawings made people laugh, but they also made them look at the problems of society around them.

Eventually he started to explore different themes with his miniatures. He remembered the beautiful scenery of his childhood, which included grasslands, mountains, and the Black Sea. These images made him realize that harmony exists in the world. Through his work, he began to express his belief that the only way people can contribute to the survival of life on earth is to find peace and harmony in their own lives. Today Igor continues to work and lives in San Diego, California.

Finding a Way continued

Read the passage on page 296. Then complete the chart below.

Problem	Igor's Solution	Other Possible Solutions	My Judgment
Igor wanted to become an artist.			
Igor had to join the army for two years but didn't want to stop doing art.			
Igor wanted to show the harsh realities of life under communism through his art.			

Name _____

Plural[s]

Read each sentence below and look at the underlined plural words. Write the singular form of each underlined word on the line provided.

1. Alma's mother used <u>ledgers</u> and <u>receipts</u> to do her accounting work.

   _____   _____

2. The <u>figurines</u> were just one of many <u>varieties</u> of <u>items</u> sold in the family store.

   _____   _____   _____

3. The <u>men</u>, <u>women</u>, and <u>children</u> of the family all helped with the work.

   _____   _____   _____

4. They painted colorful <u>costumes</u> on the tiny <u>people</u>.

   _____   _____

Write the plural form of each word on the line provided.

Plural Form

5. penny   _____

6. half   _____

7. donkey   _____

8. box   _____

9. loaf   _____

Name _____

Plurals

Remember the following patterns to form the plurals of nouns ending with *f* or *o*:

► For nouns ending with *ff*, add -*s*: sta**ffs**/sta**ffs**.
► For nouns ending with *f*, add -*s* or change *f* to *v* and add -*es*: chie**f**/chie**fs**, hal**f**/hal**ves**.
► For nouns ending with a vowel + *o*, add -*s*: ster**eo**/ster**eos**.
► For nouns ending with a consonant + *o*, add -*s* or -*es* pia**no**/pia**nos**, pota**to**/pota**toes**.

Write each Spelling Word under the heading that tells how its plural is formed.

Spelling Words

1. pianos
2. cellos
3. solos
4. altos
5. sopranos
6. staffs
7. stereos
8. potatoes
9. halves
10. chiefs
11. echoes
12. calves
13. studios
14. shelves
15. ratios
16. volcanoes
17. loaves
18. wolves
19. heroes
20. scarves

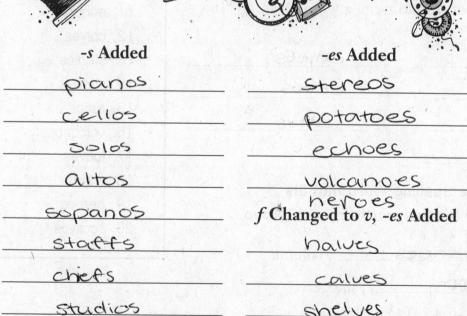

-s Added

pianos
cellos
solos
altos
sopanos
staffs
chiefs
studios
ratios

-es Added

stereos
potatoes
echoes
volcanoes
heroes

***f* Changed to *v*, -*es* Added**

halves
calves
shelves
loaves
wolves
scarves

Name _____

Spelling Spree

Word Magic **Write a Spelling Word to fit each clue.**

1. Change a vowel in *soles* to write a word for one-person performances.
2. Replace a consonant in *herds* with two vowels to write a word for brave men.
3. Add a consonant to *caves* to write a word meaning "young cattle."
4. Replace one consonant in *loans* with two letters to write a word meaning more than one package of bread.
5. Insert one vowel into *chefs* to write a synonym for *leaders*.
6. Add a vowel to *cells* to write the plural form of a large string instrument.
7. Change the ending of *alter* to write a word meaning "low singing voices."

1. _____solos_____   5. _____chiefs_____
2. _____heroes_____   6. _____cellos_____
3. _____calves_____   7. _____altos_____
4. _____loaves_____

Spelling Words

1. pianos
2. cellos
3. solos
4. altos
5. sopranos
6. staffs
7. stereos
8. potatoes
9. halves
10. chiefs
11. echoes
12. calves
13. studios
14. shelves
15. ratios
16. volcanoes
17. loaves
18. wolves
19. heroes
20. scarves

Alphabetizing **Write the Spelling Word that fits alphabetically between the two words in each group.**

8. vocabulary, _____volcanoes_____, volume
9. stacks, _____staffs_____, stagger
10. rating, _____ratios_____, rattle
11. peanuts, _____pianos_____, plants
12. scars, _____scarves_____, scavenge
13. steers, _____stereos_____, stores
14. eccentric, _____echoes_____, ecology
15. sopping, _____sopranos_____, sorrow

Name _____

Proofreading and Writing

Proofreading Circle the five misspelled Spelling Words in this dialogue based on the selection. Then write each word correctly.

Father: Well, the figurines aren't bad. Nothing like what artists can produce in their fancy studioes, but not bad — except for that shepherd. The two halfs of the mold didn't meet up right on that one.

Roberto: They're better than not bad, I think. Besides, that's not the point, is it? Now our customers can have a Nativity scene and still afford their meat, potatos, and loaves of bread.

Father: That's true. It wouldn't be much of a holiday if they were all hungry as wolfes.

Roberto: So let's place these on the store shelfs tomorrow and see how they sell.

1. pianos
2. cellos
3. solos
4. altos
5. sopranos
6. staffs
7. stereos
8. potatoes
9. halves
10. chiefs
11. echoes
12. calves
13. studios
14. shelves
15. ratios
16. volcanoes
17. loaves
18. wolves
19. heroes
20. scarves

1. ____studios____   4. ____wolves____

2. ____halves____   5. ____shelves____

3. ____potatoes____

✏️ Write a Personal Narrative Can you remember a time when you worked with others to get something accomplished? How did you feel about working as part of a team? Was your project a success?

On a separate piece of paper, write a personal narrative about a project that you did with a partner or a group. Use Spelling Words from the list.

Name _____

Mind These Meanings

Read each entry word and its definition. For each word write two sentences, using a different meaning of the word in each.

enlist (ĕn lĭst′) *v.* **1.** To engage someone for service in the armed forces. **2.** To engage the support or cooperation of.

figure (fĭg′ yər) *n.* **1.** An amount represented in numbers. **2.** An indistinct object or shape.

live[1] (lĭv) *v.* To reside or dwell.

live[2] (līv) *adj.* Alive; living.

miss (mĭs) *v.* **1.** To fail to attend or be present for. **2.** To feel or regret the absence or loss of.

needle (nēd′ l) *n.* A small slender sewing implement, pointed at one end and having an eye at the other. —*v.* To goad, provoke, or tease.

1. _____

_____

2. _____

_____

3. _____

_____

4. _____

_____

5. _____

_____

Bonus Now try writing one sentence that uses two different meanings of one word.

_____

Name _____

My or Mine?

Possessive and Indefinite Pronouns A **possessive pronoun** shows
ownership. It takes the place of a possessive noun.

► *My, your, his, her, its, our,* and *their* are used before nouns: This is my bike.

► *Mine, yours, hers, his, its, ours, yours,* and *theirs* are used alone: It is mine.

► Notice that *his* and *its* can come before a noun or be used alone.

An **indefinite pronoun** does not have a definite antecedent. It does not refer to a
specific person, place, or thing. Use a singular verb with a **singular indefinite
pronoun**. Use a plural verb with a **plural indefinite pronoun**.

Indefinite Pronouns

Singular			**Plural**	
any	everybody	nothing	all	others
anyone	everyone	somebody	both	several
anything	everything	someone	few	some
each	nobody	something	many	

**Replace the possessive noun in each sentence with a possessive
pronoun. Write the possessive pronoun after the sentence.**

1. Rebecca's family owns a store on our block. _____

2. The store was her grandparents' dream. _____

3. The store's goods come from all over the world. _____

**Complete each sentence by writing the correct form of the word
in parentheses ( ).**

4. Everyone _____ at that little place. (shops/shop)

5. Many _____ telling their friends about the store. (is/are)

6. The advertisements in the newspaper are _____. (your/yours)

7. Jessie bought _____ mom a present there. (her/hers)

8. I will shop for _____ there too. (my/mine)

Theme 5: **Doers and Dreamers**   303

Name _____

Who Is It ?

Using *Who, Whom,* and *Whose* The words *who, whom,* and *whose* are
forms of the pronoun *who.*
Use *who* as a **subject pronoun,** *whom* as an **object pronoun,** and *whose* as
a **possessive pronoun.** The different forms of *who* are often used in
questions. To check whether *whom* is correct, turn the question into a
statement. Here is an example.

    Whom has Rita called? (Rita has called *whom.*)

Whom is correct because it is the **direct object** in the sentence.

**Rita and her friends are hosting an international fair for charity.
Everyone has lots of questions! Fill in the blank in each sentence
with the correct form of the pronoun *who.***

1. _____Who_____ wants to sell holiday decorations at the fair?

2. _____Whom_____ will Rita invite to the fair?

3. _____who_____ brought the lemonade?

4. _____Whose_____ decorations are these?

5. _____Whom_____ will Carson ask for help?

6. _____whose_____ booth will do the most business?

7. _____Who_____ is selling baked goods?

8. _____whom_____ should we thank for these posters?

9. _____Whose_____ idea was it to play music?

10. _____whom_____ will Rita ask to deliver the money to the charity?

Name _____

Who's Who

Whose or Who's? A good writer is careful not to confuse the possessive pronoun *whose* with *who's*, the contraction of the words *who is*. It helps to remember that a possessive pronoun never has an apostrophe. Study these examples.

> **Incorrect**: **Whose** at the door?
> **Correct**: **Who's** at the door? (Who is at the door?)
> **Incorrect**: **Who's** house is that?
> **Correct**: **Whose** house is that? (Who owns that house?)

Ernesto's family is moving. He becomes curious about his family's history from the interesting old family photos and belongings in the attic. A list of Ernesto's questions is below. You can see that he has been confused by the difference between *who's* and *whose*. Cross out any error and write the correction above it. If a sentence has no error, write *none* above the sentence.

1. ~~Who's~~ *whose* big old trunk is that?

2. ~~Whose~~ *who's* the man wearing a hat in the big portrait?

3. *none* Whose military uniform hangs on the nail?

4. ~~Whose~~ *who's* the oldest member of our family?

5. *none* Who's going to write down our family history?

6. ~~Who's~~ *whose* journal is on the shelf?

7. ~~Who's~~ *whose* maps are these?

8. ~~Whose~~ ~~who is~~ *who's* going to put all these photographs in order?

Name _____

How-To Paragraph

A **how-to paragraph** tells how to do something. It has clear, complete instructions.

Use this page to plan and organize a how-to paragraph. First, identify your topic. Next, list the materials that are needed. Then outline each step. Finally, jot down specialized terms and ideas for helpful diagrams.

How to _____

Materials

Step 1	→	Step 2	→	Step 3

Step 6	←	Step 5	←	Step 4

Specialized Terms

Diagrams

Now write your how-to paragraph on a separate sheet of paper. In the topic sentence, describe what skill will be taught. Then tell what materials are needed. Next, explain each step clearly and in order. Include a diagram and a glossary of specialized terms.

Writing Clearly with Pronouns

You often use **pronouns** such as *he*, *she*, *they*, or *it* in your writing. Using pronouns helps you replace nouns in sentences, streamline your language, and avoid unnecessary repetition. Careful writers, however, do not use pronouns with unclear **antecedents** — the nouns to which the pronouns refer.

Unclear:

Ann and Lia bake holiday cookies. **She** asks **her** to make the dough and shape it with a cookie cutter. (Who makes the dough and shapes it, Ann or Lia?)

Clear:

Ann and Lia bake holiday cookies. **Lia** asks **Ann** to make the dough and shape **it** with a cookie cutter. (The pronoun *it* clearly refers to the dough.)

Read the following paragraph about two sisters working together to make a plaster of Paris figurine. Underline the pronouns. Then replace any pronouns with unclear antecedents with the nouns for which they stand. Write the nouns above the pronouns you underline.

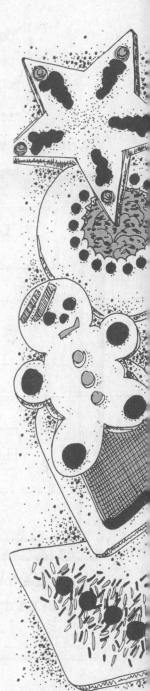

   Flor and her sister Alma make figurines. They use these supplies: a

figurine mold, soft plaster of Paris, grease, a kitchen knife, paints, and

small brushes. You find them at an arts and crafts store. First, Alma

greases the inside of the mold before closing and locking the mold's

hinges. They pour in a small amount of plaster of Paris through a hole in

the bottom of the mold until it is filled. Once the plaster has completely

hardened, she helps her gently remove it from the mold.

Name _____

A Word Exhibition

Vocabulary

palette   painstaking   canvas   portrait

pixels   conceptual   hyperrealistic   exhibition

optically   obstacles   abstract

Write each word from the box beneath the heading that tells about it.

Tools Used for Painting	Small Dots Used in Computer Art
_____	_____
_____	**Painting of a Person**
Three Styles of Art	_____
_____	**Requiring Great Care and Effort**
_____	_____
_____	**A Public Show of Artwork**
Having to Do with Vision	_____
_____	**A Word for _Difficulties_**
	_____

Now use four words from the box to write a brief paragraph about what you might see in an artist's studio.

_____

_____

_____

_____

Name _____

Comparison Chart

Write the most important ideas you learn about Chuck Close in the chart below.

Pages 500–505	Pages 506–511

After you read, compare Chuck Close's life before and after "the event." On a separate piece of paper make three lists:

▶ Things that Chuck Close did before "the event"

▶ Things that Chuck Close did after "the event"

▶ Things Chuck did both before and after "the event"

Name _____

Fact Sheet

Write some facts about Chuck Close to complete the fact sheet below.

Name: _____

Occupation: _____

Best Known for: _____

_____

Place of Residence: _____

Painting Methods:

1. _____

2. _____

3. _____

Life's Greatest Challenge:

_____

How He Overcame His Challenge:

_____

_____

Advice to Others:

_____

_____

_____

Like or Unlike?

Read the passage. Then complete the activity on page 312.

Portrait of JoeSam.

Joseph Samuels, who uses the name *JoeSam.*, is a contemporary artist who lives and works in San Francisco. He has created works in a wide range of forms, including paintings, mixed-media pieces, and sculptures. He uses a variety of materials in his work: wood, metal, old photographs, paint, and even flannel shirts.

Although he has been creating art since he was young, he hasn't always been a full-time artist. In college he studied education and psychology. For many years he worked for organizations devoted to helping others, such as Headstart. Eventually he became a full-time artist, which he says is "fabulous." His interest in teaching continues in his art. He believes that his artwork needs to show "some awareness of what's happening in the world" and that it must teach people something. One of his most famous art projects, "Black West," focuses on teaching people little-known facts about the lives of African Americans who settled the American frontier.

JoeSam. loves being an artist. He volunteers at many schools to encourage a love of art in young people. His advice to them includes these words: "Just create your art. . . . Anyone can create art." He admits that art is not a likely way for a person to make a lot of money, but he believes it is still important. He says, "Art is something you do — it's just a part of what you love, that you want to create."

Name _____

Like or Unlike? continued

Complete the exercises below.

1. Compare and contrast the careers and art of JoeSam. and Chuck
   Close. Write your answers in the Venn diagram below.

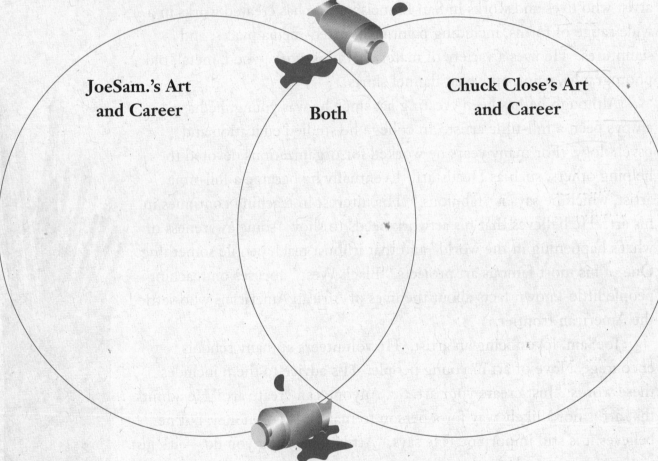

**JoeSam.'s Art
and Career**

Both

**Chuck Close's Art
and Career**

2. Write a sentence that describes one similarity between Chuck Close and JoeSam.

_____

_____

3. Write a sentence that describes one difference between these two artists.

_____

_____

Chuck Close Up Close

Structural Analysis Suffixes
-ent/-ence, -ant/-ance,
-able/-ible, -ate

Name _____

Suffix Scramble

Read each sentence. In the letter spaces, write the word from the palette that best completes each sentence. Then unscramble the circled letters to answer the question at the bottom of the page.

accident   celebrate   dictate

different   endurance   portable

reliant   rotate   separate

terrible

1. Chuck Close likes to try _ _ _ _ _ _ _ ◯ _ _ _ painting styles.

2. For some paintings, Chuck would ◯ _ ◯ _ _ _ _ a photograph into three colors.

3. Chuck likes to _ _ _ _ _ _ ◯ _ _ _ with music as he finishes a painting.

4. While giving a speech, Chuck felt ◯ _ _ _ _ _ _ _ _ _ and went to the hospital.

5. Chuck's injury can also happen to people who have been in an _ _ _ ◯ _ _ _ _ _ _.

6. "The event" will _ _ _ _ ◯ _ _ _ how Chuck paints from now on.

7. Chuck needs a lot of _ _ _ _ _ _ _ ◯ _ _ _ to hold a paintbrush for many hours.

8. After working through a whole painting, Chuck likes to _ ◯ _ _ _ _ the painting to a new position and go through it again.

What kinds of paintings does Chuck Close most often create?

◯◯◯◯◯◯◯◯◯◯

Name _____

Suffixes: *-ant/-ance;*
-ent/-ence; -able/-ible; -ate

The suffixes *-ant*, *-ent*, *-able*, and *-ible* are sometimes added to base words or word roots to form adjectives. Because the spelling of the schwa sound is not clear, you must remember the spelling pattern for each suffix.

The suffixes *-ance* and *-ence* are similar to *-ant* and *-ent*, but they form nouns instead of adjectives when added to base words or word roots. When you hear the final /ĭt/ or /āt/ sounds, think of the pattern *ate*.

Write each Spelling Word under its suffix.

-ant

brilliant
fragrant

-ance

appearance
instance
importance

-ent

excellent
client
agent

-ence

audience
sentence
difference

-able

lovable
noticeable
workable

-ible

visible
responsible

-ate

desperate
celebrate
fortunate
separate

Chuck Close Up Close

Spelling Suffixes: -ant/-ance;
-ent/-ence; -able/-ible; -ate

Spelling Spree

Word Detective Write a Spelling Word for each clue.

1. a particular case, or example
2. deserving of affection
3. an employee of the FBI
4. the way something looks
5. sweet-smelling, like a flower
6. a lawyer's customer
7. shining very brightly
8. kept apart

1. _____ 5. _____

2. _____ 6. _____

3. _____ 7. _____

4. _____ 8. _____

Syllable Spot Write the Spelling Word that has one of the
syllables in each word below.

9. sponsor
10. person
11. audibly
12. portion
13. fortify
14. fertile
15. sentiment

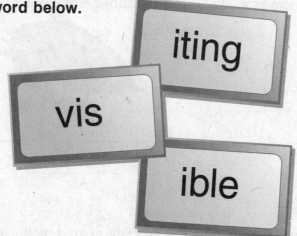

iting

vis

ible

9. _____ 13. _____

10. _____ 14. _____

11. _____ 15. _____

12. _____

Name _____

Proofreading and Writing

Proofreading Circle the five misspelled Spelling Words in
this newspaper column. Then write each word correctly.

Eye on Art

NEW YORK– An excelent exhibit of Chuck Close's newest
paintings opened here yesterday. The artist has been
partially paralyzed from the neck down since December of
1988. With courage and determination, he has found a
workible way of continuing to paint, strapping brushes to his
hands and moving his arms across the canvas. There is a
noticable difference between his current paintings and his
earlier work. The canvas seems to contain many little
images when looked at closely. When the viewer steps back,
however, a larger figure becomes visibel. The paintings are
remarkable, and art lovers will cellebrate this fine
exhibition.

Spelling Words

1. desperate
2. brilliant
3. audience
4. celebrate
5. excellent
6. visible
7. appearance
8. lovable
9. noticeable
10. sentence
11. difference
12. workable
13. instance
14. fragrant
15. fortunate
16. client
17. separate
18. agent
19. responsible
20. importance

1. _____   4. _____

2. _____   5. _____

3. _____

✏——— **Write a Description** Chuck Close is very dedicated to his art. Is
there a favorite sport, hobby, or craft that you have a great interest in?
Why do you like it? How often do you participate in this activity?

**On a separate piece of paper, write a brief description of your
favorite sport, hobby, or craft. Be sure to tell what it means to you.
Use Spelling Words from the list.**

Name _____

Find That Origin!

Read the dictionary entries. Then read the sentences. For each
underlined word, write the word origin and the meaning of the origin.
Then use the word clues to write other common English words that
have the same origin.

> **artist 1.** *n.* A person who produces works of art. **2.** *n.* A person who shows
>   skill and creativity in a job or in his or her free time. [Latin *ars*, art.]
>
> **deposit 1.** *v.* To put or set down; place. [Latin, *dē* + *pōnere*, to put.]
>
> **person** *n.* A living human being; an individual. [Latin, *persōna*, mask used
>   by actors.]

1. Chuck Close feels that the face of a <u>person</u> is a road map of her or his life.

   Origin: _____ Meaning of origin: _____

   Word clue: to pretend to act and look like someone else _____

   Word clue: This makes one person different _____
           from another.

2. Chuck likes to feel how much ink he <u>deposits</u> on a painting.

   Origin: _____ Meaning of origin: _____

   Word clue: to put off until later _____

   Word clue: a person or group who opposes _____
           another in a game

3. From a distance you can't tell how the <u>artist</u> created one of his paintings.

   Origin: _____ Meaning of origin: _____

   Word clue: made by human beings, not by nature _____

   Word clue: an object made by human beings, especially _____
           an object from an ancient time

Name _____

Too Negative!

Avoiding Double Negatives A word that means "no" is called a **negative**.
A **negative** reverses the meaning of a sentence.

   Do not use a **double negative**, or two negative words, in the same
sentence. Some common negatives are *no, none, not, nobody, nothing,*
nowhere, and *never.* Contractions using *not* are also negatives.
You will see that there is usually more than one way to correct
a **double negative**.

   Incorrect: I will not paint nothing.

   Correct: I will paint nothing. (Drop the negative *not.*)

   Correct: I will not paint anything. (Change *nothing* to *anything.*)

Most negative words have a matching positive word. Here are some
common negative-positive pairs.

hardly - almost   never - ever   no - any
neither - either   none - some

Rewrite each sentence, correcting the double negatives. There may
be more than one way to correct a sentence. Choose the one you prefer.

1. Art class was not never Pat's favorite.

_____

2. Pat thought he didn't have no talent.

_____

3. Pat had not tried no kind of painting.

_____

4. Once he tried oil painting, he didn't never want to stop!

_____

_____

5. There is not nobody in the class who likes to paint as much as Pat.

_____

_____

Short and Sweet!

Contractions A **contraction** is formed by combining two words and shortening one of them. An apostrophe (') takes the place of the letter or letters left out. The word *not* can be combined with *is*, *are*, *was*, and *were* to form contractions. Pronouns and verbs can also be combined to form contractions. The two lists below contain some of the common contractions.

Contractions formed with *not*	Contractions formed with pronouns and verbs
isn't (is not)	I've (I have)
aren't (are not)	you're (you are)
won't (will not)	she'll (she will)
can't (cannot)	they're (they are)
hasn't (has not)	it's (it is)

Underline the contraction in each sentence below. Then write the words that make up the contraction.

1. I hadn't visited an art gallery before today. _____

2. The artists aren't ones that I know. _____

3. Mr. Watkins says he'll tell us about the paintings. _____

4. He doesn't know all the artists either. _____

5. He's pointed out a landscape. _____

6. It's a painting of a lake and some deer. _____

7. Haven't we gone swimming in that lake? _____

8. Doesn't the painting make you want to be there? _____

9. I'd like to try landscape painting. _____

10. This won't be the last time I visit an art gallery. _____

Name _____

Which One's Right?

Using *it's*, *its*; *there*, *their*, *they're* A good writer is careful not to confuse *it's* and *its* and *there*, *their*, and *they're*. These words sound alike, but they mean different things and are spelled differently.

it's	contraction of *it is*	**It's** opening day at the show!
its	possessive pronoun	I know **its** location.
there	adverb; can also be used to begin a sentence	Are you going **there**? **There** are many entries.
their	possessive pronoun	Joe and Meg have **their** drawings in it.
they're	contraction of *they are*	**They're** excited about the show.

Proofread Heather's review of the school art show. Cross out the errors she has made with the words in the list above, and write your correction above each error.

The Student Art Show opened on Friday afternoon. Their are too many wonderful works to be able to mention them all. Its an honor to be able to tell you about a few of them. Shirley Jane G. entered a group of drawings of her grandmother. Each one is beautiful, and together there very moving. Mark Z.'s entry is a small sculpture. "The Phoenix" is it's title and Mark says it's his expression of hope. Students Cindy R. and David M. worked together on a large mural. They're work is called "Friends Forever." I recommend that everyone see the works of the students in the Student Art Show. You will be amazed at there talent!

Name _____

Writing a Summary

If you were asked to summarize *Chuck Close Up Close*, you would probably tell who Chuck Close is, how he paints, and what event changed his life. A **summary** is a brief account of a selection. Writing a summary is a good way to recall main ideas or events in a selection and to share what it is about.

Choose a selection you have read, such as *Under the Royal Palms* or *A Kind of Grace: The Autobiography of Jackie Joyner-Kersee*. Then fill in the graphic organizer below with the most important ideas or events in the selection.

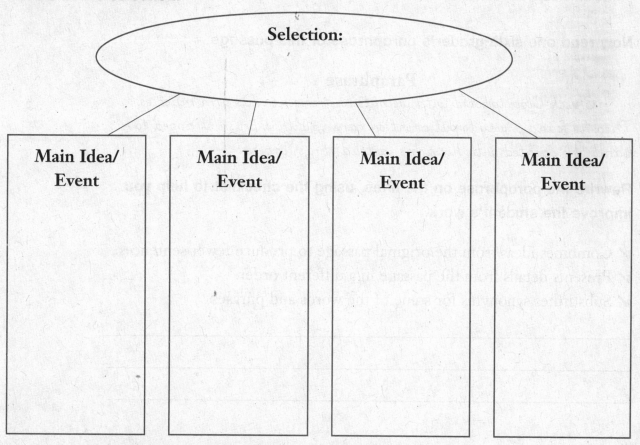

Selection:

Main Idea/ Event	Main Idea/ Event	Main Idea/ Event	Main Idea/ Event

Now write your summary of the selection on a separate sheet of paper. In the first sentence, tell who or what is being summarized. Briefly restate the main points or events in your own words. Remember to leave out details and minor events. End with a concluding sentence.

Name _____

Paraphrasing

When you **paraphrase** a passage from a book, article, or story, you put it into your own words without changing the author's meaning. A careful writer paraphrases without copying word-for-word.

Read the following passage from *Chuck Close Up Close*.

> He labored with weights, strengthening the muscles in his arms. Finally, after many long weeks of struggle, he developed a way to work. Seated in his wheelchair, with a brush strapped to his hand, he could put paint on a canvas. His arms took the place of his fingers.

Now read one sixth-grader's paraphrase of this passage.

Paraphrase

Chuck Close labored with weights to strengthen his arm muscles. Then he found a way to put paint on canvas with a brush strapped to his hand. He painted with his arms instead of his fingers.

Rewrite the paraphrase on the lines, using the checklist to help you improve the student's work.

✔ Combines ideas from the original passage to produce fewer sentences.
✔ Presents details from the passage in a different order.
✔ Substitutes synonyms for some of the words and phrases.

_____

_____

_____

Name _____

Writing an Answer to a Question

Use what you have learned about taking tests to help you write answers to questions about something you have read. This practice will help you when you take this kind of test.

Read these paragraphs from the selection _Chuck Close Up Close_.

The giant black-and-white paintings had been strikingly fresh in the late 1960s. Now he [Close] was ready to create another "problem" for himself — a new challenge. Around 1970 he invited some friends over to pose for a different set of "head shots," this time in color. He says there is a big advantage to using photographs. "If you paint from life, you have to do more than one sitting. The models gain weight, lose weight; their hair gets long; they cut it off. They're happy; they're sad. They're asleep or they're awake. But the camera provides the freshness and intimacy of one moment frozen in time."

To keep himself from making "the same old colors" on his palette, he found a way to mix the color directly on the canvas. Since color photo images are made up of three primary hues — red, blue, and yellow — he had the photographs separated into these three colors. Then he began to paint.

Now write your answer to each question.

1. How is using photographs different from using live models?

_____

_____

_____

_____

_____

_____

Name _____

Writing an Answer to a Question continued

2. How is using photographs the same as using live models?

_____

_____

_____

_____

_____

_____

3. Why did Close mix the color directly on the canvas?

_____

_____

_____

_____

_____

Name _____

Spelling Review

Write Spelling Words from the list to answer the questions.

1–10. Which ten words have the final /īz/, /ĭv/, /ĭj/, /ĭk/, /chər/, or /əs/ sound?

1. _____
2. _____
3. _____
4. _____
5. _____

6. _____
7. _____
8. _____
9. _____
10. _____

11–20. Which ten words are plurals?

11. _____
12. _____
13. _____
14. _____
15. _____

16. _____
17. _____
18. _____
19. _____
20. _____

21–30. Which ten words have the suffix -*ant*, -*ance*, -*ent*, -*ence*, -*able*, -*ible*, or -*ate*?

21. _____
22. _____
23. _____
24. _____
25. _____

26. _____
27. _____
28. _____
29. _____
30. _____

Spelling Words

1. stereos
2. chiefs
3. scientific
4. visible
5. positive
6. noticeable
7. active
8. staffs
9. echoes
10. separate
11. workable
12. courage
13. realize
14. fragrant
15. studios
16. difference
17. shelves
18. temperature
19. importance
20. departure
21. excellent
22. pianos
23. fantastic
24. halves
25. exercise
26. curious
27. appearance
28. celebrate
29. loaves
30. potatoes

Name _____

Spelling Spree

Puzzle Play **Write a Spelling Word to fit each clue. Then write the word that you make from the letters in the boxes.**

1. places where artists work __ __ __ ☐ __ __ __ __

2. having a pleasing odor __ ☐ __ __ __ __ __ __

3. two _____ of bread __ __ __ ☐ __ __

4. four quarters equal two _____ __ ☐ __ __ __

5. how hot or cold the air is

__ __ ☐ __ __ __ __ __ __ __

6. of the highest quality, superb

__ __ __ __ ☐ __ __ __

7. bravery __ __ __ ☐ __ __ __

Special Word: __ __ __ __ __ __ __

Spelling Words

1. courage
2. fantastic
3. halves
4. stereos
5. temperature
6. echoes
7. potatoes
8. noticeable
9. studios
10. difference
11. workable
12. separate
13. loaves
14. fragrant
15. excellent

The Next Word **Write the Spelling Word that belongs in each group.**

8. eye-catching, obvious, _____

9. weird, bizarre, _____

10. tape decks, CD players, _____

11. repeated sounds, reflections, _____

12. carrots, turnips, _____

13. unlikeness, variation, _____

14. doable, practical, _____

15. distinct, individual, _____

Proofreading and Writing

Spelling Words

1. active
2. realize
3. departure
4. curious
5. scientific
6. positive
7. shelves
8. chiefs
9. staffs
10. celebrate
11. visible
12. appearance
13. exercise
14. importance
15. pianos

Proofreading Circle the six misspelled Spelling Words in this speech. Then write each word correctly.

People who dream and make a difference in our world are curius. They go beyond the visibel appearanse of things to look at their true importans. It is time we realyze how valuable their deparcher from the ordinary really is.

1. _____   4. _____

2. _____   5. _____

3. _____   6. _____

Brainstorming Write Spelling Words to complete each phrase.

7. take an _____ part

8. either _____ or negative

9. _____ of bookcases

10. items in a _____ lab

11. lab workers on _____ of science projects

12. _____ in charge

13. _____ or other musical instruments

14. walking is good _____

15. _____ a success

━━━━▶ **Write a Character Sketch** **On a separate sheet of paper, write a character sketch about a doer or a dreamer. Use the Spelling Review Words.**

Name _____

Sound Bites

When a speech gets reported on television or in the newspaper, it is often not shown in its entirety. Instead, the most important or striking phrases are presented. These are called "sound bites." Choose some sound bites for the speeches below.

Speech	Sound Bites
"The Gettysburg Address"	
"A Story of Courage, Bravery, Strength, and Heroism"	
Spinelli Newbery Acceptance Speech	
Ortega Speech	
"I Have a Dream"	

Which speech did you like best? Why?

_____

_____

Name _____

Cover That Speech

You are a newspaper reporter assigned to the event at which one of these speeches was given. Write a news story about the speech.

_____

_____

_____

_____

_____

_____

_____

_____

_____

_____

_____

_____

_____

_____

_____

_____

_____

_____

_____

Name _____

New Frontiers: Oceans and Space

The selections in this theme will take you on journeys up into deep space and down into the deep sea. After reading each selection, add to this chart to show what you learned along the way.

	Adventures of Sojourner	**Franklin R. Chang-Díaz**
What kind of writing is the selection an example of?		
What is the selection about?		
In what way does the selection describe a frontier?		

Name _____

New Frontiers: Oceans and Space

	Beneath Blue Waters	Out There
What kind of writing is the selection an example of?		
What is the selection about?		
In what way does the selection describe a frontier?		

What important ideas have you learned about the oceans and about space?

_____

_____

Name _____

Exploring a Distant World

Write words from the box to complete the sentences below.

1. If you are operating a vehicle designed to explore the surface of a planet, you are controlling a _____ .

2. If you use both your eyes to see something three-dimensionally, you are seeing a _____ image.

3. If you work with individuals who have special training that enables them to build and operate complex devices, you work with _____ .

4. If you are checking something regularly, you are _____ it.

5. If a vehicle has sensitive devices that respond to light, sound, or movement, the vehicle has _____ .

6. If you use instruments to figure out where you are and where you are going, you are using them for _____ . If you use instruments to break a substance down into its parts for study, you are using them for _____ .

7. If you have figured out the likely meaning of the data collected from a planet, you have _____ the data.

8. If you plan how a vehicle turns to avoid obstacles, you plan its _____ .

Name _____

Cause and Effect Chart

Cause	Effect
Scientists had never tried to land a remote-control robot on Mars.	→	The scientists were tense about the descent and landing.
Pathfinder fired three small braking rockets.	→	
Pathfinder had a very smooth landing.	→	
The lander's camera was stereoscopic.	⇨	
	⇨	The science team almost immediately posted on the Internet the photos they were receiving.
As Sojourner approached Yogi, the alternate rover driver made a mistake in its estimate of where to turn.	⇨	
	⇨	Sojourner could not communicate with the lander.
The Pathfinder Mission was considered a great success.	⇨	

Name _____

Keep a Mission Log

Complete the mission log below to show the sequence of events in the Pathfinder mission.

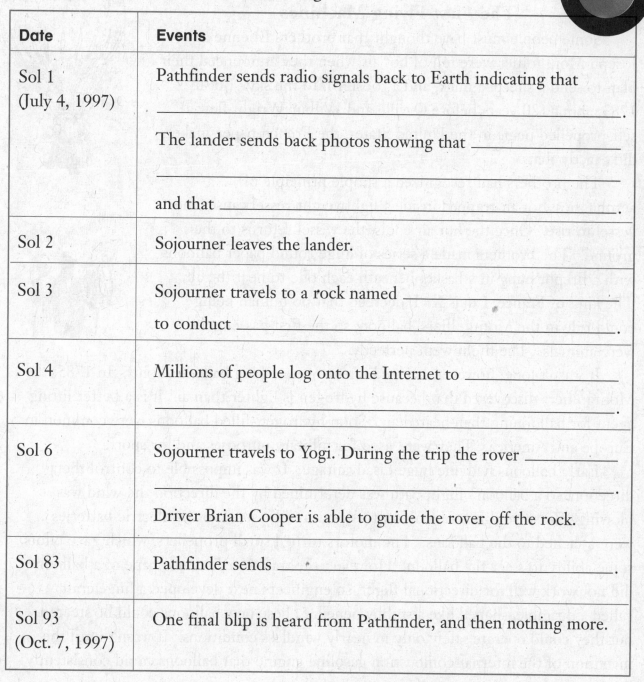

Mission Log

Date	Events
Sol 1 (July 4, 1997)	Pathfinder sends radio signals back to Earth indicating that _____. The lander sends back photos showing that _____ _____ and that _____.
Sol 2	Sojourner leaves the lander.
Sol 3	Sojourner travels to a rock named _____ to conduct _____.
Sol 4	Millions of people log onto the Internet to _____ _____.
Sol 6	Sojourner travels to Yogi. During the trip the rover _____ _____ Driver Brian Cooper is able to guide the rover off the rock.
Sol 83	Pathfinder sends _____.
Sol 93 (Oct. 7, 1997)	One final blip is heard from Pathfinder, and then nothing more.

In Search of Causes and Effects

Read the passage. Then complete the activity on page 337.

The First Flying Machines

Some people must have thought that brothers Etienne and Joseph Montgolfier were full of hot air when they announced their plan to send a sheep, a duck, and a rooster into the sky. But in 1783, about 120 years before Orville and Wilbur Wright flew a self-propelled plane in the United States, the French paper-makers did exactly that.

The brothers had recognized a simple principle of aeronautics: hot air trapped inside a lightweight vessel causes the vessel to rise. Once the hot air cools, the vessel returns to the ground. The brothers made a series of huge round paper balloons with a firepot hung in a basket beneath each one to heat the air. The king of France, Louis XVI, decreed that no human being could ride in the Montgolfiers' balloon, so the first passengers were animals. The flight went perfectly.

It wasn't long, however, before humans were taking balloon flights. In 1785, the Montgolfiers discovered that because hydrogen is lighter than air, it is a better lifting agent for ballooning than heated air. Soon hydrogen-filled balloons were common in Europe and America. They were used for military purposes and for sport.

Early balloons had one huge disadvantage. It was impossible to control their direction, so a balloon's flight path was determined by the direction the wind was blowing. To solve this problem, motors powered by steam or by electric batteries were attached to the balloons. The motors turned small propellers, which gave pilots some ability to steer the balloon. However, the traditional round shape of a balloon did not work well for directional flight, so engineers next developed a huge craft called a dirigible, shaped like a stubby pencil. These new balloons could be steered, but they could operate safely only in nearly windless conditions. It wasn't until the invention of the internal-combustion gasoline engine that balloons could consistently be navigated.

In Search of Causes and Effects continued

Complete the chart by writing the missing causes and effects. Use the information in the passage on page 336.

Cause		Effect
Air is heated and trapped inside a lightweight vessel.	→	
The air inside the vessel cools.	→	
	→	The first passengers in a hot-air balloon were farm animals.
Hydrogen was discovered to be a better lifting agent than heated air.	→	
	→	Engineers created balloons called dirigibles that were shaped like stubby pencils.
The internal-combustion gasoline engine was invented.	→	

Name _____

Puzzling Out Prefixes

Read the diary page of an aerospace engineer. Underline each word with the prefix de-, dis-, ex-, inter-, per-, pre-, or pro-.

> The moment Sojourner detached herself from the lander and rolled onto Martian soil was so exciting! The next several weeks were busy ones as she gathered data from Martian rocks for us to interpret. When we permitted her to navigate herself, we would disturb her only when it was necessary to prevent her from running into protruding parts of rocks. Soon she demonstrated that she was very good at extending her APXS against the rocks to test them.

Now write the words you underlined. Use the word parts as well as sentence clues from the diary entry to write the meaning of each word. Write the word on the short line, and its meaning on the long line next to it.

1. _____ _____
2. _____ _____
3. _____ _____
4. _____ _____
5. _____ _____
6. _____ _____
7. _____ _____
8. _____ _____

Name _____

Prefixes: *de-, dis-, ex-, inter-, per-, pre-, pro-*

The word parts *de-, dis-, ex-, inter-, per-, pre-,* and *pro-* are all prefixes. To spell a word with a prefix, find the prefix, the base word or the word root, and any ending. Then spell the word by parts.

> **de**cision   **dis**able   **ex**perience   **inter**national
> **per**mission   **pre**view   **pro**ceed

Write each Spelling Word under its prefix.

Spelling Words

1. disease
2. decision
3. proceed
4. international
5. permission
6. experience
7. disable
8. preview
9. describe
10. progress
11. product
12. exhaust
13. previous
14. demonstrate
15. extent
16. disturb
17. persuade
18. interview
19. determine
20. prepare

de-

_____

_____

_____

_____

dis-

_____

_____

ex-

_____

_____

_____

inter-

_____

_____

per-

_____

_____

_____

pre-

_____

_____

_____

pro-

_____

_____

Name _____

Spelling Spree

Changing Prefixes Change the underlined prefix in each
word to write a Spelling Word.

1. <u>in</u>tent
2. <u>de</u>duct
3. <u>com</u>mission
4. <u>in</u>scribe
5. <u>ex</u>ceed
6. <u>un</u>able
7. <u>multi</u>national

1. _____   5. _____

2. _____   6. _____

3. _____   7. _____

4. _____

Spelling Words

1. disease
2. decision
3. proceed
4. international
5. permission
6. experience
7. disable
8. preview
9. describe
10. progress
11. product
12. exhaust
13. previous
14. demonstrate
15. extent
16. disturb
17. persuade
18. interview
19. determine
20. prepare

Double Syllable Scramble Rearrange the syllables in each
item to write *two* Spelling Words. (There are no extra
syllables.)

8–9. suade pre per view
10–11. pare dis pre ease
12–13. ri ence dis pe turb ex
14–15. mine haust de ex ter

8–9. _____   10–11. _____

12–13. _____   14–15. _____

Proofreading and Writing

Proofreading Circle the five misspelled Spelling Words in this television program description. Then write each word correctly.

Spelling Words

1. disease
2. decision
3. proceed
4. international
5. permission
6. experience
7. disable
8. preview
9. describe
10. progress
11. product
12. exhaust
13. previous
14. demonstrate
15. extent
16. disturb
17. persuade
18. interview
19. determine
20. prepare

Mission to Mars! *(8 P.M. Wednesday)*

How did a team of scientists and engineers land a rover on Mars? This fascinating show is a preview of an upcoming documentary on the recent Pathfinder Mission. Beginning with NASA's deccision to make another mission to Mars possible, the program details each step of the project. The director was able to innerview many people who worked on the team. In one memorable scene, two scientists demenstrate how Pathfinder's complex parachute system allowed for a safe landing on Mars. As a result of Pathfinder, the progres made in our knowledge of Mars has increased greatly. The program also discusses previus attempts at exploration on Mars. ★★★★ 11 17 34

1. _____   4. _____

2. _____   5. _____

3. _____

Write an Opinion The Pathfinder Mission to Mars cost $266 million. Do you think it was worth it? What are some of the benefits of exploring other planets? What do we learn that we might not otherwise know? Are there other things that you think the money could be better spent on?

On a separate piece of paper, write a paragraph in which you state your opinion about the Pathfinder Mission. Use Spelling Words from the list.

Name _____

Go Figure the Relationship!

Read each analogy. Then write the word that best completes each analogy. One has been done for you.

Example: <u>Exploration</u> is to <u>explorer</u> as <u>invention</u> is to ___inventor___.

    laboratory   experiment   inventor   inconvenient

1. <u>Sojourner</u> is to <u>rover</u> as <u>Pathfinder</u> is to _____.

    commands   lander   Mars   power

2. <u>Applause</u> is to <u>clapping</u> as <u>laughter</u> is to _____.

    laughing   anger   shouting   joy

3. <u>Date</u> is to <u>calendar</u> as <u>time</u> is to _____.

    difficult   clock   dust   rough

4. <u>Excited</u> is to <u>discouraged</u> as <u>kindly</u> is to _____.

    cruelly   helpful   clear   cruelty

5. <u>Hazard</u> is to <u>danger</u> as <u>report</u> is to _____.

    send   form   writing   update

6. <u>Fail</u> is to <u>succeed</u> as <u>transmit</u> is to _____.

    computer   receive   satellite   send

Use some of the following words to write two incomplete analogies.
Challenge a partner to complete each analogy with a remaining word.

water	day	liquid	month
year	rock	week	solid

7. _____

8. _____

What's in a Phrase?

Prepositions and Prepositional Phrases A preposition shows the relationship
between a noun or a pronoun and some other word in the sentence. A noun or
pronoun that follows a preposition is the object of the preposition. A
prepositional phrase is made up of a preposition, the object of the preposition,
and all the words between them. Here is a list of some common prepositions.

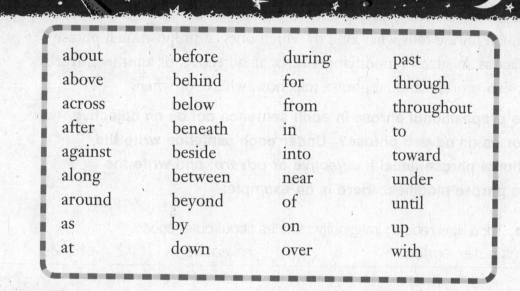

about	before	during	past
above	behind	for	through
across	below	from	throughout
after	beneath	in	to
against	beside	into	toward
along	between	near	under
around	beyond	of	until
as	by	on	up
at	down	over	with

**Write the prepositional phrase in each sentence, and circle the object of
the preposition.**

1. The twentieth century saw machines and human beings blasted into space.

   _____

2. Most of the NASA missions have been successful.

   _____

3. We have seen rocks brought back from the moon.

   _____

4. Scientist astronauts have performed experiments during space missions.

   _____

Name _____

Ways to Describe

Prepositional Phrases as Adjectives and Adverbs A prepositional phrase can act as an adjective, modifying a noun or a pronoun. As an adjective, a prepositional phrase tells what kind or which one. A prepositional phrase can also act as an adverb, modifying a verb, an adjective, or another adverb. As an adverb, a prepositional phrase tells how, where, or when.

Does the prepositional phrase in each sentence act as an adjective phrase or as an adverb phrase? Under each sentence write the prepositional phrase, label it *adjective* or *adverb*, and write the word the phrase modifies. Here is an example:

Example: Trina likes reading imaginative stories about outer space.

<u>about outer space</u>   <u>adjective</u>   <u>stories</u>

1. Every night she gazes at the stars.

_____   _____   _____

2. The lights of the night sky stir her imagination.

_____   _____   _____

3. Sometimes she points a telescope toward Mars.

_____   _____   _____

4. Trina has a book of science fiction stories.

_____   _____   _____

5. The stories take her imagination to distant planets.

_____   _____   _____

Tell Me More!

Elaborating with Prepositional Phrases A good writer adds prepositional phrases to sentences to make them say more. Here is an example.

> The space explorers landed on the distant planet.

> **Improved:** The space explorers landed <u>with a great bounce</u> on the distant planet.

Here is the beginning of a science fiction story. Show the writer how the story might be improved by adding prepositional phrases that tell more about the event described. Add at least one new prepositional phrase to each sentence. Use your imagination! Write your paragraph on the lines below.

The lander's hatch opened. The brave explorers stepped out. They had never before visited this planet. All of a sudden, they noticed a strange creature peeking at them. The creature seemed to be pointing. The explorers looked.

Name _____

Writing an Announcement

During the 1997 space mission you read about in *The Adventures of
Sojourner*, members of the Mars Pathfinder Team made a number of
announcements. An **announcement** is a short speech or notice that
gives important information about an event. You might read an
announcement on a bulletin board, on the Internet, or in a magazine,
or you might hear one at school, in an airport, on the radio, or on TV.

**Fill in the chart below with details for an announcement about an
exhibition of Mars photographs that were taken by Pathfinder and
Sojourner. Invent a date, time, and location where this event
might take place in your community. Then draw on information in
the selection to come up with details about how the photographs
were taken, what they show, and why people should see them.**

Date	
Time	
Place	
Cost	
Details about the program	

**Now write your announcement on a separate sheet of paper. State
the purpose of the announcement at the very beginning. Then
provide information that answers these questions: *who? what?
where? when? why? how?* and *how much?* Include the exact date,
time, and location of the photography exhibit as well as other details
about the program. Be sure to use clear, interesting, and friendly
language that your audience will understand.**

Name _____

Ordering Important Information

Careful writers make sure that the information in an announcement is complete and presented in a clear order. The use of sequence words, such as *first*, *next*, and *last*, helps clarify the order of events.

Someone on the staff of the *Pleasantville Times* accidentally scrambled this announcement. Before the newspaper is printed, reorder the sentences so that the announcement begins clearly and follows a logical sequence of events. Pay attention to sequence words that give clues to the order of the sentences. Then write the revised announcement on the lines below.

Blast Off!

For any questions and further information, please call the library's Special Events Coordinator, Mr. Charles Luna, at 555-4321. After the film, there will be a brief question-and-answer period. The film will be shown on Sunday, February 13, from 2 P.M. to 4 P.M., in the Armstrong Conference Room on the lower level. This award-winning documentary details the ups and downs of the 1997 Mars landing of Pathfinder and Sojourner. Pleasantville native Jim Schuyler, an alternate rover driver, will be on hand to answer questions about his role during the historic Pathfinder mission. The Pleasantville Library is sponsoring a free screening of *Mars or Bust*.

_____

_____

_____

_____

_____

_____

_____

Name _____

Revising Your Persuasive Essay

Reread your persuasive essay. What do you need to make it better? Use this page to help you decide. Put a checkmark in the box for each sentence that describes your persuasive essay.

Loud and Clear!

☐ My essay has a beginning that will capture my readers' attention.

☐ My goal is stated clearly at the beginning of the essay.

☐ I stated my reasons for my point of view and answered objections.

☐ I used facts and details to support my opinion.

☐ The essay is interesting to read and convincing.

Sounding Stronger

☐ I could make the beginning more attention grabbing.

☐ I could state my goal more clearly.

☐ I answered some objections people might raise, but I could deal with a few more.

☐ I need to add more facts and details to support my point of view.

☐ I didn't always use adverbs and adjectives correctly.

Turn Up the Volume

☐ I need a better beginning.

☐ I didn't state my goals or reasons for my opinion.

☐ I didn't answer any objections people might have.

☐ I need to add facts and details.

☐ This isn't very convincing.

Using Adverbs and Adjectives Correctly

► An adjective can modify a noun or a pronoun.
► An adverb can modify a verb or an adjective.

**Underline the correct adjective or adverb. Write
adverb or *adjective* in the space provided.**

1. I (complete/completely) endorse the Channel Magic
   channel changer. _____

2. I give my (complete/completely) endorsement of the Channel Magic
   channel changer. _____

3. Channel Magic channel changer has a (clever/cleverly) design.
   _____

4. Channel Magic channel changer is designed
   (clever/cleverly). _____

5. Channel Magic (automatic/automatically) senses when a commercial
   comes on your TV screen. _____

6. Channel Magic has an (automatic/automatically) sensor that knows
   when a commercial comes on your TV screen. _____

7. The device then makes an (instant/instantly) switch to a different
   channel. _____

8. The device then (instant/instantly) switches to a different channel.
   _____

9. Channel Magic is an (effortless/effortlessly) way to avoid commercials.
   _____

10. Using Channel Magic, you can (effortless/effortlessly) avoid
    commercials. _____

Name _____

Spelling Words

Look for familiar spelling patterns to help you remember how to spell the Spelling Words on this page. Think carefully about the parts that you find hard to spell in each word.

Write the missing letters in the Spelling Words below.

Spelling Words

1. w _____ _____ _____ d
2. th _____ _____ _____ _____ t
3. thr _____ _____ _____ _____
4. c _____ _____ _____ _____ t
5. br _____ _____ _____ _____ t
6. fin _____ _____ _____ _____
7. su _____ _____ ose
8. usua _____ _____ _____
9. eig _____ _____ _____
10. mi _____ _____ imeter
11. hap _____ _____ _____ ly
12. g _____ _____ ss
13. _____ at _____ _____ day
14. s _____ _____ ool
15. bef _____ _____ _____

Spelling Words

1. weird
2. thought
3. through
4. caught
5. brought
6. finally
7. suppose
8. usually
9. eighth
10. millimeter
11. happily
12. guess
13. Saturday
14. school
15. before

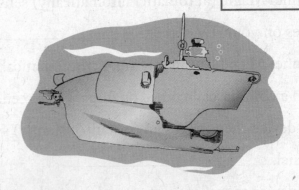

Study List On a separate piece of paper, write each Spelling Word. Check your spelling against the words on the list.

Name _____

Spelling Spree

Finding Words Each word below is hidden in a Spelling Word. Write the Spelling Word.

1. fin
2. lime
3. for
4. at
5. us
6. up
7. though

1. _____   5. _____

2. _____   6. _____

3. _____   7. _____

4. _____

Phrase Fillers Write the Spelling Word that best completes each phrase.

8. _____ in the act
9. to come in _____ place
10. a _____ whistling sound from the attic
11. to accept a gift _____
12. to make an educated _____
13. to attend summer _____
14. a trail _____ the woods
15. guests who _____ food to the party

8. _____   12. _____

9. _____   13. _____

10. _____   14. _____

11. _____   15. _____

Theme 6: **New Frontiers: Oceans and Space**   351

Name _____

Proofreading and Writing

Proofreading Circle the five misspelled Spelling Words on this computer game box. Then write each word correctly.

NEW FRONTIERS

Are you ready to experience the feelings of hurtling thru the solar system? Do you want to come face-to-face with wierd deep-sea creatures? Then *New Frontiers* is the game for you! Now there's finaly a game that lets you go millions of miles into space or thousands of feet below the ocean's surface. Who would have thot that one game could combine two worlds so well? You'll get caught up in the action befor you even realize it!

Spelling Words

1. weird
2. thought
3. through
4. caught
5. brought
6. finally
7. suppose
8. usually
9. eighth
10. millimeter
11. happily
12. guess
13. Saturday
14. school
15. before

1. _____   4. _____

2. _____   5. _____

3. _____

✏➤ **Write Movie Titles** If you were going to make movies about space or underwater exploration, what would you call them? What would they be about?

On a separate piece of paper, write four movie titles. Include a one-sentence description of each. Use Spelling Words from the list.

Name _____

Journey into Space

Write each word from the box under the heading that best describes it.

fields of scientific study

_____

_____

_____

people who ask to be admitted to the space program

_____

what each of those people would like to become

_____

skills and experiences those people need to have

_____

place for doing experiments

_____

how experiments should be done

_____

verb meaning "to imitate"

_____

verb meaning "showed clearly"

_____

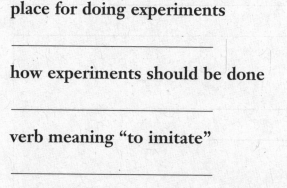

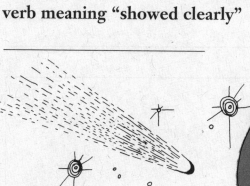

Name _____

Problem-Solution Chart

Problem		Solution
There were no astronauts as role models when Franklin was young.	→	
Franklin wanted to find out how to become an astronaut.	→	
Franklin wanted to earn money to move to the U. S.	→	
Franklin needed to learn to speak English.	→	
Franklin was not learning English in the special class he was taking.	→	
He was told he couldn't enroll at the University of Connecticut because he wasn't a U.S. citizen.	→	
Franklin was rejected in his first attempt to become an astronaut, possibly because his citizenship status was not complete.	→	

Name _____

Complete the Countdown

Complete the following sentences with information from the selection to show how Franklin Chang-Díaz became an astronaut.

1. Franklin Chang-Díaz was seven years old when _____

_____.

2. As a child, Franklin read _____ stories and played at

_____.

3. In 1967, Franklin wrote to _____ at NASA to ask

_____

4. Franklin decided he had to move to _____, so he worked

_____ to earn the money.

5. In the United States, he enrolled in school in order to

_____. He had to persuade his teachers to _____

_____.

6. His efforts earned him a scholarship to _____.

7. In college he earned degrees in _____ and

_____. Then he went to graduate school at

_____

8. In 1977 Franklin applied to NASA but _____.

9. In 1979 he applied again, this time as _____.

He was accepted, and became one of the first _____

_____.

10. Franklin became _____ in 1981. In 1986 he was on

board the _____ during its nearly flawless launch.

Name _____

Kite in Space!

Read the directions. Answer the questions on page 357.

How to Make a Kite

Materials

► two pine or spruce sticks about 30" long, 3/8" wide, and 3/16" thick
► cotton string
► colored tissue paper, or a cotton sheet, or a sheet of plastic (such as from a trash bag)
► glue or rubber cement
► a short, thin nail

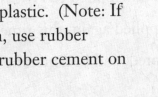

Assembly

1. Cut a notch at each end of both sticks.

2. Cross the sticks and nail them together where they cross.

3. Pass a string through one of the notches. Turn the string once around the stick, and pass it through the notch again. Rotate the frame 90 degrees. Repeat the stringing and rotating process until you are back where you started. Tie the end of the string at the starting notch.

4. Place the kite frame on the tissue paper, cloth, or plastic. Place a weight on the frame, and trim the paper, cloth, or plastic about 1/2" beyond the string outline. Apply a thin line of glue on the outermost part of the paper, cloth, or plastic. (Note: If you are using plastic instead of paper or cloth, use rubber cement instead of glue.) Do not put glue or rubber cement on the string.

5. Fold the paper, cloth, or plastic over the string and press down firmly. Allow to dry completely before handling kite.

Your kite is now ready for you to attach a string and a tail—and then to fly!

Name _____

Kite in Space! continued

Answer these questions about the directions on page 356.

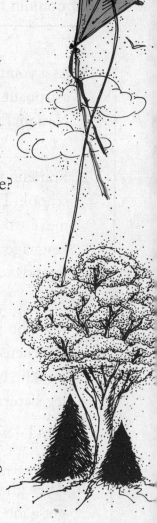

1. What is the first thing you should do in order to follow this set of directions?

   _____

2. What is the next thing you should do?

   _____

   _____

3. In what situation would you need to use rubber cement instead of glue?

   _____

   _____

4. What do you do after stringing the first notch?

   _____

   _____

5. Why is it important to do steps 1 and 2 before doing step 3?

   _____

   _____

6. What could you do if your kite did not come out right on the first try?

   _____

   _____

Name _____

A Summary of Prefixes

Each description below is a description of a scene for a documentary film about Franklin Chang-Díaz. After each description, write the words that contain the prefixes *ad–* or *ob–* .

Summary of Film Sections

1. As a young boy, Franklin dreams of the opportunity to become an astronaut. He aims to work someday in the United States for the National Aeronautics and Space Administration (NASA). (Find 1 word.)

   _____

2. Franklin moves to the United States and attends an American high school. He objects to being placed in a Spanish-speaking class and moves to an English-speaking class. He adapts quickly to the new language and his grades improve rapidly. It is obvious that Franklin intends to reach his goals. (Find 3 words.)

   _____   _____   _____

3. Franklin is admitted to college with a scholarship, but his progress is obstructed. Because of an obscure mix-up, he cannot use the scholarship until he becomes a U.S. citizen. However, the Connecticut state legislature makes an exception, and Franklin obtains the scholarship.

   (Find 4 words.) _____

   _____   _____   _____

4. After graduate school, Franklin begins work at a laboratory and tries to get a job at NASA. At first, he does not get in. On his second attempt, however, he advances to the interview stage. (Find 1 word.)

   _____

5. In Houston, he meets many adventurers like himself, but he feels that his unique background and qualifications give him an obvious advantage. This time, NASA hires him. His next assignment: to fulfill his dream of becoming an astronaut! (Find 3 words.)

   _____   _____   _____

Prefixes: *ad-* and *ob-*

The prefix *ad-* can be spelled *ac, ap, as,* or *af* to match the first consonant or consonant sound of the base word or the word root.

advice   **ac**count   **ac**quire
approve   **as**sist   **af**fair

The prefix *ob-* is spelled *oc* when the base word or word root starts with *c*.

observe   **oc**cupy

Write each Spelling Word under the spelling of its prefix.

Spelling Words

1. account
2. observe
3. addition
4. accurate
5. occasion
6. approve
7. advice
8. occupy
9. assist
10. affair
11. occur
12. acquire
13. assume
14. adjust
15. assign
16. oblige
17. accomplish
18. approach
19. according
20. obtain

ad- Spelled *ad*

_____
_____
_____

ad- Spelled *as*

_____
_____

ad- Spelled *ac*

_____
_____

ad- Spelled *af*

_____

ob- Spelled *ob*

_____
_____
_____
_____

ad- Spelled *ap*

_____
_____

ob- Spelled *oc*

_____
_____

Name _____

Spelling Spree

Finding Words Each word below is hidden in a Spelling Word. Write the Spelling Word.

> **Example:** vent *adventure*

1. cup
2. roach
3. rate
4. add
5. serve

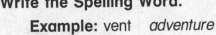

1. _____   4. _____

2. _____   5. _____

3. _____

Code Breaker Some Spelling Words have been written in code. Use the code below to figure out each word. Then write the words correctly.

6. KVXNJH   6. _____

7. BTTIKFH   7. _____

8. BUALZW   8. _____

9. BEDLNIH   9. _____

10. BZZNZW   10. _____

11. BEEKLQW   11. _____

12. KVWBNQ   12. _____

13. BUFNEH   13. _____

14. BEEKCTXNZO   14. _____

15. BPPBNI   15. _____

Code:	K	V	T	E	A	X	N	W	B	P	Z	H	C	U	F	J	L	I	Q	D	O
Letter:	o	b	p	c	j	l	i	t	a	f	s	e	m	d	v	g	u	r	n	q	h

Spelling Words

1. account
2. observe
3. addition
4. accurate
5. occasion
6. approve
7. advice
8. occupy
9. assist
10. affair
11. occur
12. acquire
13. assume
14. adjust
15. assign
16. oblige
17. accomplish
18. approach
19. according
20. obtain

Name _____

Proofreading and Writing

Proofreading Circle the five misspelled Spelling Words in this news bulletin. Then write each word correctly.

Spelling Words

It was a special occashun for NASA today, as the agency welcomed Franklin Chang-Díaz into the astronaut corps. Mr. Chang-Díaz, the first Hispanic American ever selected, impressed the selection board with his strong background in science and engineering. In addition, his performance during the required interviews and tests was outstanding, acording to an official at the agency. Don't assuem that his adventures in space will occurr anytime soon, though. Instead, NASA will asign him to a variety of projects here on Earth to prepare him for his time in orbit. We'll keep you posted on his progress.

Spelling Words

1. account
2. observe
3. addition
4. accurate
5. occasion
6. approve
7. advice
8. occupy
9. assist
10. affair
11. occur
12. acquire
13. assume
14. adjust
15. assign
16. oblige
17. accomplish
18. approach
19. according
20. obtain

1. _____   4. _____

2. _____   5. _____

3. _____

✏️ **Write a Biographical Sketch** Franklin Chang-Díaz worked hard to become an astronaut and was very dedicated to his profession. Do you know anyone with similar characteristics? What has that person done to achieve success? What do you admire about that person?

On a separate piece of paper, write a brief biographical sketch about someone you know who is similar to Franklin Chang-Díaz. Use Spelling Words from the list.

Name _____

Your Choice

Decide which word best completes each sentence. Then write the word in the blank.

unexpected	agency	emotion	science	laboratory
expectantly	agenda	mobile	conscience	labor
expectation	agility	motor	unscientific	collaborate

1. An astronaut must be able to move quickly and lightly, with great

   _____.

2. NASA and other organizations sometimes join forces to _____

   on space projects.

3. Franklin Chang-Díaz waited _____ for NASA to

   contact him after his interviews in Houston.

4. Experiments in the field of _____ may lead to important

   advances in medicine and technology.

5. The space shuttle is carried to the launch pad by a "crawler" —

   a giant _____ vehicle.

Now write a sentence using two words that you haven't used yet.

_____

_____

Name _____

Hey! It's an Interjection!

Interjections An **interjection** is a word or group of words that express
feeling. Usually an interjection appears at the beginning of a sentence.

An **interjection** can be followed by either an **exclamation point** or a **comma.**

► If the interjection stands alone, use an **exclamation point.**

► If the interjection begins a sentence, set it off with a **comma.**

   Hey! Look over here!   Oh, I didn't see you.

Here are some common interjections.

Common Interjections

| Oh | Hooray | Wow | Oh, dear | Hey |
| Well | Aha | Oh, no | Amazing | Oops |

**Here are some sentences with interjections. Write each
sentence on the line. Add the punctuation that is needed.**

1. Wow Can you imagine getting a phone call from NASA?

_____

2. Well that will never happen to me. _____

3. Oh it might. _____

4. Hey Blasting off into space would be a great experience!

_____

5. Amazing The phone is ringing!

_____

6. Aha Let me answer it!

_____

Name _____

Keep It Short!

Abbreviations An **abbreviation** is a shortened form of a word. Most, but not all, **abbreviations** begin with a capital letter and end with a period. To find the correct form of an abbreviation, consult a dictionary.

Some Common Abbreviations

Place names:					
Apt.	Apartment	Mt.	Mount or Mountain	Rd.	Road
Ave.	Avenue	St.	Street	P. O.	Post Office

Businesses:					
Co.	Company	Inc.	Incorporated	Ltd.	Limited

Titles:					
Mr.	Mister	Ms.	(any woman)	Mrs.	(married woman)
Col.	Colonel	Dr.	doctor	Capt.	Captain

States:					
OH	Ohio	NY	New York	TX	Texas

Agencies and organizations:

NASA   National Aeronautics and Space Administration

FBI   Federal Bureau of Investigation

Write the following addresses, using abbreviations. Use your dictionary if necessary.

1. Doctor Constance Kline

   45 Elmo Street, Apartment 3

   Red Apple, Pennsylvania

2. Mister Buck Rogers

   Toy Rockets, Limited

   10 Countdown Avenue

   Kubrick, Indiana

1. _____

   _____

   _____

2. _____

   _____

   _____

   _____

Suit the Occasion!

Abbreviations are suitable to use only in certain kinds of writing. For instance, it is usually not appropriate to use abbreviations in an essay or in the body of a letter.

In this draft of her essay, Lynette has used abbreviations to save time and space. Now she is ready to write another draft. Help her by writing out the words her abbreviations stand for. Cross out each abbreviation and write the word above it.

When I was only eight years old, I wanted to play music. I thought that it would be easy and that soon I would be giving concerts in NY! I was wrong.

My family lives in a small apt. on Kinsey St. in Brooklyn. In the window of a piano co. uptown there was a beautiful grand piano that I thought I needed. I had not even had one lesson! When I told my sister about the piano, she asked me if I knew how many ft long a grand piano was. She didn't really know how big the piano was, but she said that our living room was too small by at least a yd.

I thought about this problem all Aug. Then it came to me. A flute was very small, and the school lent them to students in the band. I could learn to play the flute instead! So that is what I did when we went back to school the next mo. I have learned that it is not easy to be a good musician. I am not ready to give a concert in Carnegie Hall, but next Jan. our band will travel to NJ to play in a music festival with ten other schools.

Name _____

Writing a Biography

In *Franklin R. Chang-Díaz*, you read about a boy who realizes his dream of becoming an astronaut in the NASA space program. A **biography** is a written account of important events and significant experiences in a person's life and may highlight reasons why a famous person is remembered. Before you write a biography of your own, follow these steps:

► **Choose a real person whom you admire or someone you have read about.**

► **Research important facts, dates, places, events, and accomplishments in this person's life. To gather information, use the Internet, reference or history books in your library, or, if possible, conduct a telephone or in-person interview.**

► **Record and organize major dates, locations, and events in this person's life on the timeline below.**

The Life of _____

DATE	EVENT

Now write your biography on a separate sheet of paper. Start with an anecdote or a famous quotation from this person's life. Then work from your timeline. Write about important events and experiences, using chronological order, time-clue words, and key dates. Highlight the events that you think best reveal this person's character or lifetime achievements. Finally, conclude by summarizing why this person is remembered.

Name _____

Combining Sentences with Prepositional Phrases

One way to streamline your writing is to combine short sentences that have a repeated subject but differing prepositional phrases into a single sentence with consecutive prepositional phrases.

> Dr. Chang-Díaz is a native **of Costa Rica.** He dreamed **of becoming an astronaut.** He wanted to be an astronaut with **NASA.** NASA is **in the United States.**
>
> Dr. Chang-Díaz, a native **of Costa Rica,** dreamed **of becoming an astronaut with NASA in the United States.**

Imagine you are the editor of a new reference book, *Who's Who in Space.* **Revise these sentences from a biographical sketch about Dr. Franklin R. Chang-Díaz that will appear in the book. Combine short sentences that have a repeated subject into a single sentence.**

1. Franklin R. Chang-Díaz was fascinated by space exploration as a child. He read about flying in space in newspapers. He read articles in magazines. He found thrilling tales in science fiction stories.

   _____

   _____

2. When he was a young boy, he played in a make-believe spaceship. The spaceship was made from old TV and radio parts. He put the parts inside a large cardboard box.

   _____

   _____

3. He studied science in school. He attended school in the United States. He went to school until he landed a job at a well-known lab. He got the job in 1977.

   _____

   _____

Name _____

Marvels of the Deep

Write a word from the box to answer each riddle.

1. We are scientists who study the sea. Who are we?

   _____

2. We will grab or sting any prey that floats near us. What

   are we? _____

3. I am a creature with a body that is almost like jelly. How

   would you describe me? _____

4. I am a vehicle that travels underwater. What am I?

   _____

5. I am something too deep to measure. How would you describe me?

   _____

6. We are a collection of animals. What are we?

   _____

7. As this creature swims, it moves slowly up and down with the

   currents. How does it move? It _____ .

8. I am a hard-shelled animal with jointed parts, and I live mostly in

   water. What am I? _____

Name _____

Ocean Diagram

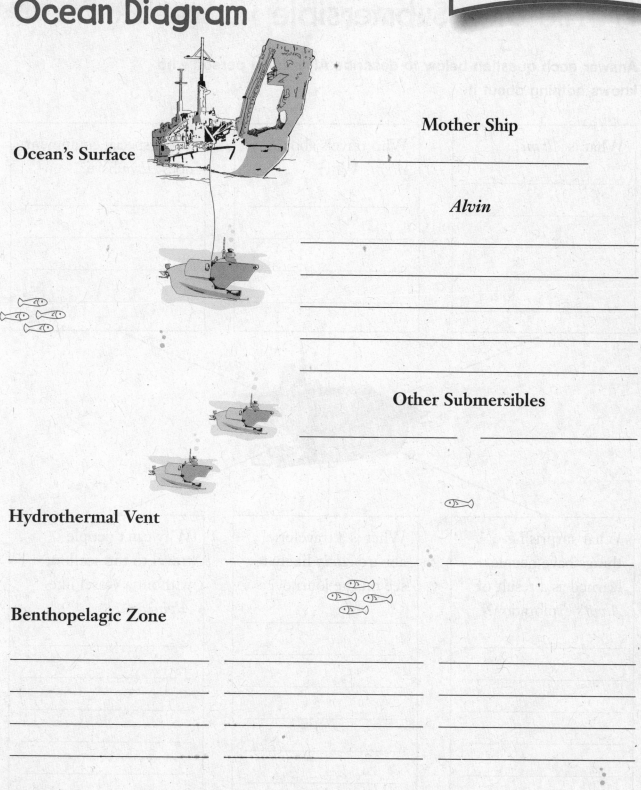

Ocean's Surface

Mother Ship

_____

Alvin

_____
_____
_____
_____
_____

Other Submersibles

_____

Hydrothermal Vent

_____ _____ _____

Benthopelagic Zone

_____ _____ _____
_____ _____ _____
_____ _____ _____
_____ _____ _____

Seafloor

Name _____

Profile of a Submersible

Answer each question below to describe Alvin for a person who knows nothing about it.

What is *Alvin?*
_____
_____
_____
_____

Who travels aboard *Alvin?* Why?
_____
_____
_____
_____

What special equipment does *Alvin* have?
_____
_____
_____
_____

What surprising things have people learned as a result of *Alvin's* exploration?
_____
_____
_____
_____
_____

What is a traveler aboard *Alvin* likely to see on the journey?
_____
_____
_____
_____
_____

Why can't people travel to the seafloor without a vessel like *Alvin?*
_____
_____
_____
_____
_____

Classified Information!

Read the passage. Then complete the activity on page 372.

Miniature Menageries at the Shore

The dark depths of the ocean are full of fascinating life forms, but interesting pockets of sea life are also visible in places much closer to us. When the tide goes out on a rocky shore, small pools of water called tide pools are left behind. A menagerie of small creatures remains in the tide pools until the tide returns.

A careful look into a tide pool can reveal an astonishing array of creatures. You might first see brightly colored starfish clinging to the tide pool's rocky walls. Starfish move across the surface of the rocks more slowly than the eye can detect, propelled by rows of tiny tube feet that act like suction cups. Their hard bodies feel spiny to the touch. Barnacles, shellfish that fasten themselves to fixed objects, cling in piles atop rocky ledges. Barnacles feed by opening their hinged centers and waving their leaf-like legs through the water. Their legs act as a filter that draws food into the soft body inside the shell, where it is digested. Barnacles are usually dull gray, blue, or black in color, and can be mistaken for rocks.

You're also likely to see several sea anemones in the pool. These soft and beautiful creatures look like flowers and might surprise you with their range of color. Sea anemones in the same tide pool might be dark red, lime green, and bright orange. Sea anemones also attach themselves to rocks. They feed by catching tiny fish with their sticky, sponge-like tentacles.

Small fish are often trapped in tide pools, forced to dart back and forth until high tide releases them. Look fast! A small brown crab skitters over the rocks and plunges into the tide pool. It grasps an unfortunate fish in it claws.

Tide pools are brimming with activity. If you have a chance to visit a rocky shore where these miniature pockets of marine life are found, be sure to take a look!

Name _____

Classified Information! continued

Read the category headings in each chart. Then classify the tide pool
creatures described in the passage on page 371 by writing their names
in the correct columns. Refer to the information in the passage.

Brightly colored creatures	Dully colored creatures

Creatures that attach themselves to rocks	Creatures that move freely

Think of two categories that haven't been named yet. Use the chart
below to classify tide pool creatures into those categories.

The *ie/ei* Shuffle

**Read each sentence below. For each underlined word, decide whether
ie or *ei* sounds like the long *e* sound in *key*, or the long *a* sound in *aim*.
Then write the word in the correct column of the chart.**

1. Around deep-sea vents on the ocean floor, a <u>menagerie</u> of animals thrives.

2. At first, the harsh environment <u>deceived</u> scientists into thinking that
   nothing could live in such a place.

3. Some of the deep-sea animals appear almost <u>weightless</u>.

4. Scientists must stay constantly alert because they can only stay on the
   sea floor <u>briefly</u>.

5. The bottom of the sea is like a dark, slow-moving <u>neighborhood</u>.

6. In the future, humans will <u>receive</u> data from remotely operated submersibles.

Like *key*	Like *aim*
_____	_____
_____	_____
_____	_____

**Now, choose four words from the chart and use them correctly in
sentences of your own.**

7. _____

8. _____

9. _____

10. _____

Name _____

Words with *ie* or *ei*

Use *i* before *e* except after *c* or in words with the /ā/ sound, as in *freight*. You must memorize exceptions to this generalization.

yield   rec**ei**pt   fr**ei**ght

► The *ei* vowel pairs in *neither, foreign, seize,* and *leisure* do not follow this generalization. Be sure to remember the spellings of these words.

Write each Spelling Word under its spelling pattern.

Spelling Words

1. freight
2. receipt
3. yield
4. review
5. belief
6. eighty
7. brief
8. ceiling
9. neither*
10. foreign*
11. shield
12. diesel
13. reign
14. fiery
15. conceit
16. veil
17. grief
18. relieve
19. seize*
20. leisure*

i Comes Before *e*

_____
_____
_____
_____
_____
_____
_____
_____

ei Follows *c*

_____
_____

ei Spells /ā/

_____
_____
_____

Other Spelling Patterns

_____
_____
_____

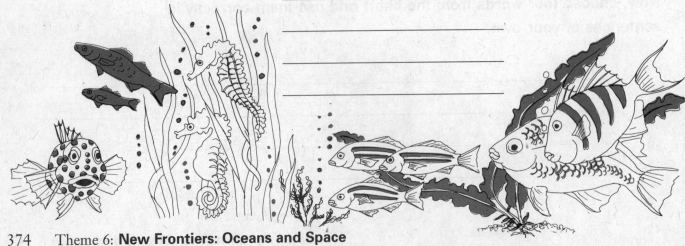

Name _____

Spelling Spree

Word Addition Write a Spelling Word by adding the beginning of the first word to the end of the second word.

1. yip + held

2. rent + sign

3. neigh + father

4. fine + ornery

5. vent + nail

6. grime + reef

7. died + weasel

1. _____

2. _____

3. _____

4. _____

5. _____

6. _____

7. _____

Spelling Words

1. freight
2. receipt
3. yield
4. review
5. belief
6. eighty
7. brief
8. ceiling
9. neither*
10. foreign*
11. shield
12. diesel
13. reign
14. fiery
15. conceit
16. veil
17. grief
18. relieve
19. seize*
20. leisure*

Word Squid Begin at the arrow and follow the letters to find eight Spelling Words. Write the words in order. Don't let the other words fool you!

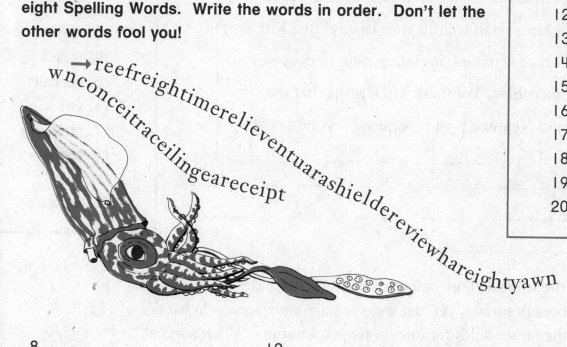

8. _____

9. _____

10. _____

11. _____

12. _____

13. _____

14. _____

15. _____

Name _____

Proofreading and Writing

Proofreading Circle the five misspelled Spelling Words in this advertisement. Then write each word correctly.

Spelling Words

Come to an Underwater Paradise!

Want to spend your vacation in a different place without traveling to a forign country? Then sieze this opportunity to come spend it under the sea! The Grand Neptune Hotel, with eighty rooms located two thousand feet below sea level, is now open for business. You can make your stay as breif as one night, or as long as two weeks. Our expert staff will fill your leizure time with a variety of activities, including rides in deep-sea submersibles. We think you'll agree that the Grand Neptune is an experience beyond beleif!

1. freight
2. receipt
3. yield
4. review
5. belief
6. eighty
7. brief
8. ceiling
9. neither*
10. foreign*
11. shield
12. diesel
13. reign
14. fiery
15. conceit
16. veil
17. grief
18. relieve
19. seize*
20. leisure*

1. _____   4. _____

2. _____   5. _____

3. _____

Write a Prediction Scientists continue to make new discoveries under the ocean's surface, yet vast areas remain unexplored. What do you think the future holds for underwater exploration? What sorts of creatures might scientists find in coming years? Will deep-sea submersibles make longer and deeper voyages possible?

On a separate piece of paper, write your prediction for the future of underwater exploration. Use Spelling Words from the list.

Name _____

Idiom and Run-on Entry Challenge

Read the sentences. If the underlined part of the sentence is a run-on entry, write its part of speech and the main dictionary entry word. If the underlined part is an idiom, write the meaning of the idiom.

black *n.* Without light. —**blackly** *adv.* —**blackness** *n.*

eventual adj. Occurring at an unspecified future time. —**eventually** *adv.*

look *v.* To turn one's gaze or attention. —*idioms.* **look after**. To take care of. **look forward to**. To think of a future event with pleasure and excitement.

successful *adj.* Having gained something desired or intended. —**successfully** *adv.*

take *v.* To acquire possession of something. — *idioms.* **take care**. To be careful. **take on**. To oppose in competition.

world *n.* 1. The earth. 2. The universe. — *idioms.* **for all the world**. In all respects; precisely.

1. Maria Jackson, the reigning tennis champion, offered to <u>take on</u> her competitors. _____

2. The creatures came into view out of the <u>blackness</u>.

   _____

3. <u>Eventually</u>, deep-sea creatures drift by some food.

   _____

4. The little octopus looked <u>for all the world</u> like Dumbo.

   _____

5. The crew <u>successfully</u> filmed a number of creatures.

   _____

6. The crew members <u>look forward to</u> their next chance to ride in *Alvin*.

   _____

Name _____

One, Two, Three, or More

Commas in a Series A list of three or more items is called a **series**.
Use a **comma** to separate all the items in a series, except the last.
Usually, a **conjunction** such as *and* or *or* appears before the last item in
the series and connects the items.

> Dogs, cats, birds, **and** fish are popular pets.

Insert commas where they belong in the following sentences.

1. Mark David and Shirley like tropical fish.

2. They buy gravel filters and plants for their aquariums.

3. Mark has goldfish angelfish guppies and snails.

4. A plaster castle a plastic diver and brightly colored gravel decorate

   David's aquarium.

5. Shirley named her goldfish George Paul John and Theresa.

**Now write this sentence, adding a series. Insert commas and a
conjunction where they belong.**

6. Three sea creatures are _____

_____

_____

Name _____

Consider the Useful Comma

More Uses for Commas Besides separating items in a series, commas
have several other uses.

▶ Use commas to set off an **appositive** from the rest of the sentence. An
  appositive is a word or a group of words that identify or explain the noun that
  they follow.

  Robert Ballard, an undersea explorer, found the wreckage of the *Titanic*.

▶ Set off an **introductory word** like *yes*, *no*, or *well* at the beginning of a
  sentence from the rest of the sentence with a comma.

  Yes, people were amazed by the discovery.

▶ Use a comma or commas to set off a noun used in **direct address**.

  Sarah, did you see the documentary?

Add commas where they belong in the sentences below.

1. Jim let's walk along the seashore today.

2. Tess my cousin goes deep-sea diving with her father.

3. I'd like to dive in *Alvin* a special deep-diving submarine to see a big
   jellyfish.

4. Well maybe someday you'll have the chance.

5. Here is a small jellyfish near the water Moesha.

6. This animal is round soft and clear.

7. Yes Jim it is an unusual creature.

8. I'd like to be an oceanographer a scientist who studies the sea.

9. Well you will need to study biology.

10. Look Jim at this crab!

Name _____

Commas for Good Reason

Proofreading for Commas A good writer proofreads carefully to be sure
that commas are correctly used. This requires close attention because
commas are so small!

**Julio is getting ready to turn in a paper to his teacher. He knows
that he needs to proofread carefully for comma errors. Help him by
proofreading the portion of his draft below. Add six commas where
they are needed. Use the proofreading marks on page 434.**

My Career as an Oceanographer

I read the story about the chemist biologist and pilot with

great interest. They dived in *Alvin* a special submarine, to study

the ocean's depths. What they found there surprised me! Yes they

found a very strange world. I thought I'd have to go to outer

space to see such an exotic place. That is why I had wanted to be

an astronaut. Now, Ms. Kovacs and Ms. Kate because of your

story I want to explore the oceans. I want to dive in the Atlantic

Ocean, the Pacific Ocean, the Mediterranean Sea and even the

Arctic Ocean.

Writing a Compare/ Contrast Essay

In *Beneath Blue Waters*, you read about similarities and differences between sea creatures in the deepest zone and those in other parts of the ocean. One way to explain similarities and differences is by writing a **compare/contrast essay.** A good essay describes both the ways things are alike and the ways they are different.

Choose two of the following deep-sea creatures from the article to compare and contrast:

► "fried egg" siphonphore, Stephalia corona

► the jellyfish, Deepstaria enigmatica

► Benthocodon pedunculata

► unnamed ctenophore

Write the names of the creatures on the lines below. Then use the Venn diagram to gather and organize details that compare and contrast the creatures' diet, size, shape, color, and so on.

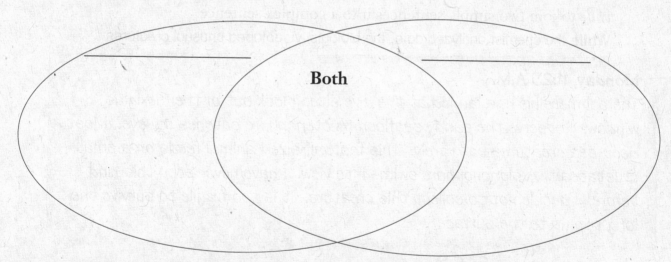

Both

On a separate sheet of paper, write a compare/contrast essay about the two deep-sea creatures you chose. In the opening paragraph, clearly state the subject being compared and contrasted. In the following paragraphs, present details from your Venn diagram. Group details that compare and details that contrast in a clear manner. Use clue words such as *similarly* or *likewise* to help readers identify likenesses and *however* or *unlike* to help them identify differences.

Name _____

Using Commas to Combine Sentences

Good writers strive to avoid using dull, choppy sentences. One way to improve the flow of your writing is to combine sentences using commas. You can combine two short, choppy sentences into either a compound or a complex sentence, depending on how the two ideas you are combining are related.

A biologist aboard the submersible Alvin tape-recorded some observations about deep-sea creatures. Revise the transcript of the biologist's notes by using commas to combine sentences as follows:

► Use a comma and a coordinating conjunction like *and, or,* or *but* to join two simple sentences into a compound sentence.

The chemist analyzed data. The biologist videotaped unusual creatures.

The chemist analyzed data, **and** the biologist videotaped unusual creatures.

► Use a comma and a subordinating conjunction like *when, because, although,* or *while* to join two simple sentences into a complex sentence.

While the chemist analyzed data, the biologist videotaped unusual creatures.

Monday, 11:23 A.M.

The submersible has landed at the dive site. I look out of the Plexiglas window. I observe the sandy seafloor. A ctenophore catches my eye. Most deep-sea creatures eat rarely. This football-sized animal feeds on a small crustacean. A siphonophore swims into view. I have never seen this kind before. I decide not to collect this creature. It is too fragile to survive the long trip up to the surface.

_____

_____

_____

_____

_____

Name _____

Mystery at Sea

Read the story below. Write words from the box to complete the story.

Vocabulary

visibility
buoy
inquiries
discount
afterdeck
bulkhead
derelict
port side

Stephanie boarded the boat, went all the way to the rear, and began setting up her camera on the _____. She could barely contain her excitement. She was about to begin making her first movie. It was going to be a mystery involving the sea. The setting was to include an old, abandoned fishing boat – a _____. She had made many _____ before finding a boat she could use.

Most owners seemed to _____ her promises that she would not harm the boat. Finally she had found an owner willing to allow her aboard—Earl Cuthbert, a friend of her uncle. His battered old boat was now carrying Stephanie toward a _____ that marked the mouth of the harbor. It was very foggy, and Stephanie hoped the _____ would improve. If the weather stayed foggy, she would not be able to get good shots of the harbor or the shore. While she waited, she decided to film Earl at work on the left, or _____ , of the boat. Just then a wave rocked the boat, and she heard a thud from below the deck. A frown crossed Earl's face. "Sounds like something bumped against a _____ in my sleeping cabin," he said. "I think we have someone else aboard."

Name _____

Conclusions Chart

	Story Clues		**Conclusions**

pages 620–621

Danny Aldo drops anchor and fishes near the buoy to wait for the fog to lift.	+	He has fished for a long time and knows what kind of fish he might catch.	=	

pages 621–622

Danny is more amazed than afraid after he sees a huge eel swim by.	+	He boards the abandoned boat to explore.	=	

pages 623–627

	+		=	Danny is responsible and honest and not afraid of being laughed at.

pages 627–628, 633

Because of the blood, Danny thinks the eel ties in with Jack Stokes's disappearance.	+	The medical examiner says the blood wasn't human blood.	=	

pages 628–632

	+		=	Danny is assured that strange sea creatures do exist, despite most people's skepticism.

Name _____

Recording Reactions

Complete each sentence below to tell about important events that happen in *Out There* and how Danny reacts to each one.

Event	How Danny Reacts to the Event
1. When Danny sees the huge eel-like creature,	_____ _____ _____
2 When he first sees the *Lotta Fun*,	_____ _____ _____
3. After seeing _____ aboard the *Lotta Fun*,	Danny begins to feel frightened.
4. When the sheriff's deputies at the Harbor Patrol _____ _____,	Danny is frustrated and angry.
5. When Danny reads stories on the Internet about _____ _____	he is convinced that what he saw is real.
6. After hearing Captain Carroll's story,	Danny is so encouraged that he _____ _____

Name _____

What Do You Conclude?

Read the passage. Then complete the activity on page 387.

Stargazing

I was perched on top of our roof with my telescope and a plastic bottle full of lemonade, ready for a long night of stargazing. I had finished all my homework and done the dishes. Mom had watched over my shoulder to make sure I got it all done. My two brothers were watching a TV show about UFOs, and Mom was on the phone. I was all alone, thinking how I would love to see a real UFO.

It was a perfectly clear night. I could pick out the Big Dipper and Orion's belt. I thought I noticed a star with a red glow that could have been the planet Mars. A plane passed by, its red lights flashing. Then I saw something that made me drop my lemonade. Emerging from the black sky was a crisp blue light shaped like a saucer. It looked as if it was headed straight for me.

I quickly ran downstairs, shouting, "Mom! Come here, you've got to see this!"

"Billy, I'm on the phone," she said.

When I told her this was serious, she ended her phone conversation in a hurry and followed me. I stood on the roof, my chest heaving, and pointed at the sky. The blue light was gone. The constellations twinkled in the darkness. Mom put her hands on her hips. "What was it you wanted me to see?" she asked.

I stuttered and pointed. "I saw . . . there was a . . . a blue light. . . ." She was staring at me with a skeptical expression. "Never mind," I said. "It was probably a shooting star."

Mom told me to come inside. When we joined my brothers, a special announcement came on TV. A reporter was standing in the middle of a field in front of an unusual-looking airplane with blue lights glowing steadily on its wings. The reporter said, "We have discovered the source of the mysterious blue lights tonight. New planes are being tested in the vicinity for a special flight show planned for October."

Name _____

What Do You Conclude?

continued

Answer these questions about the passage on page 386.

1. How does Billy feel about the stars and stargazing? How do you know?

   _____

   _____

2. Has Billy spent time studying the stars? How can you tell?

   _____

   _____

3. What does Billy think he sees in the sky? How can you tell?

   _____

   _____

4. How does Billy's mom feel when he tells her that the situation is serious?

   How do you know? _____

   _____

5. What was it that Billy saw? How do you know? _____

   _____

   _____

Name _____

Word Relatives

Read each group of words below. Decide what word part the words have in common. Choose a word from the tackle box with the same word part, and write it in the blank.

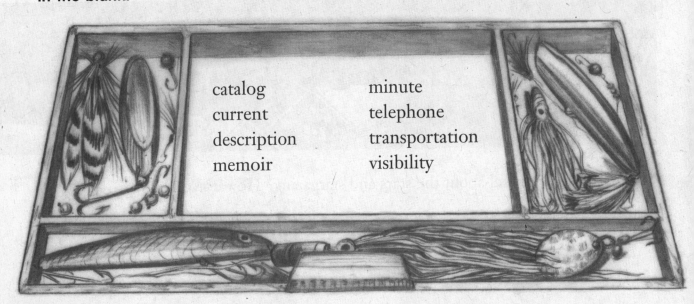

catalog   minute
current   telephone
description   transportation
memoir   visibility

1. scribe, transcribe, script   _____

2. important, reported, portable   _____

3. telescope, televise, telegraph   _____

4. revise, vision, invisible   _____

5. recur, cursive, occurrence   _____

6. logical, dialogue, analogy   _____

7. remember, memorize, commemorate   _____

8. miniature, minimize, minor   _____

Name _____

Word Parts

Many words are made up of a prefix, a base word or a word root, and a suffix. Find these parts in each word, and then spell the word by the parts.

<u>un</u>belie**v**able   in**v**ent**ion**
<u>ad</u>van**ce**ment   con**c**ent**ration**

Write each Spelling Word. Underline its prefix and circle its suffix or suffixes.

_____   _____

_____   _____

_____   _____

_____   _____

_____   _____

_____   _____

_____   _____

_____   _____

_____   _____

_____   _____

1. development
2. information
3. preparation
4. improvement
5. invention
6. advancement
7. accidentally
8. unkindness
9. concentration
10. unskillful
11. respectful
12. prevention
13. regardless
14. repetition
15. disgraceful
16. unbelievable
17. disagreement
18. imprisonment
19. encouragement
20. intermission

Theme 6: **New Frontiers: Oceans and Space**   389

Name _____

Spelling Spree

Base Word/Word Root Blanks Write a Spelling Word by placing the correct base word or word root in the blank between each item's prefix and suffix.

Example: de_____ful   delightful

1. con_____ation
2. de_____ment
3. re_____less
4. re_____ful
5. ad_____ment
6. re_____ion
7. pre_____ation
8. un_____ful

de (light) ful

1. _____   5. _____
2. _____   6. _____
3. _____   7. _____
4. _____   8. _____

Meaning Match Combine each meaning below with its prefix or suffix(es) to write a Spelling Word.

9. dis + moving elegantly and beautifully
10. to create something new + ion
11. to make better + ment
12. to keep from occurring + ion
13. inter + a special task
14. to put in jail + ment
15. something not planned + ally

9. _____   13. _____
10. _____   14. _____
11. _____   15. _____
12. _____

Spelling Words

1. development
2. information
3. preparation
4. improvement
5. invention
6. advancement
7. accidentally
8. unkindness
9. concentration
10. unskillful
11. respectful
12. prevention
13. regardless
14. repetition
15. disgraceful
16. unbelievable
17. disagreement
18. imprisonment
19. encouragement
20. intermission

Name _____

Proofreading and Writing

Proofreading Circle the five misspelled Spelling Words in this wanted poster. Then write each word correctly.

> ### WANTED
>
> Do you have any infermation about a large, eel-like creature that lives in the waters outside Dana Harbor? It may seem unbelievabel to you, but there have been several recent sightings by local fishermen. These people have stuck to their stories, regardless of the unkindnes with which the authorities have treated them. There is some disagreemint about the exact length of the creature, but most reports put it at over twenty feet. If you have a story to tell, we want to offer you every encuragement to step forward. Please contact the Dana Harbor Sighting Board at 555-8232.

Spelling Words

1. development
2. information
3. preparation
4. improvement
5. invention
6. advancement
7. accidentally
8. unkindness
9. concentration
10. unskillful
11. respectful
12. prevention
13. regardless
14. repetition
15. disgraceful
16. unbelievable
17. disagreement
18. imprisonment
19. encouragement
20. intermission

1. _____   4. _____

2. _____   5. _____

3. _____

━━━▶ **Write a Comparison and Contrast** Like the scientists in *Beneath Blue Waters*, Danny finds an unknown sea creature in *Out There*. But unlike them, Danny's report isn't taken seriously. Why do you think that might be? What makes the scientists' accounts so believable? What are some things about Danny's encounter that might make it hard to believe?

On a separate piece of paper, write a paragraph in which you compare and contrast Danny's encounter with those of the scientists. Use Spelling Words from the list.

Name _____

Which Spelling? Which Pronunciation?

**Read the dictionary entries, paying special attention to the spellings
and pronunciations. Then answer the questions.**

> **anchovy** (ăn′ chō vē *or* ăn **chō′** vē) *n.* A small sea fish related to the herring.
> **burn** (bûrn) *v.* **burned** *or* **burnt** (bûrnt). To set on fire.
> **diesel** (dē′ zəl *or* **dē′** səl) *n.* A type of internal-combustion engine.
> **toward** (tôrd *or* tə **wôrd′**) also **towards** (tôrdz or tə **wôrdz′**) *prep.*
>   In the direction of.
> **water** (wô′ tər *or* **wŏt′** ər) *n.* A compound of hydrogen and oxygen
>   occurring as a liquid.

1. What is the other way to spell *toward*? _____

2. In what single way are the two pronunciations of *anchovy* different?

   _____ Is the second

   pronunciation more like *recognize* or like *remember*? (Circle the correct

   answer.)

3 Is the first pronunciation of *diesel* more like *weasel* or like *creases*?

   (Circle the correct answer.)

4. If you are using the first pronunciation of *water*, are you saying

   WAHT ur or WAW tur? (Circle the correct answer.)

5. What are the two ways to spell the past tense of *burn*?

   _____

Name _____

Please, Quote Me!

Punctuating Dialogue There are a number of rules for punctuating dialogue. Study the list below.

Rules for Punctuating Dialogue
▶ Use **quotation marks** to set off dialogue from the rest of the sentence.
▶ Begin the first word of a quotation with a capital letter.
▶ Place punctuation marks inside the closing quotation marks.
▶ Use commas to separate most quotations from the rest of the sentence.
▶ When a quotation is interrupted in the middle, end the first part of the quotation with quotation marks. Begin the second part with quotation marks. Use commas to separate the quotation from the speaker.
▶ Begin a new paragraph with each change of speaker.

Write each sentence, using correct punctuation and capitalization.

1. Tom said Sea adventure stories are exciting _____

   _____

2. I took a trip said Miranda on a whale watching boat _____

   _____

3. Three whales came very close to our boat she said _____

   _____

4. Have you ever visited the New England Aquarium asked Tom _____

   _____

5. Tom said it's fun to watch the seals _____

   _____

Name _____

Put It in Print!

Capitalization in Titles When you write the titles of books, magazines, newspapers, songs, movies, and other works, you must treat them in special ways. Here are some rules to study.

Titles in Writing or in Print

► Capitalize the first, the last, and each important word.

► Capitalize forms of the verb *be*, including *is*, *are*, and *am*.

► Capitalize words like *and*, *in*, *of*, *to*, *a*, and *the* only when they are the first or last word in a title.

► When you use a word processor, put titles of books, movies, magazines, and newspapers in italic type.

► When you write with a pen or pencil, underline titles of books, movies, magazines, and newspapers.

► When you write the title of a song, poem, article, or short story, put the title in quotation marks. Punctuation that follows a title usually goes inside the quotation marks.

Write the following sentences, correcting the capitalization and punctuation of each title.

1. I took a book called deep-sea fishing out of the library.

   _____

2. Sarah can recite Edgar Allan Poe's poem the raven.

   _____

3. Will you do a book report on ghost ship?

   _____

4. Read the article called back to basics.

   _____

5. Circle game is my favorite song. _____

Finishing Touches

Proofreading for Capitalization and Punctuation A good writer proofreads work before turning it in to make sure that all words that should be capitalized are capitalized and that all sentences, quotations, and titles are properly punctuated.

Proofread this portion of Laurie's account of her trip to the library with her friend Zack. Use the proofreader's marks on page 434. Find and correct ten errors in capitalization and punctuation.

Zack and I went to the kenner Memorial Library the public library in our town last Saturday. It is only two blocks away from our apartment building on High Street. The librarian, Ms Conway, knows Zack and me, and she knows what we like to read.

Last Saturday, Ms. Conway said "Laurie I want to show you a book called The houseboat Mystery. "Thanks, Ms. Conway" I said.

Name _____

Writing an Answer to an Essay Question

An **essay question** is a test question that asks for a written answer of one or more paragraphs. An essay question may ask you to write about an experience, give a personal opinion about an issue and back it up with reasons and examples, explain a process, or persuade readers to do or think something.

Think about Danny's experiences on the day he saw the giant eel. Then prepare to answer this essay question:

If you see something unbelievable, how would you know whether to trust your eyes? Should you tell others about what you saw? Why or why not?

Organize your answer by filling in the planning chart. First, read the essay question carefully, identifying key words that tell you what kind of answer is needed. Next, jot down main ideas and details you might include. Finally, number your ideas, beginning with *1*, to arrange the order in which you will present them.

Key Words/ Their Meaning
Main Ideas
Details

On a separate sheet of paper, write your answer to the essay question. Begin by restating the question. Then write your main ideas and details in a logical order. When you finish, check to make sure that your response answers the question.

Keeping to the Point

Good writers stay on the subject they are writing about. Whether you are writing to respond to an essay question or for another purpose, make sure that you include only information about the topic at hand without repeating ideas or straying from the topic.

Proofread the following passage from a web site about unusual ocean sightings like the one Danny Aldo experienced in *Out There*. Draw a line through any sentences that give unnecessary information or stray from the point.

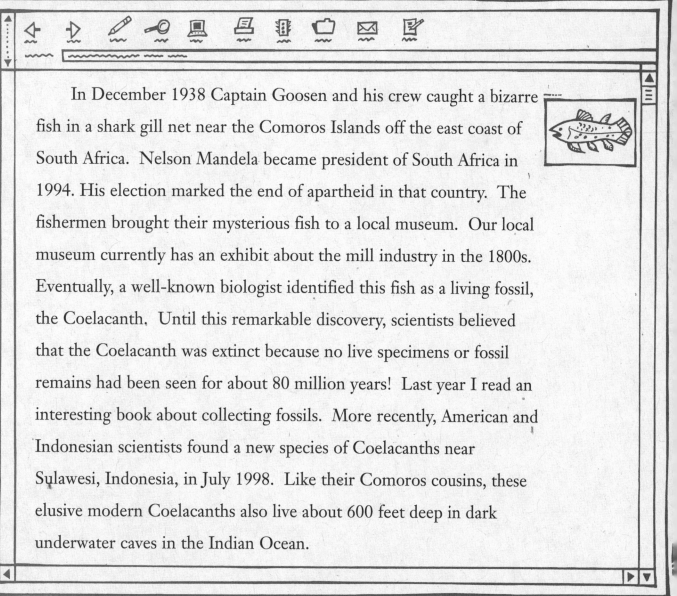

In December 1938 Captain Goosen and his crew caught a bizarre fish in a shark gill net near the Comoros Islands off the east coast of South Africa. Nelson Mandela became president of South Africa in 1994. His election marked the end of apartheid in that country. The fishermen brought their mysterious fish to a local museum. Our local museum currently has an exhibit about the mill industry in the 1800s. Eventually, a well-known biologist identified this fish as a living fossil, the Coelacanth. Until this remarkable discovery, scientists believed that the Coelacanth was extinct because no live specimens or fossil remains had been seen for about 80 million years! Last year I read an interesting book about collecting fossils. More recently, American and Indonesian scientists found a new species of Coelacanths near Sulawesi, Indonesia, in July 1998. Like their Comoros cousins, these elusive modern Coelacanths also live about 600 feet deep in dark underwater caves in the Indian Ocean.

Name _____

Writing a Persuasive Essay

Use what you have learned about taking tests to help you write an essay to persuade someone to agree with your opinion. This practice will help you when you take this kind of test.

Curiosity drives humans to explore space. In *The Adventures of Sojourner: The Mission to Mars That Thrilled the World*, you read about the unmanned exploration of Mars. Some people think that humans should go to Mars, and some think only unmanned spacecraft should go there. Write an essay to persuade a general audience that humans should explore Mars.

_____

_____

_____

_____

_____

_____

_____

_____

_____

_____

_____

_____

_____

_____

_____

_____

Name _____

Writing a Persuasive Essay

continued

Read your essay. Check to be sure that

- the introduction states your goal clearly
- you have at least three strong reasons to support your goal
- you have facts and examples to back up each reason
- your voice is confident and persuasive
- your conclusion sums up the important points
- there are few mistakes in capitalization, punctuation, grammar, or spelling

Now pick one way to improve your essay. Make your changes below.

_____

_____

_____

_____

_____

_____

_____

_____

_____

_____

_____

_____

_____

_____

_____

Name _____

Spelling Review

**Write each Spelling Word. Then underline the seven words
that begin with the prefix *en-*, *re-*, *un-*, *inter-*, *ac-*, or *dis-*, and
that also end with a suffix.**

1. _____
2. _____
3. _____
4. _____
5. _____
6. _____
7. _____
8. _____
9. _____
10. _____
11. _____
12. _____
13. _____
14. _____
15. _____
16. _____

17. _____
18. _____
19. _____
20. _____
21. _____
22. _____
23. _____
24. _____
25. _____
26. _____
27. _____
28. _____
29. _____
30. _____

Spelling Words

1. encouragement
2. relieve
3. observe
4. extent
5. freight
6. decision
7. regardless
8. review
9. assist
10. preview
11. unbelievable
12. reign
13. acquire
14. disable
15. intermission
16. ceiling
17. occur
18. demonstrate
19. addition
20. accidentally
21. brief
22. interview
23. disgraceful
24. disagreement
25. belief
26. obtain
27. approve
28. affair
29. persuade
30. product

Name _____

Spelling Spree

Alphabet Puzzler Write the Spelling Word that fits alphabetically between the two words shown.

1. assign, _____, assort

2. dirt, _____, disadvantage

3. rehearse, _____, reindeer

4. interlude, _____, intermix

5. achieve, _____, agent

6. interrupt, _____, introduce

7. refuse, _____, register

8. debate, _____, defeat

Analogies Write a Spelling Word that completes each analogy.

9. *Conflict* is to *harmony* as _____ is to *agreement*.

10. *Review* is to *repay* as _____ is to *prepay*.

11. *Truth* is to *fact* as *opinion* is to _____.

12. *Final* is to *finally* as *accident* is to _____.

13. *Show* is to *tell* as _____ is to *explain*.

14. *Help* is to *assist* as *ease* is to _____.

15. *Persuasion* is to _____ as *decision* is to *decide*.

Spelling Words

1. disable
2. relieve
3. belief
4. regardless
5. decision
6. interview
7. intermission
8. assist
9. accidentally
10. disagreement
11. demonstrate
12. preview
13. affair
14. persuade
15. reign

Name _____

Proofreading and Writing

Proofreading Circle the six misspelled Spelling Words from this website. Then write the words correctly.

> Our goal is to acuire information about space. Perhaps we will discover the full exstent of the universe. Maybe we will find new ways to ship frieght from Earth to other planets. In adition, we would like to obzerve Earth's weather from the moon, and to develop at least one new praduct to help predict the weather.

Spelling Words

1. approve
2. encouragement
3. addition
4. brief
5. extent
6. observe
7. product
8. obtain
9. occur
10. review
11. freight
12. acquire
13. ceiling
14. unbelievable
15. disgraceful

1. _____   4. _____

2. _____   5. _____

3. _____   6. _____

Computer Glitch! This e-mail message is missing some words. Write Spelling Words to complete the message.

> I'm coming home as soon as I 7. _____ a plane ticket. It's 8. _____ to me how quickly time passes! I miss you and don't need much 9. _____ to visit. What I hope will 10. _____ while I'm home is that the school will 11. _____ my project idea. The committee still has to 12. _____ and vote on my proposal. My proposal was 13. _____, only five pages; I hope I wrote enough. My project is about small oil spills and sealife. I think it's 14. _____ that people are so careless about the ocean.
>
> By the way, the seashell mobile you gave me is hanging from my dorm room 15. _____. I love it!

7. _____   10. _____   13. _____

8. _____   11. _____   14. _____

9. _____   12. _____   15. _____

➤ **Write a Web Page** On a separate sheet of paper, write a paragraph about the ocean for your website. Use the Spelling Review Words.

Student Handbook

Contents

How to Study a Word

1. LOOK at the word.
► What does the word mean?
► What letters are in the word?
► Name and touch each letter.

2. SAY the word.
► Listen for the consonant sounds.
► Listen for the vowel sounds.

3. THINK about the word.
► How is each sound spelled?
► Close your eyes and picture the word.
► What familiar spelling patterns do you see?
► Did you see any prefixes, suffixes, or other word parts?

4. WRITE the word.
► Think about the sounds and the letters.
► Form the letters correctly.

5. CHECK the spelling.
► Did you spell the word the same way it is spelled in your word list?
► If you did not spell the word correctly, write the word again.

Words Often Misspelled

affectionate
again
all right
a lot
always
another
anyone
anything
anyway
applicable

beautiful
because
before
believe
brought
bureau

cannot
can't
captain
catastrophe
caught
clothes
coming
cousin

didn't
different
don't

eighth
embarrass
enough
essential
everybody
everything
everywhere

family
fatigue
favorite
field
finally
forfeit
friend

getting
going
guess
guy

happened
happily
haven't
heard
height
here

illustrator
indictment
instead
interpret
irreplaceable
its
it's

knew
know

might
millimeter
morning

o'clock
once

pennant
people
perceive
perspiration
pneumonia
pretty
probably

questionnaire

really
received
reversible
right

Saturday
school
someone
sometimes
stopped
stretch
sufficient
suppose
suppress
swimming

that's
their
there
there's
they're
thought
through
to
tonight
too
two

usually

weird
we're

whole
would
wouldn't
write
writing

your
you're

Words Often Confused

affect
effect

alley
ally

ascent
assent

bauble
bubble

bellow
below

bisect
dissect

bazaar
bizarre

bland
blend

confidant
confident

decent
descent

desert
dessert

eclipse
ellipse

hurdle
hurtle

illegible
ineligible

eminent
imminent

moral
mortal

pastor
pasture

sleek
slick

Passage to Freedom

Long Vowels

/ā/ → g**a**z**e**, tr**ai**t
/ē/ → th**eme**, pr**ea**ch, sl**ee**ve
/ī/ → str**i**v**e**
/ō/ → qu**o**t**e**, r**oa**m
/yōō/ → m**u**t**e**

Spelling Words

1. theme	11. strain
2. quote	12. fade
3. gaze	13. league
4. pace	14. soak
5. preach	15. grease
6. strive	16. throne
7. trait	17. fume
8. mute	18. file
9. sleeve	19. toast
10. roam	20. brake

Challenge Words

1. microphone
2. emphasize
3. refugee
4. pertain
5. coax

My Study List

Add your own spelling words on the back. →

Courage
Reading-Writing Workshop

Look for familiar spelling patterns in these words to help you remember their spellings.

Spelling Words

1. your	8. we're
2. you're	9. to
3. their	10. too
4. they're	11. that's
5. its	12. knew
6. it's	13. know
7. wouldn't	

Challenge Words

1. pennant
2. bureau
3. interpret
4. forfeit
5. perspiration

My Study List

Add your own spelling words on the back. →

Hatchet

Short Vowels

/ă/ → cr**a**ft
/ĕ/ → d**e**pth
/ĭ/ → f**i**lm
/ŏ/ → b**o**mb
/ŭ/ → pl**u**nge

Spelling Words

1. depth	11. prompt
2. craft	12. pitch
3. plunge	13. else
4. wreck	14. cliff
5. sunk	15. pledge
6. film	16. scrub
7. wince	17. brass
8. bomb	18. grill
9. switch	19. stung
10. length	20. bulk

Challenge Words

1. habitat
2. cobweb
3. tepid
4. magnetic
5. deft

My Study List

Add your own spelling words on the back. →

Take-Home Word List

Name _____

 My Study List

1. _____
2. _____
3. _____
4. _____
5. _____
6. _____
7. _____
8. _____
9. _____
10. _____

Review Words

1. swift
2. tense
3. bunch
4. grasp
5. ditch

How to Study a Word

Look at the word.
Say the word.
Think about the word.
Write the word.
Check the spelling.

Take-Home Word List

Name _____

My Study List

1. _____
2. _____
3. _____
4. _____
5. _____
6. _____
7. _____
8. _____
9. _____
10. _____

How to Study a Word

Look at the word.
Say the word.
Think about the word.
Write the word.
Check the spelling.

Take-Home Word List

Name _____

 My Study List

1. _____
2. _____
3. _____
4. _____
5. _____
6. _____
7. _____
8. _____
9. _____
10. _____

Review Words

1. greet
2. boast
3. brain
4. code
5. squeak

How to Study a Word

Look at the word.
Say the word.
Think about the word.
Write the word.
Check the spelling.

Take-Home Word List

Take-Home Word List

Courage
Spelling Review

Spelling Words

1. wince	16. craft
2. league	17. throne
3. strive	18. rhythm
4. routine	19. vault
5. prompt	20. avoid
6. strain	21. depth
7. meant	22. roam
8. foul	23. reply
9. hoist	24. stout
10. naughty	25. squawk
11. bulk	26. gaze
12. theme	27. sleeve
13. mute	28. ravine
14. sponge	29. sought
15. bloom	30. annoy

See the back for Challenge Words.

My Study List
Add your own
spelling words
on the back. ➡

The True Confessions of Charlotte Doyle

The /ou/, /o͞o/, /ô/, and /oi/ Sounds

/ou/ ➡ st**ou**t
/o͞o/ ➡ bl**oo**m
/ô/ ➡ v**au**lt, squ**aw**k,
   s**ou**ght, n**augh**ty
/oi/ ➡ av**oi**d, ann**oy**

Spelling Words

1. bloom	11. mound
2. stout	12. groove
3. droop	13. foul
4. crouch	14. hoist
5. annoy	15. gloom
6. vault	16. trout
7. squawk	17. noun
8. avoid	18. roost
9. sought	19. clause
10. naughty	20. appoint

Challenge Words

1. bountiful
2. adjoin
3. nauseous
4. turquoise
5. heirloom

My Study List
Add your own
spelling words
on the back. ➡

Climb or Die

More Vowel Spellings

/ē/ ➡ rout**ine**
/ĕ/ ➡ sw**ea**t
/ī/ ➡ **cy**cle
/ĭ/ ➡ rh**y**thm
/ŭ/ ➡ sh**o**ve
   (*o consonant e*)

Spelling Words

1. cycle	11. sponge
2. sweat	12. apply
3. rhythm	13. threat
4. rely	14. myth
5. pleasant	15. deny
6. routine	16. leather
7. cleanse	17. rhyme
8. shove	18. thread
9. reply	19. meadow
10. meant	20. ravine

Challenge Words

1. endeavor
2. oxygen
3. nylon
4. realm
5. trampoline

My Study List
Add your own
spelling words
on the back. ➡

Take-Home Word List

Name _____

 My Study List

1. _____
2. _____
3. _____
4. _____
5. _____
6. _____
7. _____
8. _____
9. _____
10. _____

Review Words

1. breath
2. measure
3. typical
4. deaf
5. crystal

How to Study a Word

Look at the word.
Say the word.
Think about the word.
Write the word.
Check the spelling.

412

Take-Home Word List

Name _____

My Study List

1. _____
2. _____
3. _____
4. _____
5. _____
6. _____
7. _____
8. _____
9. _____
10. _____

Review Words

1. scoop
2. moist
3. haul
4. loose
5. hawk

How to Study a Word

Look at the word.
Say the word.
Think about the word.
Write the word.
Check the spelling.

412

Take-Home Word List

Name _____

My Study List

1. _____
2. _____
3. _____
4. _____
5. _____
6. _____
7. _____
8. _____
9. _____
10. _____

Challenge Words

1. cobweb
2. tepid
3. refugee
4. coax
5. nylon
6. endeavor
7. oxygen
8. nauseous
9. bountiful
10. heirloom

How to Study a Word

Look at the word.
Say the word.
Think about the word.
Write the word.
Check the spelling.

412

The Girl Who Married the Moon

Homophones
Homophones are words that sound alike but have different spellings and meanings.

Spelling Words

1. fir	11. manor
2. fur	12. manner
3. scent	13. who's
4. sent	14. whose
5. scene	15. tacks
6. seen	16. tax
7. vain	17. hangar
8. vein	18. hanger
9. principal	19. died
10. principle	20. dyed

Challenge Words

1. phase
2. faze
3. burrow
4. burro
5. borough

My Study List
Add your own spelling words on the back. ➡

What Really Happened? Reading-Writing Workshop

Look for familiar spelling patterns in these words to help you remember their spellings.

Spelling Words

1. tonight	9. clothes
2. everywhere	10. height
3. everybody	11. always
4. another	12. right
5. because	13. might
6. whole	14. really
7. people	15. everything
8. cousin	

Challenge Words

1. essential
2. questionnaire
3. affectionate
4. illustrator
5. embarrass

My Study List
Add your own spelling words on the back. ➡

Amelia Earhart: First Lady of Flight

Vowel + /r/ Sounds
/ûr/ ➡ sk**ir**t, **ur**ge, **ear**th
/ôr/ ➡ th**or**n, c**our**t
/är/ ➡ ch**ar**t
/îr/ ➡ fi**er**ce

Spelling Words

1. fierce	11. whirl
2. sword	12. mourn
3. court	13. rehearse
4. snarl	14. curb
5. thorn	15. earnest
6. earth	16. starch
7. skirt	17. purse
8. chart	18. birch
9. urge	19. pierce
10. yarn	20. scorn

Challenge Words

1. circumstances
2. turmoil
3. absurd
4. territory
5. sparse

My Study List
Add your own spelling words on the back. ➡

Take-Home Word List

Name _____

 My Study List

1. _____
2. _____
3. _____
4. _____
5. _____
6. _____
7. _____
8. _____
9. _____
10. _____

Review Words

1. pearl
2. stir
3. inform
4. pour
5. scar

How to Study a Word

Look at the word.
Say the word.
Think about the word.
Write the word.
Check the spelling.

Take-Home Word List

Name _____

My Study List

1. _____
2. _____
3. _____
4. _____
5. _____
6. _____
7. _____
8. _____
9. _____
10. _____

How to Study a Word

Look at the word.
Say the word.
Think about the word.
Write the word.
Check the spelling.

Take-Home Word List

Name _____

My Study List

1. _____
2. _____
3. _____
4. _____
5. _____
6. _____
7. _____
8. _____
9. _____
10. _____

Review Words

1. berry
2. bury
3. soar
4. sore

How to Study a Word

Look at the word.
Say the word.
Think about the word.
Write the word.
Check the spelling.

Where the Red Fern Grows

VCV, VCCV, and VCCCV Patterns

VC|V:	**bal**	**ance**
V|CV:	**mi**	**nus**
VC|CV:	**law**	**yer**
V|CCV:	**au**	**thor**
VCC|V:	**meth**	**od**
VC|CCV:	**sup**	**ply**

Spelling Words

1. balance
2. lawyer
3. sheriff
4. author
5. minus
6. method
7. item
8. require
9. supply
10. whisper
11. spirit
12. tennis
13. adopt
14. instant
15. poison
16. deserve
17. rescue
18. journey
19. relief
20. laundry

Challenge Words

1. enhance
2. delete
3. precious
4. structure
5. decade

My Study List
Add your own spelling words on the back. ➡

What Really Happened?
Spelling Review

Spelling Words

1. chart
2. starch
3. hangar
4. manner
5. gallon
6. whirl
7. curb
8. vein
9. similar
10. rural
11. sword
12. purse
13. hanger
14. manor
15. direction
16. mourn
17. who's
18. scent
19. channel
20. passenger
21. pierce
22. thorn
23. vain
24. struggle
25. frighten
26. rehearse
27. whose
28. sent
29. familiar
30. calendar

See the back for Challenge Words.

My Study List
Add your own spelling words on the back. ➡

Dinosaur Ghosts

Final /ər/, /ən/, and /əl/

/ər/	➡	messeng**er**, direct**or**, simil**ar**
/ən/	➡	weap**on**, fright**en**
/əl/	➡	strugg**le**, chann**el**, ment**al**

Spelling Words

1. struggle
2. director
3. weapon
4. similar
5. mental
6. frighten
7. channel
8. messenger
9. familiar
10. acre
11. error
12. gallon
13. rural
14. calendar
15. elevator
16. stumble
17. youngster
18. kitchen
19. passenger
20. quarrel

Challenge Words

1. agricultural
2. colonel
3. predator
4. corridor
5. maneuver

My Study List
Add your own spelling words on the back. ➡

Take-Home Word List

My Study List

1. _____
2. _____
3. _____
4. _____
5. _____
6. _____
7. _____
8. _____
9. _____
10. _____

Review Words

1. matter
2. novel
3. mayor
4. consider
5. dozen

How to Study a Word

Look at the word.
Say the word.
Think about the word.
Write the word.
Check the spelling.

Take-Home Word List

My Study List

1. _____
2. _____
3. _____
4. _____
5. _____
6. _____
7. _____
8. _____
9. _____
10. _____

Challenge Words

1. territory   6. predator
2. absurd   7. colonel
3. turmoil   8. faze
4. phase   9. burro
5. burrow   10. corridor

How to Study a Word

Look at the word.
Say the word.
Think about the word.
Write the word.
Check the spelling.

Take-Home Word List

My Study List

1. _____
2. _____
3. _____
4. _____
5. _____
6. _____
7. _____
8. _____
9. _____
10. _____

Review Words

1. protect
2. effort
3. actor
4. credit
5. merchant

How to Study a Word

Look at the word.
Say the word.
Think about the word.
Write the word.
Check the spelling.

The Challenge

Endings and Suffixes
divide + ed = divid**ed**
grace + ful = grace**ful**

Spelling Words

1. graceful
2. divided
3. advanced
4. privately
5. replacement
6. excitement
7. adorable
8. heaving
9. forgiveness
10. mileage
11. barely
12. forceful
13. scarcely
14. blaming
15. entirely
16. usable
17. sincerely
18. amusement
19. lifeless
20. manageable

Challenge Words

1. deflated
2. disciplined
3. consecutively
4. silhouetted
5. refinement

My Study List
Add your own spelling words on the back. ➡

417

Last Summer with Maizon

Words with -ed or -ing
map**ped**   pilot**ing**
fit**ting**   begin**ning**

Spelling Words

1. mapped
2. piloting
3. permitting
4. beginning
5. bothered
6. limited
7. forgetting
8. reasoning
9. preferred
10. equaled
11. wondering
12. slipped
13. listening
14. fitting
15. pardoned
16. shoveling
17. favored
18. knitting
19. answered
20. modeling

Challenge Words

1. propelling
2. equipped
3. transmitted
4. recurring
5. beckoned

My Study List
Add your own spelling words on the back. ➡

417

Growing Up
Reading-Writing Workshop

Look for familiar spelling patterns in these words to help you remember their spellings.

Spelling Words

1. bland
2. blend
3. below
4. bellow
5. pastor
6. pasture
7. moral
8. mortal
9. bauble
10. bubble
11. bisect
12. dissect
13. assent
14. ascent

Challenge Words

1. imminent
2. eminent
3. illegible
4. ineligible

My Study List
Add your own spelling words on the back. ➡

417

Name _____

 My Study List

1. _____
2. _____
3. _____
4. _____
5. _____
6. _____
7. _____
8. _____
9. _____
10. _____

How to Study a Word

Look at the word.
Say the word.
Think about the word.
Write the word.
Check the spelling.

418

Name _____

My Study List

1. _____
2. _____
3. _____
4. _____
5. _____
6. _____
7. _____
8. _____
9. _____
10. _____

Review Words

1. ordered
2. planned
3. spotted
4. winning
5. gathering

How to Study a Word

Look at the word.
Say the word.
Think about the word.
Write the word.
Check the spelling.

418

Name _____

My Study List

1. _____
2. _____
3. _____
4. _____
5. _____
6. _____
7. _____
8. _____
9. _____
10. _____

Review Words

1. breathless
2. collapsed
3. valuable
4. retirement
5. government

How to Study a Word

Look at the word.
Say the word.
Think about the word.
Write the word.
Check the spelling.

418

Lost Temple of the Aztecs

The /sh/ Sound
/sh/ ➡ poli**sh**, mo**ti**on
offi**ci**al, mi**ssi**on

Spelling Words

1. glacier
2. motion
3. pressure
4. direction
5. caution
6. partial
7. ancient
8. polish
9. station
10. shallow
11. official
12. edition
13. musician
14. mention
15. mission
16. portion
17. session
18. selfish
19. establish
20. cushion

Challenge Words

1. expedition
2. diminish
3. recession
4. beneficial
5. technician

My Study List
Add your own spelling words on the back. ➡

Growing Up Spelling Review

Spelling Words

1. method
2. author
3. answered
4. forgiveness
5. complicate
6. supply
7. beginning
8. heaving
9. scarcely
10. include
11. relief
12. forgetting
13. amusement
14. excitement
15. consumer
16. balance
17. slipped
18. advanced
19. control
20. impolite
21. minus
22. listening
23. adorable
24. immediate
25. involve
26. lawyer
27. preferred
28. graceful
29. conversation
30. community

See the back for Challenge Words.

My Study List
Add your own spelling words on the back. ➡

The View from Saturday

Prefixes: *in-* and *con-*
in + active = **in**active
in + volve = **in**volve
in + polite = **im**polite
in + mense = **im**mense
con + trol = **con**trol
con + test = **con**test
con + ment = **com**ment
con + pete = **com**pete

Spelling Words

1. computer
2. impolite
3. control
4. include
5. immigrant
6. compete
7. consumer
8. involve
9. immediate
10. comment
11. infection
12. concert
13. import
14. conversation
15. community
16. incomplete
17. immense
18. contest
19. inactive
20. complicate

Challenge Words

1. imply
2. consequence
3. comprehensive
4. inadequate
5. communicate

My Study List
Add your own spelling words on the back. ➡

Name _____

 My Study List

1. _____
2. _____
3. _____
4. _____
5. _____
6. _____
7. _____
8. _____
9. _____
10. _____

Review Words

1. concern
2. insist
3. compare
4. improve
5. convince

How to Study a Word

Look at the word.
Say the word.
Think about the word.
Write the word.
Check the spelling.

Name _____

 My Study List

1. _____
2. _____
3. _____
4. _____
5. _____
6. _____
7. _____
8. _____
9. _____
10. _____

Challenge Words

1. precious
2. enhance
3. beckoned
4. propelling
5. deflated

6. consecutively
7. refinement
8. communicate
9. imply
10. consequence

How to Study a Word

Look at the word.
Say the word.
Think about the word.
Write the word.
Check the spelling.

Name _____

 My Study List

1. _____
2. _____
3. _____
4. _____
5. _____
6. _____
7. _____
8. _____
9. _____
10. _____

Review Words

1. vanish
2. nation
3. condition
4. migration
5. confession

How to Study a Word

Look at the word.
Say the word.
Think about the word.
Write the word.
Check the spelling.

The Royal Kingdoms of Ghana, Mali, and Songhay

Unstressed Syllables
prob l lem ➔
  /**prŏb´** ləm/
ex l am l ple ➔
  /ĭg **zăm´** pəl/

Spelling Words

1. company
2. success
3. position
4. problem
5. policy
6. difficult
7. document
8. quality
9. surprise
10. physical
11. crisis
12. awake
13. example
14. ignore
15. accept
16. parallel
17. admiral
18. desire
19. garage
20. ambulance

Challenge Words

1. efficient
2. utensil
3. morale
4. ethical
5. potential

My Study List
Add your own spelling words on the back. ➔

The Great Wall

Adding -ion or -ation
connect, connec**tion**
situate, situa**tion**
admire, admir**ation**

Spelling Words

1. construct
2. construction
3. connect
4. connection
5. combine
6. combination
7. cooperate
8. cooperation
9. attract
10. attraction
11. admire
12. admiration
13. situate
14. situation
15. examine
16. examination
17. contribute
18. contribution
19. explore
20. exploration

Challenge Words

1. negotiate
2. negotiation
3. insulate
4. insulation

My Study List
Add your own spelling words on the back. ➔

Discovering Ancient Cultures
Reading-Writing Workshop

Look for familiar spelling patterns in these words to help you remember their spellings.

Spelling Words

1. decent
2. descent
3. affect
4. effect
5. desert
6. dessert
7. slick
8. sleek
9. alley
10. ally
11. confident
12. confidant
13. hurdle
14. hurtle

Challenge Words

1. bizarre
2. bazaar
3. ellipse
4. eclipse

My Study List
Add your own spelling words on the back. ➔

Take-Home Word List

Name _____

 My Study List

1. _____
2. _____
3. _____
4. _____
5. _____
6. _____
7. _____
8. _____
9. _____
10. _____

How to Study a Word

Look at the word.
Say the word.
Think about the word.
Write the word.
Check the spelling.

Take-Home Word List

Name _____

My Study List

1. _____
2. _____
3. _____
4. _____
5. _____
6. _____
7. _____
8. _____
9. _____
10. _____

Review Words

1. inspect
2. inspection
3. create
4. creation

How to Study a Word

Look at the word.
Say the word.
Think about the word.
Write the word.
Check the spelling.

Take-Home Word List

Name _____

My Study List

1. _____
2. _____
3. _____
4. _____
5. _____
6. _____
7. _____
8. _____
9. _____
10. _____

Review Words

1. industry
2. orphan
3. president
4. absent
5. attention

How to Study a Word

Look at the word.
Say the word.
Think about the word.
Write the word.
Check the spelling.

Doers and Dreamers
Reading-Writing Workshop

Look for familiar spelling patterns in these words to help you remember their spellings.

Spelling Words

1. anyone
2. captain
3. all right
4. beautiful
5. enough
6. family
7. someone
8. stretch
9. favorite
10. guy
11. a lot
12. friend
13. sometimes
14. anyway
15. anything

Challenge Words

1. irreplaceable
2. suppress
3. sufficient
4. catastrophe
5. perceive

My Study List
Add your own spelling words on the back. ➡

A Kind of Grace

Final /īz/, /ĭv/, /ĭj/, /ĭk/, /chər/, and /əs/

/īz/	➡	advert**ise**, organ**ize**
/ĭv/	➡	act**ive**
/ĭj/	➡	us**age**
/ĭk/	➡	trag**ic**
/chər/	➡	signa**ture**
/əs/	➡	nerv**ous**

Spelling Words

1. advertise
2. serious
3. scientific
4. active
5. usage
6. signature
7. realize
8. nervous
9. temperature
10. college
11. tragic
12. positive
13. fantastic
14. exercise
15. jealous
16. organize
17. courage
18. curious
19. departure
20. storage

Challenge Words

1. chronic
2. merchandise
3. unanimous
4. legislature
5. visualize

My Study List
Add your own spelling words on the back. ➡

Discovering Ancient Cultures
Spelling Review

Spelling Words

1. ancient
2. pressure
3. connect
4. cooperate
5. problem
6. shallow
7. partial
8. connection
9. cooperation
10. ambulance
11. official
12. cushion
13. combine
14. success
15. example
16. edition
17. mission
18. combination
19. position
20. physical
21. musician
22. construct
23. admire
24. difficult
25. surprise
26. establish
27. construction
28. admiration
29. accept
30. crisis

See the back for Challenge Words.

My Study List
Add your own spelling words on the back. ➡

Name _____

 My Study List

1. _____
2. _____
3. _____
4. _____
5. _____
6. _____
7. _____
8. _____
9. _____
10. _____

Challenge Words

1. expedition   6. negotiate
2. diminish   7. morale
3. beneficial   8. insulation
4. insulate   9. potential
5. utensil   10. negotiation

How to Study a Word

Look at the word.
Say the word.
Think about the word.
Write the word.
Check the spelling.

Name _____

 My Study List

1. _____
2. _____
3. _____
4. _____
5. _____
6. _____
7. _____
8. _____
9. _____
10. _____

Review Words

1. message
2. public
3. future
4. sensitive
5. dangerous

How to Study a Word

Look at the word.
Say the word.
Think about the word.
Write the word.
Check the spelling.

Name _____

 My Study List

1. _____
2. _____
3. _____
4. _____
5. _____
6. _____
7. _____
8. _____
9. _____
10. _____

How to Study a Word

Look at the word.
Say the word.
Think about the word.
Write the word.
Check the spelling.

Doers and Dreamers
Spelling Review

Spelling Words

1. active
2. curious
3. stereos
4. potatoes
5. difference
6. realize
7. scientific
8. echoes
9. workable
10. studios
11. exercise
12. temperature
13. chiefs
14. separate
15. noticeable
16. courage
17. positive
18. staffs
19. celebrate
20. importance
21. fantastic
22. halves
23. visible
24. fragrant
25. loaves
26. departure
27. shelves
28. pianos
29. appearance
30. excellent

See the back for Challenge Words.

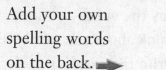

My Study List
Add your own spelling words on the back. ➡

Chuck Close, Up Close

> **Suffixes:** *-ant/-ance; -ent/-ence; -able/-ible; -ate*
> /ənt/ → brilli**ant**, excell**ent**
> /əns/ → import**ance**, sent**ence**
> /əbəl/ → lov**able**, vis**ible**
> /ĭt/ → desper**ate**
> /āt/ → separ**ate**

Spelling Words

1. desperate
2. brilliant
3. audience
4. celebrate
5. excellent
6. visible
7. appearance
8. lovable
9. noticeable
10. sentence
11. difference
12. workable
13. instance
14. fragrant
15. fortunate
16. client
17. separate
18. agent
19. responsible
20. importance

Challenge Words

1. portable
2. irresistible
3. resemblance
4. magnificent
5. elaborate

My Study List
Add your own spelling words on the back. ➡

Under the Royal Palms

> **Plurals**
> staff   chief   half
> staffs   chiefs   halves
>
> ster**eo**   pian**o**   potat**o**
> ster**eos** pian**os** potat**oes**

Spelling Words

1. pianos
2. cellos
3. solos
4. altos
5. sopranos
6. staffs
7. stereos
8. potatoes
9. halves
10. chiefs
11. echoes
12. calves
13. studios
14. shelves
15. ratios
16. volcanoes
17. loaves
18. wolves
19. heroes
20. scarves

Challenge Words

1. patios
2. maestros
3. tuxedos
4. vetoes
5. mementos

My Study List
Add your own spelling words on the back. ➡

Name _____

My Study List

1. _____
2. _____
3. _____
4. _____
5. _____
6. _____
7. _____
8. _____
9. _____
10. _____

Review Words

1. abilities
2. countries
3. duties
4. enemies
5. lilies

How to Study a Word

Look at the word.
Say the word.
Think about the word.
Write the word.
Check the spelling.

Name _____

My Study List

1. _____
2. _____
3. _____
4. _____
5. _____
6. _____
7. _____
8. _____
9. _____
10. _____

Review Words

1. terrible
2. science
3. distance
4. remarkable
5. constant

How to Study a Word

Look at the word.
Say the word.
Think about the word.
Write the word.
Check the spelling.

Name _____

My Study List

1. _____
2. _____
3. _____
4. _____
5. _____
6. _____
7. _____
8. _____
9. _____
10. _____

Challenge Words

1. legislature
2. visualize
3. unanimous
4. patios
5. vetoes
6. tuxedos
7. portable
8. irresistible
9. resemblance
10. magnificent

How to Study a Word

Look at the word.
Say the word.
Think about the word.
Write the word.
Check the spelling.

Franklin R. Chang-Díaz

Prefixes: *ad-* and *ob-*

advice	**ac**count
acquire	**ap**prove
assist	**af**fair
observe	**oc**cupy

Spelling Words

1. account
2. observe
3. addition
4. accurate
5. occasion
6. approve
7. advice
8. occupy
9. assist
10. affair
11. occur
12. acquire
13. assume
14. adjust
15. assign
16. oblige
17. accomplish
18. approach
19. according
20. obtain

Challenge Words

1. applicant
2. accumulate
3. obscure
4. affiliated
5. obstinate

My Study List
Add your own spelling words on the back. ➡

427

New Frontiers: Oceans and Space
Reading-Writing Workshop

Look for familiar spelling patterns in these words to help you remember their spellings.

Spelling Words

1. weird
2. thought
3. through
4. caught
5. brought
6. finally
7. suppose
8. usually
9. eighth
10. millimeter
11. happily
12. guess
13. Saturday
14. school
15. before

Challenge Words

1. fatigue
2. pneumonia
3. applicable
4. indictment
5. reversible

My Study List
Add your own spelling words on the back. ➡

427

The Adventures of Sojourner

Prefixes: *de-, dis-, ex-, inter-, per-, pre-, pro-*

describe	**inter**national
determine	**per**mission
disable	**pre**view
exhaust	**pro**ceed

Spelling Words

1. disease
2. decision
3. proceed
4. international
5. permission
6. experience
7. disable
8. preview
9. describe
10. progress
11. product
12. exhaust
13. previous
14. demonstrate
15. extent
16. disturb
17. persuade
18. interview
19. determine
20. prepare

Challenge Words

1. deliberate
2. perception
3. expertise
4. interdependent
5. procure

My Study List
Add your own spelling words on the back. ➡

427

Take-Home Word List

Name _____

My Study List

1. _____
2. _____
3. _____
4. _____
5. _____
6. _____
7. _____
8. _____
9. _____
10. _____

Review Words

1. providing
2. disagree
3. explain
4. detail
5. program

How to Study a Word

Look at the word.
Say the word.
Think about the word.
Write the word.
Check the spelling.

Take-Home Word List

Name _____

My Study List

1. _____
2. _____
3. _____
4. _____
5. _____
6. _____
7. _____
8. _____
9. _____
10. _____

How to Study a Word

Look at the word.
Say the word.
Think about the word.
Write the word.
Check the spelling.

Take-Home Word List

Name _____

My Study List

1. _____
2. _____
3. _____
4. _____
5. _____
6. _____
7. _____
8. _____
9. _____
10. _____

Review Words

1. address
2. object
3. accident
4. adventure
5. arrive

How to Study a Word

Look at the word.
Say the word.
Think about the word.
Write the word.
Check the spelling.

New Frontiers: Oceans and Space

Spelling Review

Spelling Words

1. decision	16. product
2. interview	17. addition
3. obtain	18. approve
4. brief	19. relieve
5. unbelievable	20. regardless
6. disable	21. demonstrate
7. persuade	22. assist
8. occur	23. review
9. freight	24. ceiling
10. disagreement	25. intermission
11. preview	26. extent
12. observe	27. affair
13. acquire	28. belief
14. reign	29. accidentally
15. encourage-ment	30. disgraceful

See the back for Challenge Words.

Out There

> **Word Parts**
> **un**believ**able**
> **ad**vance**ment**
> **in**ven**tion**
> **con**cen**tr**ation

Spelling Words

1. development	12. prevention
2. information	13. regardless
3. preparation	14. repetition
4. improvement	15. disgraceful
5. invention	16. unbelievable
6. advancement	17. disagreement
7. accidentally	18. imprisonment
8. unkindness	19. encourage-ment
9. concentration	
10. unskillful	20. intermission
11. respectful	

Challenge Words

1. precision
2. reputation
3. distinction
4. immeasurable
5. inevitable

Beneath Blue Waters

> **Words with *ie* or *ei***
> y**ie**ld
> rec**ei**pt
> fr**ei**ght

Spelling Words

1. freight	11. shield
2. receipt	12. diesel
3. yield	13. reign
4. review	14. fiery
5. belief	15. conceit
6. eighty	16. veil
7. brief	17. grief
8. ceiling	18. relieve
9. neither	19. seize
10. foreign	20. leisure

Challenge Words

1. retrieve
2. deceit
3. wield
4. eerie
5. hygiene

My Study List
Add your own spelling words on the back. ➡

My Study List
Add your own spelling words on the back. ➡

My Study List
Add your own spelling words on the back. ➡

Name _____

My Study List

1. _____
2. _____
3. _____
4. _____
5. _____
6. _____
7. _____
8. _____
9. _____
10. _____

Review Words

1. piece
2. view
3. niece
4. pier
5. mischief

How to Study a Word

Look at the word.
Say the word.
Think about the word.
Write the word.
Check the spelling.

Name _____

My Study List

1. _____
2. _____
3. _____
4. _____
5. _____
6. _____
7. _____
8. _____
9. _____
10. _____

Review Words

1. enjoyment
2. delightful
3. reaction
4. comfortable
5. conviction

How to Study a Word

Look at the word.
Say the word.
Think about the word.
Write the word.
Check the spelling.

Name _____

My Study List

1. _____
2. _____
3. _____
4. _____
5. _____
6. _____
7. _____
8. _____
9. _____
10. _____

Challenge Words

1. interdependent
2. expertise
3. applicant
4. obstinate
5. retrieve
6. immeasurable
7. inevitable
8. deceit
9. precision
10. reputation

How to Study a Word

Look at the word.
Say the word.
Think about the word.
Write the word.
Check the spelling.

Problem Words

Words	Rules	Examples
bad badly	*Bad* is an adjective. It can be used after linking verbs like *look* and *feel*. *Badly* is an adverb.	This was a <u>bad</u> day. I feel <u>bad</u>. I play <u>badly</u>.
borrow lend	*Borrow* means "to take." *Lend* means "to give."	You may <u>borrow</u> my pen. I will <u>lend</u> it to you for the day.
can may	*Can* means "to be able to do something." *May* means "to be allowed or permitted."	Nellie <u>can</u> read quickly. <u>May</u> I borrow your book?
good well	*Good* is an adjective. *Well* is usually an adverb. It is an adjective only when it refers to health.	The weather looks <u>good</u>. She sings <u>well</u>. Do you feel <u>well</u>?
in into	*In* means "located within." *Into* means "movement from the outside to the inside."	Your lunch is <u>in</u> that bag. He jumped <u>into</u> the pool.
its it's	*Its* is a possessive pronoun. *It's* is a contraction of *it is*.	The dog wagged <u>its</u> tail. <u>It's</u> cold today.
let leave	*Let* means "to permit or allow." *Leave* means "to go away from" or "to let remain in place."	Please <u>let</u> me go swimming. I will <u>leave</u> soon. <u>Leave</u> it on my desk.
lie lay	*Lie* means "to rest or recline." *Lay* means "to put or place something."	The dog <u>lies</u> in its bed. Please <u>lay</u> the books there.

Problem Words continued

Words	Rules	Examples
sit set	*Sit* means "to rest in one place." *Set* means "to place or put."	Please <u>sit</u> in this chair. Set the vase on the table.
teach learn	*Teach* means "to give instruction." *Learn* means "to receive instruction."	He <u>teaches</u> us how to dance. I <u>learned</u> about history.
their there they're	*Their* is a possessive pronoun. *There* is an adverb. It may also begin a sentence. *They're* is a contraction of *they are*.	<u>Their</u> coats are on the bed. Is Carlos <u>there</u>? <u>There</u> is my book. <u>They're</u> going to the store.
two to too	*Two* is a number. *To* means "in the direction of." *Too* means "more than enough" and "also."	I bought <u>two</u> shirts. A squirrel ran <u>to</u> the tree. May we go <u>too</u>?
whose who's	*Whose* is a possessive pronoun. *Who's* is a contraction for *who is*.	<u>Whose</u> tickets are these? <u>Who's</u> that woman?
your you're	*Your* is a possessive pronoun. *You're* is a contraction for *you are*.	Are these <u>your</u> glasses? <u>You're</u> late again!

Read each question below. Then check your paper. Correct any mistakes you find. After you have corrected them, put a check mark in the box next to the question.

☐ 1. Did I spell all words correctly?

☐ 2. Did I indent each paragraph?

☐ 3. Does each sentence state a complete thought?

☐ 4. Are there any run-on sentences or fragments?

☐ 5. Did I begin each sentence with a capital letter?

☐ 6. Did I capitalize all proper nouns?

☐ 7. Did I end each sentence with the correct end mark?

☐ 8. Did I use commas, apostrophes, and quotation marks correctly?

Are there other problem areas you should watch for? Make your own proofreading checklist.

☐ _____

☐ _____

☐ _____

☐ _____

☐ _____

☐ _____

Mark	Explanation	Examples
¶	Begin a new paragraph. Indent the paragraph.	¶The space shuttle landed safely after its five-day voyage. It glided to a smooth, perfect halt.
∧	Add letters, words, or sentences.	My friend eats lunch with me evry day. (best / e)
∧ (comma)	Add a comma.	Carlton my Siamese cat has a mind of his own.
⟨⟨ ⟩⟩	Add quotation marks.	Where do you want us to put the piano? asked the gasping movers.
⊙	Add a period.	Don't forget to put a period at the end of every statement⊙
℘	Take out words, sentences, and punctuation marks. Correct spelling.	We looked at and admired the model airaplanes.
/	Change a capital letter to a small letter.	We are studying about the Louisiana Purchase in History class.
≡	Change a small letter to a capital letter.	The Nile river in africa is the longest river in the world.
∼	Reverse letters or words.	To complet the task successfully, you must follow carefully the steps.